W9-CCX-314

CONTENTS

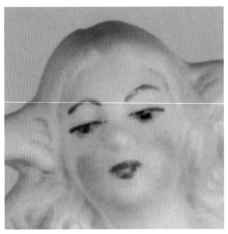
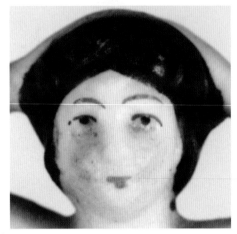

Which hand-painted face is new and which is old? See Page 24.

Which are the fake Hillbilly Frog cookie jars and which is the original? See Page 91.

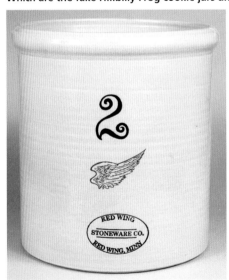

Which is the fake Red Wing crock and which is the original? See Page 284.

Guide to
Fakes&
REPRODUCTIONS

Authentic or fake?
Can you make the right choice?

Features 800 Color Photos

MARK CHERVENKA

©2007 Mark Chervenka

Published by

700 East State Street • Iola, WI 54990-0001
715-445-2214 • 888-457-2873
www.krausebooks.com

Our toll-free number to place an order or obtain
a free catalog is (800) 258-0929.

Library of Congress Catalog Number: 2006935564
ISBN: 978-0-89689-460-0

Designed by Kay Sanders
Edited by Kristine Manty

Printed in China

INTRODUCTION

Fakery has been a profitable career path for thousands of years.

The only change over the centuries is how money changes hands. In 5th century BC, poor Herodotus endured ocean storms and camel caravans only to slake his tourist's lust for souvenirs on fake canopic jars. Today, Mr. H. could be eating goat cheese and sipping ouzo in his villa only a mouse click away from cheats of equal distinction. And PayPal and Visa save the cost of renting an extra camel for lugging all those awkward pouches of silver and gold.

The truth is, fakes and forgeries are as ancient as collecting. One of the earliest examples of systematic imitation is a 5,000-year-old Egyptian papyrus in the Stockholm Museum. In it, a master forger gives apprentices step-by-step details on how to turn colorless rocks into valuable gemstones to meet upper-class demand.

One of the most profitable fakes during the Crusades was relatively worthless silver coins represented as "the ones given to Judas by the Romans." But like forgers of all ages, medieval hucksters cared more about money than religion. They cheerfully provided dusty manuscripts absolutely proving a drinking vessel descended from either Jesus Christ, Mohammed or Abraham according to a prospective buyer's interest. And Michelangelo, Da Vinci and Cellini all brag about fobbing workshop knockoffs of Greek and Roman antiquities to Renaissance Italian merchants with more money than taste.

No friends, complaints today are simply echoes of those from the distant past. Only the medium of exchange is different. Buyers are now cheated in dollars and euros when centuries past, collectors bemoaned losses of talents, scudi and gulden.

Fakes will always be with us. You can either learn what the fakers already know or ignore the problem.

It's your choice.

Mark Chervenka

"The fault, dear Brutus, is not in our stars,
But in ourselves, that we get ripped off in online auctions."
Anonymous 2007

BLACK
MEMORABILIA

There are reproductions of black memorabilia in just about every category of collecting: cast iron, toys, kitchen items, textiles, wood, etc. It's impossible to list or show them all in the space available so we have limited our selection to some of the more confusing items. Although there is a tremendous variety of reproductions available, there are some general rules of thumb that are useful to keep in mind.

When examining ceramic items, keep in mind that virtually all original 1930 to 1950s ceramic pieces made in Japan were made with at least some cold painted (not paint fired-on in a kiln or oven) over glaze decoration. Most all of these painted originals show at least some wear to the cold paint. The vast majority of ceramic reproductions of these pieces are decorated entirely under the glaze, not cold painted over the glaze. There are no signs of normal paint wear, as found in the vintage originals.

Many pieces sought by black memorabilia collectors today were originally made for routine utilitarian everyday use around the house, especially kitchen items. In other words, many vintage items were designed for a specific practical function. Many reproductions are designed as "collectibles" and lack the essential elements to make them serve the purpose for which the originals were designed. Range shakers, for example, should logically have filling holes that make practical sense. Spouts of pitchers and teapots should allow liquid to pass smoothly. Handles and knobs should fit the human hand.

NEW   OLD

The original decanter was made in the 1950s; the fake in the late 1990s. But which is old? The fake decanter is on the left; the original is on the right. The bottles are the telltale clue, as shown below.

NEW   OLD

The bottle held by the new butler is perfectly smooth.

The bottle held by the vintage butler is molded with basket-like grooves.

Be particularly wary of all items that include images on paper. Now that almost everyone has a home computer, scanner, and color printer, the number of do-it-yourself paper forgeries has exploded. It's relatively simple to scan an original image in a reference book or auction catalog, alter the image, print it out, and apply it to genuinely old recipe boxes, toys, clock faces and other items. Such digital images can also be produced as iron on images that can be applied to fabrics and transfers that can be applied to curved surfaces.

Coon Chicken Inn

The Coon Chicken Inn restaurant chain was founded by Maxon Lester Graham in the Salt Lake City, Utah, area around 1924. The restaurants, which featured fried chicken, soon expanded into Seattle, Washington, and Portland, Oregon. The last remaining Coon Chicken Inn location closed in 1957. The company's grinning bell hop trademark was originally used on many items including

O.P.CO.
SYRACUSE
- CHINA -
P-3

A new Coon Chicken Inn decoration applied to a 10" dinner platter. The new transfer decoration is applied over the glaze; original Coon Chicken Inn restaurant china is decorated under the glaze.

The faked platter in the photo above is marked with a Syracuse China back stamp. The P-3 date code is for March 1935. The mark alone is not a reliable test of age or authenticity.

A new three-piece set consisting of individual-sized sugar, butter pat and creamer. No old counterparts are known. Some, but not all, of these fakes are being marked "Made in Occupied Japan."

MADE IN OCCUPIED JAPAN

The faked Occupied Japan mark on the three-piece set shown above.

restaurant china, menus, matchbooks, toothpick holders, cups, bowls and many other pieces all of which are highly collectible.

Some of the most confusing new Coon Chicken Inn items are pieces of faked restaurant china. There are two ways to catch almost all of these fakes: by determining whether the decoration is overglaze or underglaze, and examining the back stamp. Decorations on all original Coon Chicken Inn restaurant china—and virtually all other restaurant china—are underglaze. Overglaze decorations would be scratched by utensils and subject to wear by continuous washing. Putting the decoration under the glaze helps preserve and protect the design.

How can you tell if a decoration is overglaze or underglaze? Underglaze decorations are applied directly on the fired bisque. The glaze that covers the bisque seals the decoration. The entire finished surface appears glassy smooth. Underglaze decorations may have a slight swelling above the decoration, but rarely show sharply outlined borders or design details. Overglaze decorations are applied to china bodies, which have already been glazed. The typical overglaze decoration generally shows obvious edges and borders around the design. This is often best seen by tilting the china at an angle under a bright light. The well defined edges of most overglaze decorations can also be easily detected with your fingernail.

There are at least three known confusing marks appearing on new transfer decorated Coon Chicken Inn china: the "Syracuse China P-3" back stamp (on P. 9); a stamp reading "Shenango China USA by Interface" and a back stamp reading "Shenango China New Castle PA, USA, Anchor Hocking." Both of the Shenango marks never existed until well after the restaurants went out of business. Any Coon Chicken Inn piece with the Shenango marks is automatically a fake.

A new Coon Chicken Inn transfer applied to a genuinely old ca. 1930s brown and white stoneware jug. No genuine Coon Chicken Inn items in stoneware have ever been found.

Another mark being faked on new Coon Chicken Inn china is "Made in Occupied Japan." That mark is found on all three pieces of a three-piece set of a personal-sized creamer, sugar and butter pat, shown on P. 10. Both the shapes and the mark are pure fantasies. No similarly shaped authentic sets with the Coon Chicken Inn trademark are known. No authentic Coon Chicken Inn ceramic items have ever been found marked Made in Occupied Japan. This set is sold through the reproduction wholesale trade with a wide variety of faked names and symbols, particularly the names and trademarks of railroads.

New Coon Chicken Inn decorations are also being applied to stoneware and crockery. One of the regularly appearing items is a 5-inch diameter crockery "lard tub" being sold as Roseville. Around the side of the new crock is the bell hop trademark with "Coon Chicken Inn, Seasoned Lard For Frying." The Roseville attribution comes from the mark of Robinson Ransbottom Pottery Co. of Roseville, Ohio, in business today. The company's molded mark is "RRP CO Roseville, Ohio." Sellers either deliberately or mistakenly imply that "Roseville, Ohio" indicates the piece is a vintage product of Roseville Pottery, which closed in the mid-1950s. Roseville Pottery was made in Zanesville, Ohio, and has no connection with Robinson Ransbottom Pottery made in Roseville, Ohio.

The new RRP crocks are appearing with a variety of black-related advertising including Aunt Jemima products. As far as we could determine, Robinson Ransbottom is not applying the new advertising at the factory; someone else is buying the new crocks and adding the advertising. There are no old counterparts to any of the RRP lard tubs with black-related subjects. All such pieces are modern fantasy products.

All glass tumblers and glass ashtrays are modern fantasy items. No vintage glass tumblers and ashtrays were ever made with the Coon Chicken Inn trademark.

The fantasy Coon Chicken Inn paper header on this bag of marbles was made with a home computer and color printer. No old counterpart exists.

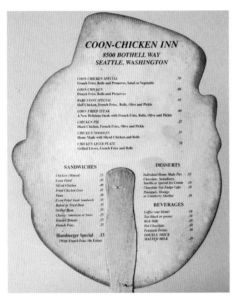

A new mass-produced menu in the form of a fan on a flat wood handle. The paper is stained by the manufacturer to appear old. Menus are one of the most widely reproduced Coon Chicken Inn items.

The reverse side of the new menu fan. Note the staining applied at the factory to make the menu appear old.

At least one (and maybe more) online seller is applying new Coon Chicken Inn decorations to genuinely old brown and white stoneware from the 1920s and 1930s. This includes items like covered jars, pitchers and jugs, such as the one on P. 11. There are no old counterparts to these items. No authentic pre-1957 Coon Chicken Inn bell hop decorations are applied to such stoneware. All the new decorations are applied overglaze. Almost any old piece of crockery of stoneware may turn up with the new decorations. It is hard to predict what shapes might be in the market.

Any glass item with the Coon Chicken Inn trademark should be purchased with extreme caution. ML Graham, grandson of the restaurant's founder, has flatly stated that all glass tumblers, for example, are fakes. "In all the original artifacts that we have of my grandparents' inns," said Graham, "there are no glass tumblers or glass ashtrays. I have seen many of them offered for sale, but they are all reproductions."

Several variations of new Coon Chicken Inn glass tumblers have been in the market for years. Some of the bell hop trademarks are simple black outlines with yellow trim. Others, like the example on P. 12, are more colorful. Some new tumblers are marked with various glass company names such as Anchor Hocking. Sellers sometimes claim such company marks indicate age, but those marks have no bearing on age. Anchor Hocking, Libbey and other manufacturers all commonly mark their new table glass. Forgers are simply applying new transfers to modern glass tumblers.

Other new glass with Coon Chicken Inn decorations include salt and pepper shakers in clear glass and colored glass, individual-size clear glass creamers, half-pint clear glass milk bottles and round clear glass ashtrays. Like the new tumblers, these other shapes in glass may also be marked with names of various glass makers, but those marks are no indication of age.

New paper items are one of the most frequently faked of all Coon Chicken Inn pieces. The new paper fakes fall into two broad categories: mass produced pieces made on printing presses and sold by reproduction wholesalers; and the smaller run do-it-yourself fakes printed on home- and office-quality inkjet and laser printers. Reproduction wholesalers have mass-produced menus in various forms for years. Virtually all Coon Chicken Inn hand fans in the market today are fakes. Similarly, the majority of Coon Chicken Inn postcards and posters found today are also mass-produced products distributed by reproduction wholesalers.

Do-it-yourself paper fakes are more difficult to categorize because they come in almost countless forms limited only by forgers' imaginations. The Coon Chicken Inn trademark has been found on everything from paper headers on "advertising" marbles to faces of watches and alarm clocks. Other frequently found homemade paper fakes include letterheads and envelopes, paper inserts inside glass paperweights and backs of pocket mirrors. New paper inserts have also been placed in men's rings and money clips.

Hambone Cigars

Back in October 2001, ACRN reported a fake 10-inch porcelain plate advertising J.P. Alley's Hambone 5¢ Cigars. At that time, no information was available on any old counterparts. A family descendant with connections to the original Hambone brand recently offered ACRN additional information on this subject.

The Hambone brand was manufactured for J.P. Alley by W.C. Frutiger & Co. of Red Lion, Pennsylvania. Frutiger was a cigar factory, which specialized in private labels. It was in operation from the early 1900s until the factory closed in the late 1960s. For federal tax purposes, the Frutiger factory was licensed as Factory #417 in the First District of Pennsylvania.

The family member who contacted ACRN provided an example of the original Hambone artwork shown on P. 15, above right. The piece shown is a 7-inch cardboard sign printed in color on both sides. It was designed to be suspended from ceilings in tobacco shops and other retail locations where cigars were sold. This form of sign was widely used to advertise cigars from the 1920s to 1950s and is referred to in the trade as a "drop."

The family member who contacted ACRN confirmed the porcelain plate is a modern fake. It is unlike anything associated with the original Frutiger factory or original Hambone brand advertising.

New glass jar with new paper label, "J.P. Alley's Hambone Cigars." The original Hambone cigar was manufactured by W.C. Frutiger & Co. of Red Lion, Pennsylvania.

A fantasy 10" porcelain plate, "Hambone Cigars." Some new plates have fake Buffalo Pottery marks.

The fantasy "Hambone Cigars" plate was copied from this original cardboard hanging sign. All porcelain plates are new; no vintage counterparts exist.

The new paper in the Hambone label fluoresces brightly under long wave black light. Paper made since the 1950s with modern bleaches and chemicals almost always fluoresce under long wave black light. Paper made before the 1940s rarely fluoresces.

New range-size shakers are a close copy of vintage originals by Pearl China. You can separate old from new by overall size, decoration and filling holes.

The whites of the eyes, the lips and the headscarf on the original cook, at right, are all cold painted over the glaze.

The whites of the eyes, the lips and the headscarf on the new cook, left, are all applied under the glaze.

Filling holes in the bases of all old shakers, right, are very nearly a perfectly smooth 1" circle. New filling holes, left, in the 1990s reproductions are only about the size of a dime.

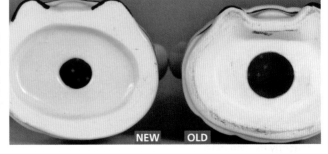

Kitchen and Household Items

Some of the best vintage kitchen shakers were made by Pearl China. The most expensive are the range-size male chef and female cook. Because of the value of originals, this set has been reproduced since the early 1990s. New and improved copies began appearing in 2004. The quickest way to identify the reproductions is to look at the holes in the base where original shakers were filled with salt or pepper. Filling holes in original range-sized shakers are nearly 1-inch in diameter

NEW

These new 6" figural ceramic banks are copied from a vintage original. The fakes started appearing in early 2003. Bases of the new ceramic banks are rubber stamped with a forged "MADE IN OCCUPIED JAPAN" mark.

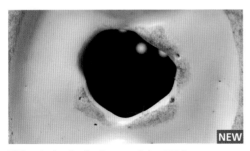

NEW

NEW

Filling holes in the bases of the 2004 reproductions of the cooks shakers on P. 16 are very irregular and out-of-round and frequently missing glaze.

This is the forged "Made in Japan" mark on the base of the new ceramic banks, above.

and are smooth rimmed, nearly perfect circles. Filling holes in reproductions are very distinctive. They are either particularly rough and irregular and or only about the size of a dime. These types of filling holes appear only on the fake range shakers, never on the originals. Trim on original Pearl range shakers—like the whites of eyes and red lips—were applied with paint over the glaze. Those details on the reproductions are under the glaze.

As a final check, measure a suspected shaker. Original figures are almost always one-quarter to one-half inch larger than the reproductions. Original chefs are 7-1/2 inches, original cooks are 6-3/4 inches; reproduction chefs are 7 inches; reproduction cooks are 6-1/2 inches.

One of the more confusing ceramic pieces recently reproduced is a new ceramic mammy bank now being sold with "Made in Occupied Japan" stamped on the base, shown on P. 17. The new banks are copied from a vintage ceramic bank made in Japan from the late 1930s through the mid-1950s. Vintage originals sell for $60-$95; the new copies wholesale for $10 each.

There are several ways to separate new from old. The most obvious difference is that the reproductions have a hole, or trap, in the base to remove the coins. Originals have closed bases and had to be broken open to get the money. New banks are decorated under the glaze; old banks are cold painted over the glaze. No vintage bank in this style has ever been found with an Occupied Japan mark.

Another hard-to-detect fake is the pincushion shown on P. 19. The upper body is cast in a white resin that looks very similar to plaster. It has been chipped at the factory in a random pattern to let the white resin show through the paint just like natural paint wear appears. The cushion is made from old-appearing patterns in a fabric that has been discolored by brown staining. Pins are included and are of various sizes and heads.

If you encountered this piece online or at a show, how can you tell it's new? About the only substantial clues we discovered were revealed under black light. The apron in particular, and the red paint to a lesser extent, both fluoresced brightly under long wave black light. New thread also fluoresced brightly. This piece is absolutely one of the harder to detect pieces of new black memorabilia we've encountered. It's currently retailing for only $20.

New mammy pin cushion, about 6" x 6". The fabric in the new cushion is stained and soiled to suggest age.

Despite the stained new fabric appearing brown in room lighting, the apron fluoresces bright white under black light. The paint on the lips also fluoresces.

CHINA AND PORCELAIN

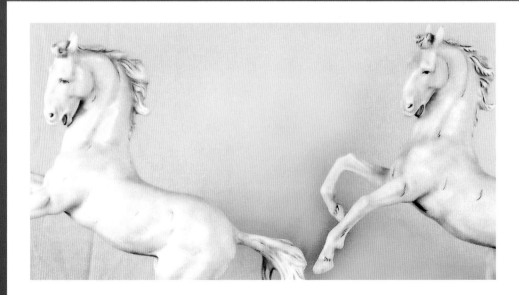

New bisque figures are being made in original German molds dating from the late 19th through the first third of the 20th century. Subjects now being made in the old molds include bathing beauties, snowbabies, black figures, animals, half-dolls, character figures including Mickey Mouse and Kewpies, piano babies, Santas, and figures in blimps, early airplanes and early autos. Shapes include jars, dolls, toothpick holders, vases, figures, holiday ornaments, doll heads and parts and a variety of other vintage forms.

The great majority of the old molds were originally used by the Weiss, Kuhnert & Co. factory of Grafenthal, Germany which began business in 1891. After World War II, the factory was nationalized by the East German communist government (German Democratic Republic). The firm continued to manufacture goods under various names through the postwar years but struggled after the decline of communism in the late 1980s.

The Weiss, Kuhnert molds were discovered in a warehouse by Roland Schegel, a German, and Susan Bickert of the United States. The two became partners and formed The German Doll Company in 1998 to put the molds back in production. The company contracted with Walendorf Porcelain Factory to manufacture new bisque figures from the old molds. Since new pieces are made from original molds, they carry the same molded marks as vintage pieces made from the same molds. The new examples, the mermaid figures on P. 23, for example, have "Germany" plus a four digit number molded in the bases. These marks are virtually identical to those commonly found on genuinely old German bisque.

The German Doll Company, to its credit, does at least apply a blue ink backstamp (shown on P. 22 at bottom right) to bases of the new bisque. Unfortunately, the ink stamps are easily removed with ordinary items found in your kitchen or a craft store. With the ink stamp removed, only the original-appearing molded marks remain. Marks alone are no longer a reliable single test of determining age.

Molded detail also appears about the same on new pieces as old pieces. There is some slight differences but no more than old pieces differ from other old pieces. Molded detail is more closely related to when a particular piece was made in a mold's life. Pieces made in a new mold generally have sharper detail than those made after the mold has been in use for a long time regardless of the year of production. Painted details are also very similar between new and old. Hand-painted details on the new mermaid faces in the photos on P. 23 are about the same quality as hand-painted details on old faces. New pieces are decorated in soft subdued colors very similar to vintage pieces.

So far, there is no easy way to separate old from new. Probably one of the best clues to age is the feel of the surface. Virtually all old pre-1940 German bisque is very smooth to the touch. The vast majority of new bisque, especially reproductions of antique bisque, is much rougher. Although this is not easily described in words or photos, the difference is quite obvious with a little experience. Seek out and handle some pieces known to be old. You shouldn't have too much trouble detecting the new pieces you'll now find showing up at malls, shows and auctions. But even checking the smoothness of the surface is not a completely reliable test of age. Several common abrasives make new surfaces feel almost identical to old surfaces and leave no visible traces of tool marks or other telltale signs. The new bisque, like many other reproductions, is a legitimate product and honestly sold as new by the manufacturer. But after being slightly altered, the new pieces are crossing into the antique market and offered as old. New figures are currently being distributed throughout Europe and the United States. You can expect to find pieces offered for sale anywhere. Don't assume pieces you find in a London, England street fair or on a Berlin, Germany Web site are automatically beyond suspicion.

This is the impressed mark "Germany 7240" on the back of the new mermaid in the top photo, P. 23. This style of mark is virtually identical to marks on vintage German bisque made ca. 1880-1930.

This is the mark of The German Doll Co. It is on the bottoms of new bisque mermaid pieces. It appears as a blue ink stamp. Actual size is 3/8" tall.

New bisque mermaid on alligator from original mold. Blond hair, hand-painted features; 3" tall. Impressed mark, "Germany 7245," on the back.

New bisque mermaid on seashell. Hand-painted features; 3" tall. Impressed with "Germany" and a four-digit number on the back.

New bisque piece by the German Doll Company, marked with an impressed "Germany" created in the old mold. Also stamped with the new blue logo, center right.

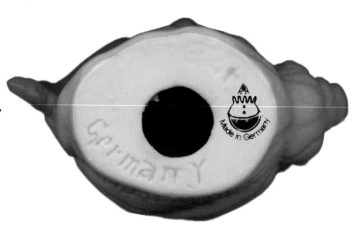

The new blue stamp has been removed leaving only the apparently old impressed mark "Germany."

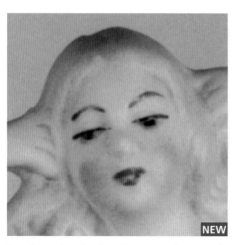

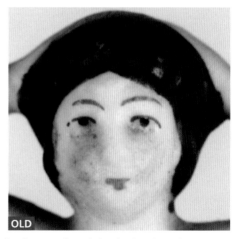

Details are hand painted on new pieces as shown in the new face, left. The brushstrokes on the new face are about the same as those appearing on the old face, right. Actual size of both faces are about 3/8" from chin to top of head.

"Delft"

"Delft" has traditionally been a term to describe earthenware coated with a white tin glaze, hand painted with blue decoration, and fired at a low temperature. This type of ware was first made in Italy in the 15th and 16th centuries as an attempt to imitate the white-bodied *porcelain* then being imported at great cost from China. Early decorations were similar to those on Oriental samples. By the mid-19th century, production had spread into Europe.

The word Delft is taken from the Dutch city of Delft, which became one of the leading manufacturers of white-bodied ware with bold blue decorations. Delft made from the mid-19th century forms the majority of authentic pieces in the antiques market today. It is a hard-bodied material, not the soft-bodied material of earlier 16th and 17th century Delft. Although not entirely accurate, the term Delft today is commonly used to describe almost any blue-decorated ceramics with Dutch scenes.

Generic Delft plaques and plates like the examples shown on the following pages have been offered in antique reproduction wholesale catalogs virtually unchanged for more than 30 years. Most reproduction Delft has backstamps and marks that deliberately suggest pieces are much older than their recent manufacture. The great majority of marks on the reproduction Delft do not have any old counterparts. They are entirely fantasy marks.

Separating new from old is fairly simple. First, as a general rule, any mark that includes the word "Delfts" with an "s" is new—that is, less than 30 to 40 years old. Some of the most commonly found new marks are shown on the following pages. Always beware of generic names used in marks, such as "Delfts," "Staffordshire," "Flow Blue" and other similar names. Such words are used by collectors to describe *categories* of wares, not specific companies. Reproduction manufacturers try to capitalize on that name recognition by creating marks incorporating those words.

Another way to separate new from old is based on how the pieces are decorated. All old pieces of Delft—mid-19th century through the 1920s—have *hand-painted* decoration with obvious brush strokes. The imitations made for the interior decoration and reproduction trades are *transfer-decorated* and do not show brush strokes. Most-machine printed transfers are made of dots and lines. Examining the decoration with a 10X loupe will clearly show what method of decoration was used.

New Delft is one of the most widespread reproductions. It appears in paid admission antique shows to flea markets in farm fields. Usually, the only difference is the asking price.

Prices at "better" shows are generally $250 to $500 for the large plaques; open-air entrepreneurs seem to be content with a more modest $50 to $100. Current wholesale for most new 16-inch plaques is $16 to $20.

New "Delft" platters from antique
reproduction wholesalers. Reproductions
like these have been offered virtually
without a change since the early 1960s.

Typical group of new Delft platters as shown in a 1970s reproduction wholesale catalog.

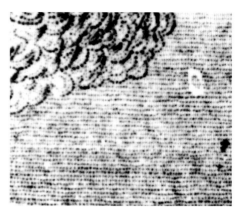

A close up of dot pattern in the transfer decoration applied to a typical piece of new Delft. Vintage Delft is decorated by hand painting, not transfers.

Virtually all genuine 19th century Delft, like this plaque, is hand painted with obvious brush strokes. With few exceptions, almost all Delft reproductions are decorated with transfers (decals), not painted.

Imitation artist "signatures" are found on many Delft reproductions. The new signatures are applied as a transfer, not hand painted like original artist signatures.

A new mark from the 1960s to 1970s. Note that "Delfts" ends in an "s." Mark reads, "Made for Royal Copenhagen by Boch."

A new mark used from the mid-1970s through the late 1980s. Note that "Delfts" ends in an "s." Mark reads, "Royal Sphinx Maastricht, Made in Holland, Delfts." Signature under Sphinx is "P. Regout." This new mark is loosely based on an original turn-of-century Maastricht mark shown in the photo at bottom right on P. 28.

New mark used since the late 1980s. "Delfts" has been removed from the bottom of the mark. This mark is on a wide variety of reproductions like Blue Willow, Pink Luster, Imari, Flow Blue and others.

Mark on new Delft made for the decorator trade in 2004. Note that Delfts still includes an "s." Although the mark includes "Handpainted," everything other than the rims were decorated with transfers. "Handpainted" never appears on any vintage pieces of Delft.

MADE IN HOLLAND

Vintage mark of De Sphinx pottery, Maastricht, Holland; found on a variety of transfer decorated wares, ca. 1890 to 1920s. This mark was copied for the fantasy new mark shown in the photo at bottom right on P. 27.

Regimental German beer steins

Perhaps no other collectible is so shrouded in myth, misinformation and mistaken identity as German regimental steins. These pieces have been steadily reproduced since the 1960s. Most experts agree reproductions far out number authentic examples, yet few buyers other than stein specialists know how to identify the fakes.

The majority of authentic German regimental beer steins were produced between about 1890 and 1914.

During this time, military service was compulsory in German. Most men would take basic training between ages 17 and 20 and then enter the reserves until age 40. A group of men would enter a unit together, stay in the same unit for training and be discharged as a unit. This sense of togetherness fostered the custom of buying souvenirs with the unit name, insignias and decorations as a keepsake of military service. Many souvenir items were available such as pipes, clocks, flasks and especially steins. Rosters of names from your unit, or regiment, could be added to the steins and these became known to collectors as "regimental steins."

Two reproduction regimental German beer steins. Reproductions like these have been in the market since the 1960s.

A vintage regimental German beer stein. New steins are close copies but details of construction and decoration are reliable tests of age.

Authentic ca. 1890-1914 steins were available in pottery, porcelain, glass and metal. Regardless of what the stein was made of, almost all had pewter lids. The most common sizes are half-litre and one-litre. The beginning of World War I effectively ended the production of regimental steins as labor and materials were diverted to the war.

The great majority of mass-produced new regimental steins sold by reproduction wholesalers are made of porcelain. Although there are other reproductions out there, this discussion will cover only porcelain reproductions since those are the most common.

One of the first tests you can conduct is to look inside the stein while holding the base up to a light. Many original porcelain steins and almost all reproduction porcelain steins have a lithophane in the base. If the lithophane

One of the typical lithophane scenes in bases of reproduction. Female nudes and erotic lithophanes are never found in vintage regimental steins.

One of the most common lithophanes found in new regimental steins made ca. 1960-1980. No vintage regimental stein has lithophanes with nudes or erotic scenes.

shows a nude woman, a partially undressed woman or a man and woman in an erotic scene, the stein is almost certainly a reproduction. No lithophanes with nudes or erotic scenes ever appear in vintage regimental steins.

Typical original regimental lithophanes feature a man and his wife or sweetheart, one or two women reading a letter, or drinking and tavern scenes. Although some new lithophanes may be somewhat similar to vintage images, new lithophanes almost always lack detail, are poorly designed and almost always look awkward.

Next to erotic lithophanes, the most obvious sign of a new regimental stein is a "bump" on the inside of the handle. Similar bumps are never found on original handles; original handles are smooth on the inside. About 80 to 90 percent of new regimental steins have the bump.

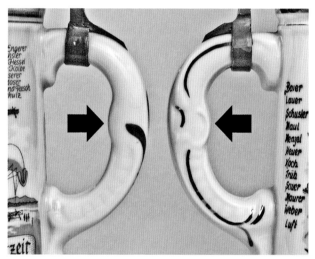

The great majority of new regimental steins have "bumps" on the inside of the handle. Smooth handles are a guarantee of age, but bumps are a warning sign of a reproduction.

Owners' names on new steins like this example are applied with a decal (transfer). The owner's name on authentic regimental steins is hand painted.

The outside of a genuinely old metal lid, right, is almost always darker than the inside of the lid, shown below right. Many new lids, like the one at left, are the same color on both the outside and inside, shown below left. There is less oxidation of the inside than the outside in normal use. Although not a guarantee of authenticity, a lid that is darker on the outside than it is on the inside is usually a positive sign of age.

Many new lids, like the example at left, are the same color on both the inside and outside. This is because the entire lid has been treated with chemicals to "age" the lid with a dark patina. The inside of an original lid, right, is almost always lighter than the outside of the lid.

Most new regimental steins have 19th and early 20 century dates. This new stein is dated 1910.

The same rosters are often repeated among new steins regardless of the branch of service depicted. The roster found on a cavalry stein, for example, may also be used on a stein purportedly from an infantry regiment. In these examples, the roster from the left is repeated in the stein on the right.

This new roster includes the first name of each solider fully spelled out (Fritz, Kurt, Hans, etc). Authentic rosters virtually never include first names spelled out.

This new example combines symbols of three services: the infantry (soldier), air service (airplanes) and navy (anchor). Service symbols and insignias are never combined on authentic steins.

Historical mistakes are common on new steins. The Graf Zeppelin was a civilian passenger airship built in 1928, 10 years after WW I ended in 1918. Why does it appear on a regimental stein dated 1910?

Original metal lids are generally cast and fairly heavy. Many new lids are stamped and quite thin. Many new lids, especially those intentionally misrepresented, are chemically treated to create a dark patina. The inside of these new treated lids look the same as the outside, usually uniformly dark. The exposed outside surface of original lids is generally darker than the protected inside surface, which is lighter. While a lighter color inside a lid does not guarantee a stein is old, a lid of uniformly even color inside and out is generally a sign of a fake.

New lids are made in relatively few designs. Manufacturers typically use the same lid and simply change the finial from stein to stein. If a seller offers several steins and all the lids are the same, it could be a sign the steins are new. Finials on vintage lids match the branch of service shown on the body of the stein. A horse-mounted cavalry figure, for example, would never be used as a finial if naval or infantry symbols were on the stein body.

Lists of names, or rosters, are frequently repeated on new steins. If the roster from an infantry stein is repeated on an artillery stein, both steins are obviously suspicious. Some new rosters include first names. Rosters on original regimental steins virtually never include first names, usually only last names and rank. Generally, the stein owner's name, prominently featured by itself somewhere on the stein, should also be found in the roster on authentic regimentals. Original rosters can have as few as three to four names but rarely more than 90 to 100 names. The number of names also varies on new rosters so the number of names is not a reliable test of authenticity. Original rosters can be either hand painted or a transfer. Rosters on mass produced reproductions are always a transfer.

The stein owner's name is hand painted on original steins but applied with a transfer on the reproductions. Within a group of new steins, the same owner's name often appears on steins from different branches of service. The spelling of German cities on many new steins has been converted to English. For example: Munich is the English spelling of München; Cologne is the English version of Koln. Authentic steins will have the German spelling. Don't be confused by dates from the late and early 20th centuries. Virtually all reproduction steins have such dates in one or more locations prominently featured around the top rim or front of the body. Dates may also be worked into the decorations on the sides.

Decorations in many new steins have mistakes obvious to anybody with an elementary knowledge of history and geography. In the photo on P. 34 of the Graf Zeppelin, for example, "Graf Zeppelin" appears on the airship in huge letters relative to the size of the ship. First, military combat airships were never painted with such large names. Second, the Graf Zeppelin was a civilian passenger ship constructed in 1928. WW I ended in 1918. How could "Graf Zeppelin" appear

Decorations on virtually all new regimental steins, like this example, are applied entirely as decals (transfers). Decorations on virtually all authentic regimental steins include at least some hand painting particularly to highlight details on uniforms such as buttons, buckles, insignias and medals.

New regimental steins as shown in a 1972 reproduction wholesale catalog. All these steins have lithophanes with nude scenes in the bottom.

GW/2402 MILITARY STEINS

on a stein purportedly made before 1918? Finally, the flag on the airship is the flag of Yugoslavia, not Germany.

One of the most common mistakes in decorations on reproductions is the mixing of the different branches of service. The new decoration shown on P. 34, for example, combines three different branches of service. The solider is dressed in an infantry uniform but stands next to an anchor-a naval symbol-and airplanes circle in the background. Decorations on authentic regimental steins always depict one and only one service branch. Any decoration that combines two or more branches is virtually certain to be a reproduction.

The majority of authentic porcelain regimental steins were not marked with a country or manufacturer. Reproduction porcelain steins can be found unmarked or marked "Germany" or "West Germany." Any piece marked West Germany, of course, proves the piece was made after 1945. However, since East and West Germany have reunited, the single word "Germany" is again used as a mark. When considering regimental steins, marks alone are not a reliable test of age.

No mass-reproduced regimental stein has ever been found that is completely authentic. There are always mistakes in uniforms, headgear, unit insignias, dates and location of service and other details. Regimental stein specialists have access to German and Bavarian military records. If there is still a question after applying the general guidelines offered here, consult a regimental specialist who has access to those records.

Authentic porcelain regimental steins are virtually never marked Germany. Most, but not all, new porcelain steins made from about 1960 through the 1980s are marked "West Germany" or "Germany."

Royal Dux

Duxer Porzellanmanufaktur, or Dux Porcelain Manufactory, was started in 1860 by Eduard Eichler in what was then Duchov, Bohemia. The pottery and porcelain figures produced there are now generally referred to as "Royal Dux." Many original 19th century molds have remained in production throughout the company's over 150-year history and continue to be used into the 21st century. Collectors need to separate not only new and old pieces of genuine Royal Dux, but weed out the many fakes and forgeries in the market.

Two Royal Dux 12" horses. Both have the same raised pink triangle mark, yet the one on the right is about twice as old as the new piece on the left. The pink triangle mark on the horse at left is shown at the top of P. 39. The mark on the original horse is shown below.

1st Period, ca. 1860-WWI

A line drawing of the oldest raised triangle mark. "Royal Dux Bohemia" appears around an oval with the letter "E" in the center. The letter in the triangle changes over the years.

A photo of the earliest raised triangle mark. Note that all lettering is impressed.

2nd Period, ca. 1919-WWII

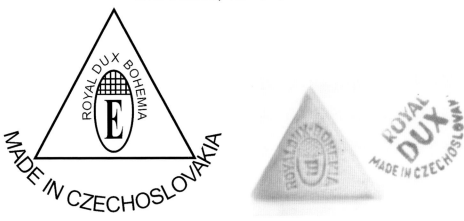

Around 1919, "Made in Czechoslovakia" was added. The letter "E" and "Royal Dux Bohemia" remain in the triangle. "Made in Czechoslovakia" may be ink stamped or impressed; the exact location of the words varies. The mark is shown here in a line drawing and a photo.

3rd Period, ca. 1947-1990

The letter "E" is removed from the pink triangle and replaced by the letter "D." "Royal Dux Bohemia" continues to appear around the oval. The raised pink triangle remains the same color and size. The mark is shown here in a line drawing and a photo.

Marks begin to be stamped in black, blue or dark green ink. This mark includes "D" and "Royal Dux Bohemia" in the triangle. The lettering "Hand Painted, Made in Czechoslovakia" runs around the triangle.

4th Period, since 1990

After 1990, "Czech Republic" and symbols for copyright, ©, and registration, ®, begin to appear in marks. More pieces begin to be marked with ink stamps. Marks begin to vary widely.

The raised pink triangle is used less frequently on pieces made after 1990, but is still in use.

Since the 1990s, many pieces are marked with paper labels like this in addition to ink backstamps.

Pieces made since 1990s are again being marked "Made in Czechoslovakia." If the mark in the triangle is "D," it's new. If the mark appears without a triangle, it cannot be taken as a guarantee of age.

A frog paperweight in shiny glaze, trimmed in gold. This is marked with raised pink triangle with "D" (at top right) and stamped ink mark (shown at right). Note the modern ® symbol.

This new 6-1/2" vase made since 2000 is marked with a gold foil label "Royal Dux Bohemia" and a green ink backstamp "Royal Dux Made in Czechoslovakia," both shown at right.

This is the forged raised triangle found on the vase shown at right. This triangle is made of white clay painted dark pink. The white clay shows through in the lower left part of the triangle. All original pink triangles are made of pink clay with the color throughout the body of the triangle. Old raised pink triangles are never painted.

A new 16" vase with Art Nouveau nude, marked with the forged triangle at top left. This vase is a crude pottery with vase walls nearly one-half inch thick. Genuine Royal Dux is porcelain rarely over one-eighth inch thick except for bases of statuary, which are made slightly thicker.

The new figurine above is made of thick heavy pottery and has the forged mark at right. Original Royal Dux is porcelain and rarely over one-eighth inch thick. The forged raised pink triangle is carefully made of pink clay and is a thick, rough-textured slab unlike the thin original pink triangles with a smooth finish.

Generally, most factory pieces can be dated by examining the company's traditional triangle mark. The best known form of the Royal Dux triangle is probably the raised ceramic pink triangle found on bases. But authentic marks may also be impressed or ink stamped depending on when the piece was produced.

Appearing in all genuine factory triangles, regardless of age or how they are applied, is "Royal Dux Bohemia." That lettering appears around an oval shaped symbol in the center of the triangle. A crosshatch, or grid-like pattern, is at the top of the oval. Even though the country of Bohemia disappeared at the end of WW I, "Royal Dux Bohemia" remains in the mark to this day.

Authentic factory-made Royal Dux can be divided into four broad periods of production: 1860 to WW I; 1919 to WW II; 1947 to 1990 and from 1990 to the present. Each of the four periods of production can be roughly identified by changes in the triangle mark. In the first period, 1860 to WW I, the letter "E," for Eichler, the founder's surname, appears in the center of the triangle. The letter in the triangle changes over the years so it's important to keep in mind that "E" is the earliest mark. A convenient way to remember this is by word association: "E is for Early." See photos on pages 38-41.

Following the end of WW I, Bohemia was united with Slovakia and Moravia to form Czechoslovakia. This change was reflected in the phrase "Made in Czechoslovakia," which began appearing in Royal Dux marks around 1919. "Made in Czechoslovakia" never appears in the triangle, but is impressed or ink stamped near the triangle. The letter "E" and "Royal Dux Bohemia" continue to appear in the triangle.

At the end of WW II, Russia continued to occupy Czechoslovakia and nationalized Czechoslovakian industries including Royal Dux. Around 1946-47, the factory was renamed Duchcovsky Porcelain after the regional name of Duchov. The letter "E" was removed from the triangle at this time and replaced by the letter "D" representing Duchov. "Made in Czechoslovakia" was discontinued in marks.

With the collapse of the Soviet Union in the early 1990s, Royal Dux returned to private ownership and Czechoslovakia renamed itself "Czech Republic." Royal Dux marks continued to use the "D" inside the triangle. Printed marks, though, begin to include not only "Made in Czech Republic" but also began using "Made in Czechoslovakia," previously used only on pre-WW II pieces.

Here are a few general guidelines that will help you identify most 1990s pieces. First, any piece marked with the modern copyright symbol, ©, or modern registered symbol, ®, are from the 1990s. Any piece marked "Czech Republic" cannot be older than 1990-1991 at most. Pieces with a gold foil label with a letter D in the center are also from the 1990s. Pieces marked "Made in Czechoslovakia"—made before or after 1990—can in no instance possibly date before 1919 at the earliest, the end of WW I. Any piece with a "D" in the triangle cannot date any earlier than 1947 at the earliest.

Generally, pieces with a letter "E" impressed in a raised pink triangle with no other marks other than shape numbers or decorators marks, are still very likely to have been made before 1919. Pink triangles on these pieces are generally bisque. Pieces with "E" impressed in a raised pink triangle and also marked "Made in Czechoslovakia" impressed or ink stamped, most likely date between the world wars, 1919-1939.

Besides separating confusing marks and pieces made at the Royal Dux factory, buyers must also contend with fakes and forgeries. Some fakes are quite ambitious, going so far as to copy the raised pink triangles. There are several clues to help you detect these and most other forged triangles. First, all authentic pink Royal Dux triangles—whether from the 19th, 20th or 21st century factories—are made from a separate piece of pink clay. The pink color is throughout the body of the triangle. Many fake triangles are simply painted pink, not made of pink clay. Most fake triangles are cast with the entire new object, not made separately and applied. Marks on authentic triangles are generally sharp and well defined; marks on many forged triangles are blurred and illegible. The depth to which letters are impressed on most fake triangles vary greatly. Letters in genuine triangles are impressed to almost exactly the same depth across the triangle.

Marks on any piece offered as pre-1919 Royal Dux must be examined very carefully. Even if you believe you can correctly date a piece, you should still request a written receipt that includes the approximate date of production. Nobody can say with any certainty what marks may have been applied to factory-made Royal Dux since the mid-1990s.

Transfer Ware
Ironstone, Flow Blue, Staffordshire

Flow Blue, Blue Willow, Ironstone and Staffordshire are all names of various wares decorated with underglaze transfer designs, many in cobalt blue. Many new pieces have patterns identical, or at least very similar, to authentic 19th century patterns. New pieces are also made in 19th century shapes such as tea caddies, toothbrush holders, pitchers and wash basins and others. Almost all the reproductions are also marked with symbols, trade names and words found in original 19th century marks. In other words, it is increasingly common to find more reproduction transfer ware with original appearing patterns on close copies of 19th century shapes and with what appear to be marks of well-known 19th century manufacturers. Knowing just a few basic differences between new and old will help you detect and avoid the great majority of these confusing copies.

Decorating ceramics with printed transfers was developed in the middle of the 18th century as a substitute for expensive hand painting. Low cost, mass-produced transfer ware made decorated china affordable to middle-class families. Many transfer pieces are blue because cobalt blue was the best and least expensive pigment capable of withstanding the high temperatures of 18th and 19th century kilns. Blue was also the color of decoration used in expensive hand-painted porcelain imported from China. From a distance, factory-made blue transfer resembled porcelain used by the wealthy upperclass. Of all the blue transfer ware, only Flow Blue was made slightly different than the other blue transfer wares. The ink and ceramic blanks of Flow Blue were deliberately designed to allow the ink to "flow," or spread, into the blank. The spreading ink creates the typical blurred or distorted Flow Blue effect.

Contrary to a commonly held opinion, shape is not always a positive proof of age. Many reproductions are direct copies of original 19th century shapes like chamber pots, toothbrush holders, sugar jars, and even rare shapes like shaving basins. The general exceptions are fantasy shapes, shapes and forms never made in the 19th century. Typical fantasy shapes include pieces like the Flow Blue reamer and Blue Willow oil lamp shown in this section. Other exceptions are not so easily detected and require specialized knowledge. Original Ringtons Tea teapots, for example, are a low, oblong shape. New Ringtons teapots, like the one on P. 49 and a similarly shaped new teapot with a longer spout not shown, are unlike any original shape. Fortunately, the new Ringtons Tea items can be detected by other features such as glaze, construction and marks.

For example, virtually all vintage blue transfer wares are fully glazed. This includes inside and outside surfaces and top and bottom rims and rims of lids. This is logical for practical daily use—unglazed areas would permit water to get behind the glaze and destroy the surface. Dirt and grease could also penetrate unglazed areas and make dinnerware impossible to clean. Reproductions aren't made for practical use, though; they are made as "antiques," objects to be looked at, not used. That's why the vast majority of new blue transfer pieces are not glazed in critical areas.

With few exceptions, most blue transfer reproductions have broad, unglazed standing rims. It is not uncommon on even relatively small shapes, such as hatpin holders, to have unglazed rims a 1/2 inch to 3/4 inch wide. Despite most reproductions having glaze over the new marks, the glaze does not extend to the new flat standing rims. The vast majority of originals are fully glazed and rest on very narrow, raised standing rims seldom wider than 1/8 inch,

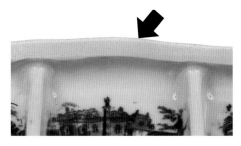 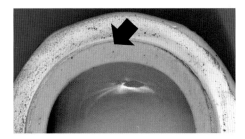

Inside rims on vintage pieces are generally glazed. Inside rims of most reproductions, like these two examples, are not glazed. An inside rim of a toothbrush holder is shown at left; the inside rim of a teapot is at right.

A new food mold, 6-1/2" x 4". No food molds are known in 19th century blue transfer ware. The inset shows the mold design, a turkey or peacock-like bird.

A new 11" platter has a seal with a Latin motto.

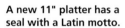

This new two-piece reamer is a fantasy shape, since no old pieces in this shape exist.

A new Ironstone-style 12" plate, available in several single colors including blue, pink and brown transfer design.

sometimes only 1/16 inch on small items.

Unglazed rims on new lids are especially obvious. It is not unusual for new lids to have a 1/2 inch wide unglazed rim. The top rims in new teapot bodies are also usually unglazed. Apparently, any area which doesn't show in the reproductions is left unglazed. All the items with lids shown in this section—chamber pot, reamer, tea jars, etc.—have wide, unglazed rims on their lids with matching wide unglazed rims on which they rest.

New glazes on the majority of the reproductions generally have a definite blue to blue-green tint. Glazes on original 19th century blue transfer wares in good condition generally have white backgrounds without a strong color tint. Originals that do have a tint are usually off-white or gray, not the obvious blue-green of the reproductions. The blue-green tint is most obvious on the earthenware-bodied reproductions made in China since the mid-1990s. Many Japanese-made reproductions in true porcelain show virtually no tint.

One final factor to consider when evaluating construction is to inspect all handles, knobs and finials. These features on originals are solid; they were made as separate pieces and attached to the main body. Many, but not all, reproductions with blue transfers are made by slip casting. Slip cast pieces are made in a one-piece mold, which includes handles, knobs and finials as part of the overall piece. Slip cast handles, knobs and finials are hollow; there will be a hole where they join the body or a lid. This is particularly true of reproductions from Japan and Europe. Recent imports from China do have separately applied solid handles, knobs and finials like originals. That is why it is always important to use several tests before making a judgment on age and authenticity.

The majority of new marks are either direct copies of originals or based on the general appearance of originals. Perhaps the most striking difference between new and old marks is size. Many new marks average 2 inches to 3 inches across

A new 8" Blue Willow sugar pot. The background is factory "distressed" to an off-white, slightly brown color.

New version of very rare original shape. Called either a shaving basin or barber's bowl, the crescent-shaped opening would be placed against a man's neck under his chin. The bowl held warm water.

A new 8" covered box; the shape is copied from a 19th century toothbrush holder.

Blue transfer reproductions from the 1970s to 1980s frequently have hollow handles. These are formed by slip casting. Handles on original pieces are solid. This is only a partial test; blue transfer reproductions made in China since the mid-1990s have solid handles like originals.

Virtually all new blue transfer ware has an overall blue or blue-green tint in the glaze. Backgrounds of original blue transfer ware, Blue Willow, Flo Blue or Staffordshire, are essentially white overall without blue or blue-green tints. Above are the undersides of typical new and old plates: new on top; old, bottom.

The bottom of a typical reproduction with unusually wide unglazed standing rim. This unglazed rim is about 3/4" in width, about average for the reproductions.

A new 8" Blue Willow tea jar with the new Ringtons mark, shown below.

A new 8" Blue Willow teapot marked Ringtons on the base as shown at right. This is a fantasy shape; originals are low and oblong-shaped.

The new mark on the teapot shown at left and new jar, above. This new mark is nearly identical to an original mark used from 1928 to 1955. The original mark includes "Maling Ware." See P. 53.

These reproduction transfers are virtually exact copies of old original patterns of Blue Willow, above, Flow Blue, right, and Ironstone, below.

New 8" jar, a multicolored transfer print similar to original Ironstone-type decoration.

New Blue Willow pattern 4-1/2" dia. oil burning lamp. The oil lamp is a fantasy shape; no 19th century counterpart exists.

regardless of the size of the piece on which they appear. Virtually no original mark approaches those dimensions. Most authentic marks on 19th century blue transfer wares are rarely over 1 inch. In other words, old marks are almost always about the size of a quarter and virtually never larger than a half-dollar. Any mark larger than a half-dollar is extremely suspicious and almost certain to be new.

The next most obvious group of new marks is those that include modern symbols such as trademark (™), registered trademark (®) and copyright (©). Any mark with those symbols is almost certainly to have been made since the 1950s, definitely made after 1900, usually not used until the 1920s at the earliest. Those symbols are particularly useful when dating the products of legitimate potteries that are in business today under the same name as their Victorian founders such as Masons, Ridgway, Royal Doulton, and others. Other obviously modern terms to avoid are "detergent proof," "oven safe," "dishwasher safe," and, of course, "microwave safe."

The next test is to look for generic names in the mark. No one ever walked into a 19th century china shop and said, "Excuse me, my good man, kindly direct me to the Flow Blue." Flow Blue, Historical Staffordshire and other names are generic terms coined by modern antiques collectors. Such terms were never used in original 19th century marks. These words have been included in fake marks to suggest age and quality.

The only exception is "Ironstone," which was originally a late-18th century trade name. By the mid-19th century, however, it entered the language as a generic term and has continued in that use to the present day. Original 19th century marks with "Ironstone" virtually never appear without a company name, such as "Mason's," "Woods & Sons" and other vintage makers.

The absence of key words in a mark is a valuable clue to age. For example, virtually all authentic 19th century blue transfer wares, with the exception of Blue Willow, are marked with the country of origin and company name. Marks on most, but not all, authentic 19th century Flow Blue, Historical Staffordshire and Ironstone also include pattern names. Pattern and company names were an important part of original marks because they helped customers order replacements and add to a service.

With few exceptions, marks on reproductions have no country of origin and no company name. The vast majority of new pieces are from China and that country's name usually appears as a removable paper label, which is quickly removed in the secondary market. Marks with no country of origin, pattern name or company name are almost certain to be of recent manufacture.

A new two-piece chamber pot, or slops bucket; 12" tall, 12" across handles.

OLD

OLD

Original Ringtons marks almost always include "Maling Ware" and "England," shown at left. So far, neither "Maling Ware" and "England" appears in any fake Ringtons mark. Almost all original Ringtons jars and tea pots have the company "R" and "T" monogram, at right, on the underside of the lids. This monogram has been missing in the reproductions.

NEW

Marks on new blue transfer ware are very large, frequently 2" to 3" across. Many new marks completely cover the bases of reproductions. See photos at right and below for a comparison to typical vintage marks.

OLD

Typical vintage marks, like these examples, are rarely over 1" across.

A new fantasy mark. No old mark includes terms used by present day antique collectors such as "Flo Blue."

A fantasy mark on ceramic reproductions from Japan. Used on pieces decorated with a wide variety of transfers including Flo Blue, Blue Willow, Ironstone, and Delft. The mark appears in dark blue, pink and brown.

Another new fantasy mark, blue underglaze. "Ironstone China" in banner. No company name, pattern name or country of origin.

New mark, blue underglaze. No factory or pattern name, no country of origin. The appearance of "Ironstone" in a mark is not a reliable indicator of age.

Contemporary mark of Mason's Ironstone. Identical to 19th century mark except for modern © symbol near the pattern name. "England" or "Made in England" did not appear within the old mark, only near the mark.

A mark found on new Touraine pattern Flow Blue. This new mark is the same as the old Stanley Pottery Co. mark, but "England" has been removed. See photo at right for the original.

Original mark on vintage Touraine pattern Flow Blue made by Stanley Pottery Co. The old mark includes the word "England." Both old and new include the British Registration number, 329815, issued in 1898. The original mark is about seven-eighths inch, top to bottom. The new mark is slightly smaller.

This mark found on new pieces with the Waldorf pattern is practically identical to marks on vintage pieces of Waldorf. The pattern name appears in a banner at top; the company name, New Wharf Pottery, appears below. Notice that the new mark does not include "England."

This original mark found on vintage pieces of Waldorf pattern made by New Wharf Pottery. The old mark includes the word "England." If you find a piece of Waldorf by New Wharf without "England," be very suspicious of the age.

NEW **OLD**

The new Dunn Bennett mark found on the new Iris pattern is not like any old Dunn Bennett mark yet found. Note that the new mark does not include "England."

Vintage Dunn Bennett beehive mark, used ca. 1875-1907. Marks vary slightly but almost always include "England" which is missing in the new mark.

This new mark resembles the authentic ca. 1912 mark of T. Rathbone & Co. The "pattern" name "Victor" appears in the banner below the swan. The new mark is very crude compared to the original. Also note the letter "I" at the end of "Co." The letters in the new mark look almost hand drawn rather than printed. Also notice the unusual ampersand between "R" and "Co." Although it almost certainly is being made in China, note the use of the word "England" in the new mark. A typical original T. Rathbone mark is shown in the photo below.

NEW

Genuine ca. 1912 mark of T. Rathbone & Co. There is usually a pattern name in the banner below the swan but not in this example. England generally appears near the authentic mark.

OLD

New "Chelsea" mark on Flow Blue reproductions (blurred from glaze.) No original counterpart to this mark is known.

Copy of British Royal Arms mark on reproductions from China. Latin motto in center shield; "Victoria Ware" in lower banner; "Ironstone" below. No country or company name. This mark has been found up to 3" wide.

Fantasy mark, no known old counterpart. "Stone Ware" in center shield, "Victoria" in banner. Very large, over 2" tall. Underglaze in blue. No company name or country of origin.

Copy of British Royal Arms mark on reproductions from China. "Victoria" in shield, "Ironstone" below. Note removable paper label at top. No country or factory name.

Copy of British Royal Arms mark used by Blakeney Pottery LTD, England. "Victory" in shield. Mark in use since 1968 on reproductions.

One of the most confusing new marks includes the name of a 19th century manufacturer, "E. & C. Challinor." Virtually identical copy of an original 19th century mark used ca. 1862-1991. New mark is 2-1/2" wide by 1-1/4" tall. The old original mark is rarely over 1-1/2" wide. Most, but not all original Challinor marks also include "England."

CIVIL WAR

B uyers need to be particularly cautious when evaluating American Civil War artifacts offered for sale. The increasing popularity of Civil War reenactments has led to an ever growing number of reproductions. Participants in the reenactments try to be as historically accurate as possible in their uniforms, weapons, personal effects and camping equipment. More and more of these otherwise legitimate replicas are being deliberately altered with the application of artificial patina, simulated wear and other modifications by unethical sellers and represented as period pieces in the antiques and collectibles market.

Many of these altered and modified pieces are complete fantasy products. That is to say, the pieces exist only as reproductions. No old counterparts were ever made. Similarly, many altered pieces are fabricated to appeal to Civil War collectors by adding specific features and details that have special appeal to collectors.

Since the late 1990s, for example, there has been a steady supply of faked brass belt buckles with various emblems and insignia of both Union and Confederate troops. Some enterprising forger decided to make these buckles even more attractive by adding a minnie ball. These new buckles with an embedded minnie ball are now sold as "battlefield relics" implying that the ball struck the buckle in a Civil War battle. Careful examination has shown that the buckles were first punched with the appropriate-sized hole and the ball pounded into the hole. In some cases, the minnie balls are genuinely old pieces either scavenged from battlefields or purchased from surplus vintage stock. The forger has used new buckles with a CS insignia knowing that Confederate States relics are generally scarcer and worth more than relics with Union insignias.

Very accurate copies of Civil War equipment made for re-enactment hobbyists, like this new wood canteen, are frequently drifting into the collectors' market.

Two CS, Confederate States, brass belt buckles with embedded vintage mini balls. Which is old? Neither; both are fakes. Many Civil War fakes, like these buckles, are one-of-a-kind forgeries. Don't expect all fakes to be identical in appearance.

Identification discs, silver pins

About the same time as the buckles began appearing, another group of creative fakes based on scarce original identification discs was filtering into the collectors' market. Identification tags, like the so-called "dog tags" of later wars, were never officially issued by armies of either side in the American Civil War. Without tags, soldiers killed in combat were difficult to identify and families could not be notified.

Soldiers of both sides resorted to making their own identification tags. Besides using odd scraps of wood, metal and other common materials, some tags were fashioned of commonly circulated coins. Identification tags made from coins are referred to by collectors as "ID discs." Original ID discs from a famous soldier, a solider in an historical unit or a soldier who fought in an important battle can sell for $5,000 to $12,000. In the late 1990s, multiple examples of ID discs made of silver dollars engraved with the name "Pender" began to surface. Since then other coins have been found inscribed with a variety of names. All of these recently found ID discs, sold at prices ranging from $200 to $1,000, are modern fakes.

According to Nancy Rossbacher, managing editor of *North South Trader's Civil War Magazine*, all the names found on the fake ID discs are of soldiers who actually existed. Dorsey Pender, for example, eventually reached general's rank. He died of a wound received in the second day's fighting at Gettysburg. Other names on the new coin ID discs include Col. Joseph Mayo, Jr., Robert F. Bunting of the 8th Texas Cavalry, James B. Washington and A.L.P Vairin. So far only ID discs related to Confederate forces have been reported. No discs have been reported with Union soldiers' names or Federal units. In addition to silver dollars, fake ID discs have also been made in the shape of silver half-dollars.

Peter Bertram, editor of *The Confederate Medals, Badges, Medals and Ribbons Newsletter*, has done an extensive analysis of the fake ID coin discs. He has noted several features by which the fakes can be detected. First, all the fake ID discs are smaller in diameter and weigh less than authentic coins. The new pieces are also oval in shape and have inconsistent reeding (the milling around the rim of the coins). A genuine US silver dollar, for example, is uniformly 38.1 millimeters in diameter, weighs 26.73 grams, is perfectly round and has a fully reeded rim. The fake silver dollar Mayo disc illustrates these points. Its oval shape is 36 millimeters wide by 37 millimeters high; its weight, 22 grams; and has only remnants of reeding around the edge.

One of the strongest indications of a fake disc is their extreme and uneven wear. If the discs were actually made during the Civil War, the coins could have been only two or three years old at the time of engraving, still relatively new for a metal coin. Yet the coins found with the engraved names exhibit the equivalent of many, many years of heavy use normally found on coins

A fake ID disc engraved "Lt. Col. Dorsey Pender, 1st North Carolina Regiment, CSA."

Obverse of the disc shown above, with a silver casting which imitates a die struck seated Liberty silver dollar. This is complete with an 1860 date and a New Orleans mint mark.

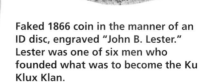

Faked 1866 coin in the manner of an ID disc, engraved "John B. Lester." Lester was one of six men who founded what was to become the Ku Klux Klan.

circulated in daily commerce. If the coins were actually used as ID discs and worn by a neck chain or carried as a pocket piece, there should be relatively little wear. Extreme wear is inconsistent with their purported original use which would have kept the relatively new coins in good condition.

Engravings on the fake discs are relatively well done and appear similar to period work. One clue that the engraving might be new is that authentic ID discs are almost always engraved with the letters "CS," not the letters "CSA," which are on the fakes. Similar faked coins have also been engraved with the names of founders of the Ku Klux Klan. Authentic Klan items are of interest to Civil War collectors because of the connection with Southern soldiers.

Like the fake Civil War identification discs, names used on the faked Klan items are historically accurate. One of the KKK discs, for example, is engraved with the name of Nathan Bedford Forrest. Forrest is best known to the public as the brilliant, if eccentric, Civil War Confederate cavalry commander. A slave trader, land speculator and cotton buyer before the war, Forrest made up for his lack of military experience with unorthodox, creative tactics. Less well known is that Forrest was the first Grand Wizard, or highest official of the KKK, who headed the first Klan convention in Nashville, Tennessee in 1867. Another important Klan name which also appears on a fake coin is Corporal John B. Lester. Lester was one of six men who met in Pulaski, Tennessee in 1866 to form the secret club that in a short time would become the KKK. Like the general ID discs discussed earlier, the engraved names on KKK "coins" are not made from genuinely old coins. The "coins" are cast, not die stamped as authentic coins are made. The same clues used to detect the fake ID discs can be used to catch the faked KKK discs.

While the new silver coins have at least some connection to vintage counterparts, there is an entire series of silver badges and pins with Civil War related subjects and themes that are pure fantasies. Among the pieces in this series are two badges. One is stamped with a steam locomotive with the words "Western Atlantic RR, Confederate States of America." The other badge is stamped "Andersonville Guard 2, Confederate States of America." A figural pin in the shape of a KKK hood with "KKK" was also made. These three items, and all other pieces in this series, are marked "Coin Silver" on the back.

During the 19th century, Coin Silver appeared almost exclusively on elegant hand made silver holloware and flatware from the 1830s to the late 1850s. It would be extremely unlikely that that mark would ever appear on small utilitarian items like pins or badges. It is equally illogical that the Confederate States, always in desperate need of financial resources to finance the war, would issue silver badges to prison guards and railroad workers. No vintage counterparts to the pins and badges are known.

Original research and images of new identification discs and badges in this chapter appear courtesy of Peter Bertram and Nancy Dearing Rossbacher.

Fake railroad badge stamped "Western Atlantic RR, Confederate States of America." No authentic counterpart known; marked "Coin Silver" on back.

A fake badge, above, stamped "Andersonville Guard 2, Confederate States of America". No authentic counterpart is known. The badge is marked "Coin Silver" on back, left.

Photos, prints and other images

Among the most sought after Civil War collectibles are original photographs and period prints. The great majority of original photographs during the Civil War were produced on tintypes. Tintypes were cheap to make and produce and sturdy enough to be mailed home from distant battlefields. A vintage tintype was a thin sheet of steel which was Japanned, or lacquered, then coated with a photographic emulsion. The tintype was placed in a camera and the emulsion exposed to the subject. The developed tintype was then placed in a simple folding paper holder or a more expensive hinged case.

The demand for and high price of original tintypes has inspired some fairly sophisticated fakes. The best of the fakes are made from genuinely old but common inexpensive tintypes. The original image is scraped off the old tintype and then coated with modern photographic emulsion. A regular 35mm camera is then used to capture a Civil War image on black and white film. Common sources of images are reference books about the Civil War and auction catalogs of vintage tintypes. After the film is developed, you place the film negative in an ordinary photographic enlarger in a darkroom. You project the negative down on the freshly coated tintype and develop the image as any ordinary black and white paper print. The result is a new image on the reconditioned genuinely old tintype.

There are several ways to identify fake tintypes made in this manner. First, look at the image with a 10X loupe. If a forger has taken a picture of a black and white image printed in a book, the printed image will be composed of black dots. By varying the size and spacing of the dots, the eye can be fooled into seeing various shades of gray. Tintypes are continuous tone images with smooth renderings of all shades from black to almost white. You would never find an authentic tintype composed of tiny black dots. If the image on a tintype is composed of tiny dots, it's a fake.

Really clever forgers of tintypes go the extra step and photograph an authentic tintype they might have in their own collection or which might appear in a public exhibit. A photograph of a photograph will be continuous tone; you will not see the black dots found in images printed in a book. Most fakes made this way can be caught by removing them from any frame or paper folder they might be in. When original vintage tintypes were exposed, the metal sheets were held by bulky frames. The edges of original tintypes hidden by the frame were not exposed and appear as random shapes and widths on vintage tintypes. Fake tintypes processed in a modern enlarger without being held in a bulky frame are almost always evenly exposed from edge to edge with no black border.

A further more drastic test for fakes exposed on reconditioned old tintypes is to rub the emulsion on the image side. Rubbing through the emulsion on vintage tintypes will reveal a black Japanned, or lacquered, surface. Rubbing through the emulsion on all but the most sophisticated reconditioned fakes will show a white background. Obviously, this test is potentially destructive. With rare Civil War images selling for thousands of dollars, though, it may be an option worth

A new image of Civil War soldiers made on a genuinely old tintype. The image is then displayed in a genuinely old frame.

Examination with a 10X loupe will reveal a series of black dots if an image has been photographed from a book or auction catalog.

Genuine vintage tintypes were held by crude frames during exposure. This authentic tintype shows the irregular black border, arrows, hidden by the holding frame.

A faked image of U.S. Grant on a reconditioned tintype. The developed image goes entirely acrosss the metal plate; there is no evidence of the plate holder. Rubbing through the emulsion exposes a white background.

The front of a new Union photo case which is a copy of the vintage "Eagle at Bay" original.

The new Eagle at Bay case can be detected by circular mold marks along the inner edges. No similar molding marks appear on originals.

Be alert for genuinely old images placed in new cases with Civil War themes to suggest both pieces are old. An original ambrotype gives this new case a look of respectability.

These Library of Congress images are two of the Civil War portraits appearing on the new Stanhopes. They are Confederate States generals John Bell Hood, left, and Thomas "Stonewall" Jackson, right.

considering. Carefully rubbing the very edge of the plate will generally not affect the important image area. For the protection of both the buyer and seller, do not disturb the emulsion without the written permission of the seller or agent.

Some forgers try to further confuse buyers by combining old and new images in old and new cases. It's common, for example, to try and pass off a faked image by displaying it in a genuinely old case. Similarly, a genuinely old image will enhance the appearance of a reproduction case.

The cases most commonly associated with Civil War portraits are molded a mixture of shellac and wood fiber known by the generic name thermoplastic. This material was first developed by Samuel Peck in the early 1850s. Peck's own brand name for the material was Union which refers to the union of shellac and wood (the name does not refer to the northern states during the Civil War). All of these molded hinged holders of tintypes, ambrotypes and daguerreotypes have come to be collectively be called Union Cases after Peck's process. Most have elaborate designs that make them highly sought after in their own right and also for the display of vintage images. Cases are usually a deep reddish brown or black in color. There are a number of reproduction Union cases with Civil War themes being manufactured. One of the most confusing is a direct copy of a vintage original "Eagle at Bay" first made by Littlefield, Parsons & Co. in 1862. It is 3-1/4" x 3-5/8", made of a reddish brown modern plastic that looks and feels like an original case.

The front is molded with an eagle perched by a Civil War-era mortar and cannon balls under an American flag surrounded by patriotic emblems. The easiest way to identify this new case is to look for a series of molding marks. These appear as circular depressions along the inner edges of the case. They are particularly noticeable around the hinges. No similar molding marks exist on original cases. An original Eagle at Bay case can sell for several hundred dollars; the reproduction was purchased from a distributor for $16.

One of the more difficult to detect reproductions of Civil War images are new Stanhopes. Stanhopes are miniature photographic images viewed through a magnifying lens. First introduced in the mid-1800s, Stanhopes were at the height of their popularity from about 1860 to 1920. An American company, Stanhope Microworks began manufacturing new Stanhopes in the late 1990s. There are now at least 23 Civil War images available as new Stanhopes including generals from both Union and Confederate forces and presidents Abraham Lincoln and Jefferson Davis.

The new Stanhopes can be used to replace damaged vintage Stanhopes, be placed into modern objects or inserted into genuine vintage objects which never originally held a Stanhope. Customers may also order new custom Stanhopes by sending the company any image they want miniaturized. The company also sells a number of stock items including Stanhopes of Civil War generals mounted in genuinely old minnie balls, the bullets fired by Civil War-era muskets. For $129, customers can order a minnie ball with their choice of General Robert E. Lee, General Nathan Bedford Forrest or General George Pickett.

Prices for new stock images range from about $70 to $150. Costs for mounting the new Stanhopes varies depending on whether the Stanhope is mounted in new objects sold by the company or installed in an object, either new or old, supplied by the customer. Some of the new objects the company offers for mounting its new Stanhopes include canes, knives, violin bows, pens and jewelry. But the new Stanhopes can be mounted in any object. A hole is simply drilled in the object and the new Stanhope inserted. Some of the first new images the company made were permanently marked SMW but Stanhope Microworks owner Michael Sheibley said that has been discontinued. "We do not do anything with the intention of fooling anybody," said Sheibley, "but marks detract from the product." Sheibley said the mark never appeared on special orders and custom work.

Although the new Stanhopes are perfectly legitimate new products honestly offered by the manufacturer, many new Stanhopes have been offered by unethical sellers in the secondary market as vintage goods. Unless the new Stanhope is marked, it is very difficult for the average collector or dealer to separate vintage Stanhopes from new pieces by Stanhope Microworks. Those who want to purchase only vintage images are probably best advised to carefully consider the subject matter. While there are authentic 19th and early 20th century vintage Stanhopes

Confederate States cavalry officer Nathan Bedford Forrest is one of the Civil War generals appearing on new Stanhopes.

One of the stock items into which new Stanhopes are being placed are genuinely old musket balls like this example.

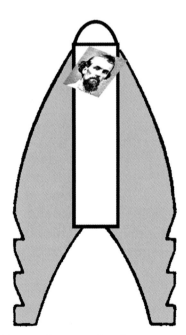

This illustrated cross section shows a new Stanhope inserted into the drilled musket ball. The bulb-shaped convex magnifying lens is on the top.

mounted in minnie balls, subjects in those vintage pieces are quite different from the new Stanhopes in minnie balls. The vast majority of authentic period Stanhopes found in minnie balls are scenic views of battlefields, not portraits of individual generals. The battlefields depicted in authentic Stanhopes are almost always either Gettysburg or Antietam. Several of these authentic battlefield Stanhopes do include some generals but only when they are incorporated with battlefield views, not as individual portraits. As a broad rule, any Stanhope image with a personal portrait of a general or historic figure from the Civil War should be considered suspect until the seller can prove otherwise. This is particularly true of more obscure figures like George Thomas, Abner Doubleday and John Breckinridge and similar figures largely unknown to the general public. Such figures generally are recognized only by Civil War collectors which can be a niche target of unethical sellers in the secondary market.

Here is a list of Civil War images known to appear in new Stanhopes:

Thomas "Stonewall" Jackson—profile

Thomas "Stonewall" Jackson—surrounded by staff

Robert E. Lee on Traveler (his horse)

Robert E. Lee—head/shoulders

Robert E. Lee—and sons

Abner Doubleday

John Mosby

Ambrose Burnside

Armstrong Custer

George Pickett

Pierre Beauregard

George Thomas

James EB Stuart

Wade Hampton

James Longstreet

John Bell Hood

John Buford

John Breckenridge

John Reynolds

Joshua Lawrence Chamberlain

Nathan Bedford Forrest

Jubal Early

Richard Ewell

Abraham Lincoln

Jefferson Davis

Confederate Water Battery at Yorktown, Virginia

Coca-Cola Fantasies

The script Coca-Cola trademark is probably one of the most recognizable corporate symbols ever created.

Since its creation in 1886, the Coca-Cola trademark has appeared on thousands of items now all avidly collected by Coke enthusiasts.

This popularity has led to almost as many reproductions as there are legitimate Coca-Cola items. Many of the most confusing reproductions are the so-called fantasy items. A fantasy item is an article that has no vintage counterpart; no old version ever existed. Most fantasy products are created by the reproduction wholesale trade, but may also be made by individuals. Unlike authentic items which can generally be located in reference books, fantasy items are hard to trace because there are no originals on which to make a comparison. Many buyers leap to the false conclusion that, since an item doesn't appear in a book, the item must be "rare and unlisted." If you can't locate a particular item in a reference book or sales catalog, keep in mind that you might be looking at a fantasy item, not a rare piece.

The items on the following pages are some of the more unusual recent reproduction and fantasy items to come into the market.

Many collectors incorrectly think the only Coca-Cola items being reproduced are related to soda fountains or grocery stores. Reproductions and fantasies with the Coca-Cola trademark and logo are made in all sorts of shapes and forms. Items like this "advertising" marble, above, and "rare" vendor's license, right, have no vintage counterparts. They exist only as fakes.

Doorknobs

Genuinely old door knobs in porcelain and glass are being etched with trademarks and logos of highly collectible companies including Coca-Cola. The etching is about one-sixteenth of an inch deep below the surrounding surface. No old Coca-Cola doorknobs are known that resemble these new products. New knobs with the Coca-Cola logo are known in both glass and white porcelain.

A genuinely old clear glass 2-1/4" door knob set that has recently had "Drink Coca-Cola" etched into it.

Two recently etched knobs like the one shown above, are sold as part of this old door hardware.

Door stop

This new 8-1/2 inch cast iron figure of a soda fountain attendant holds a tray with the Coca-Cola trademark and wears a red Coca-Cola button. It is frequently represented as a vintage doorstop. No old original like this piece was ever produced.

A fantasy cast iron figure holding a tray molded with the Coca-Cola trademark. It is commonly sold as a vintage doorstop in online auctions.

Jar

In 2002, the Anchor Hocking glass company made a 7-1/4 inch tall, 6-inch Coca-Cola square glass jar. There is a Coke bottle on one side and the profile of a woman drinking from a bottle on the other. It is three-quarts in volume. No old counterpart to this jar exists; it is a fantasy item.

Three-quart clear pressed glass jar with screw-on metal lid. The reverse side features a Coke bottle. There is no permanent mark to indicate the date of production.

Marbles

Fantasy marbles with all types of advertising including Coca-Cola are now widespread in the market. Some of the most common marble-related fakes are bags of marbles. Forgers are making paper or cardboard headers on laser and inkjet printers and stapling them to bags of new marbles. Although Coca-Cola and other beverage companies did use bags of marbles in promotions, the style of original headers on beverages is different from the new example shown here. Headers on vintage bags of marbles given away with soft drinks were made as "bottle hangers." Bottle hanger headers have a large hole to fit over, or hang, on bottle necks. You need to be careful, though. Some new bottle hanger-styles have been faked with Coca-Cola images. For additional tests to catch new bags of marbles, see "Marbles" chapter on P. 254.

A new 7/8" marble with a six-pack of Coca-Cola. No similar vintage marble was ever made.

A fantasy Coca-Cola header on a new bag of marbles. Vintage bags of marbles from soft drink companies had a large hole in the header to hang the bag on the bottlenecks.

Match safes with photos

Reproductions of hinged metal match safes with images of women used in vintage Coca-Cola advertisements have been circulating for a number of years. The forgery begins with a genuinely old but inexpensive metal advertising match safe. The original advertisement with relatively little value is removed and replaced by a highly valued Coca-Cola image from early trays and signs. The Coca-Cola images are scanned from reference books, processed on home computers and produced on inkjet and laser printers.

The original hinged match safes with vintage images has the Coca-Cola logo embossed in the metal on the backside. The fakes made from lookalike match safes do not have the logo embossed in the metal. Vintage originals can be worth $600 and up.

A faked metal match safe with a new image of a Coca-Cola advertisement. The fakes do not have Coca-Cola embossed in the metal on the back side.

Push plate

This fantasy Coca-Cola push plate dated 1901 has been in the market since the 1970s. You won't find this piece in most books on Coca-Cola collectibles because it was never made by or authorized by Coca-Cola. It's a fantasy item.

Logically, vintage advertising push plates had to be very strong and well made to stand up to the heavy daily use of commercial doors. By contrast, the new piece is made from very thin stamped tin. The gold finish on the new piece is frequently mistaken for brass or bronze. In the 1970s these pieces wholesaled for only a few dollars each and that is about what they are worth today.

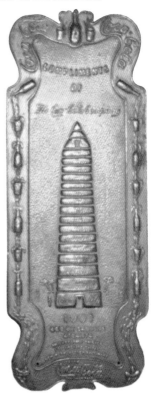

This fantasy Coca-Cola door push plate first appeared in the 1970s. No old counterpart exists.

Sterling Fob

A fake sterling watch with the Coca-Cola trademark is virtually identical to original fobs made around 1907. Both new and old are embossed on the front with a woman holding a Coca-Cola tumbler. On the back is embossed "Drink Coca-Cola, in bottles 5¢." Originals were available in three materials: brass with gold or silver plating, sterling silver and 10k gold. Original sterling fobs are valued at $250; new sterling fobs are $9 each wholesale. The best way to separate new and old sterling fobs is to look at the location of "STERLING." On originals, "STERLING" appears horizontally at the bottom center of the fob. On fakes, "STERLING" is stamped diagonally in the lower right hand corner.

The front of the new sterling silver Coca-Cola watch fob. The new fob is virtually identical to original fobs issued by Coca-Cola ca. 1907.

NEW

On new sterling fobs, "STERLING" is stamped on a slant in the lower right hand corner.

OLD

On original sterling fobs, "STERLING" is stamped horizontally in the bottom center of the fob.

Tokens

All Coca-Cola tokens marked "L.A. Stamp" are fantasy items; no originals ever existed. The faked mark is meant to suggest the legitimate vintage mark of the Los Angles Rubber Stamp Company which is "L.A. RUB. STAMP CO."

Fantasy L.A. Stamp pieces have plagued buyers for over 20 years. Over 30 fantasy L.A. Stamp pieces are known featuring many of the most popular collecting fields including Coca-Cola, railroads, saloons and military themes. L.A. Stamp tokens may be found in brass, lead, copper and white metal.

Fantasy Coca-Cola token marked L.A. Stamp. No old counterparts exist.

COOKIE JARS

Reproductions have been a problem for cookie jar buyers since the early 1990s. The Little Red Riding Hood jar, originally sold by Hull Pottery, has become so widely reproduced that the new jars far out number original examples.

Generally, the easiest way to catch most reproductions is to simply measure the jar. The great majority of reproduction jars are made in new molds which are made by copying an old jar. The object from the new mold is always smaller than the original from which the new mold was made. As a result, new cookie jars can be one-half to one inch shorter than original jars. Diameters are also proportionately reduced.

Another clue that a jar is a reproduction is an inappropriate type of decoration. Trim on the original McCoy mammy cookie jar, for example, was cold painted over the glaze. Some reproductions of that jar have the trim applied under the glaze. Just check reference books on cookie jars to learn what decorations are correct for particular jars and companies.

A reproduction Turnabout cookie jar with Mickey on one side, left; Minnie on the reverse, right. The new jar is 12-1/2" tall; the original jar is 14-1/2" tall.

You should also get in the habit of double checking which company made which jars. Reproductions of jars originally made by Hull and Shawnee, for example, may be found marked "McCoy." Although there was a company named Brush-McCoy, all cookie jars marked Brush-McCoy are fakes; no cookie jars were made at the original Brush-McCoy pottery. How marks are applied can also be a clue to age. The name "Smiley" on original Shawnee Pottery jars was always applied with a sharp-edged stencil or transfer. "Smiley" on some of the reproduction jars has been quite obviously hand painted. Original Shawnee jars were commonly marked with "USA" impressed in the base; many reproduction Shawnee jars are marked with a raised "USA."

The photos and captions on the following pages show how to separate many old and new cookie jars with side by side comparisons.

American Retro

American Retro Inc. is an American giftware distributor which claims to "have secured possession of all the original Brush molds that are still in existence." Beginning in 2004, the company began reissuing some of the more popular Brush Pottery including Cow with Cat in several colors, Formal Pig in two colors, Humpty Dumpty (cowboy), Humpty Dumpty (beanie) and the Hillbilly Frog, covered in detail at the end of this section on pages 90 and 91.

American Retro cookie jars are widely sold in gift shops and in online auctions. Prices average about $25 per jar. All of the new jars are marked "American Retro" and haven't caused any serious problems when they drift into the secondary collectibles market. Just be aware there are reproductions of Brush Pottery jars out there. Always ask for details and photos of any marks when buying without a firsthand examination.

Shawnee

Many new cookie jars in designs originally made by Shawnee are now appearing marked "McCoy." Any Shawnee designed character jars—like Mugsy, Winnie Pig, Smiley and others—found marked "McCoy" are obviously fakes.

Brush McCoy

The original Brush-McCoy Pottery operated between about 1911 to 1925. It was formed by combining the companies of Nelson McCoy and George Brush. McCoy sold his interest and around 1925 the name was changed to Brush Pottery reflecting Brush's sole ownership. Brush Pottery is credited with being among the first American potteries to produce cookie jars. It introduced its first in 1929. Cookie jars continued to be an important part of the company's production until it closed in 1982. Keep in mind that it was Brush Pottery that made the cookie jars, not Brush-McCoy.

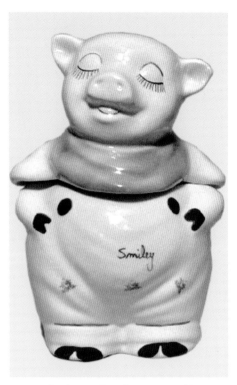

The Smiley name is hand painted on the new jar. Smiley on original jars were virtually always applied as a transfer or through a stencil, not hand painted.

A reproduction Smiley character cookie jar. The original was made by Shawnee Pottery.

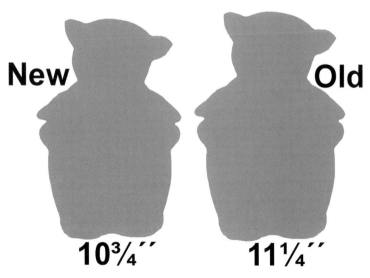

New 10¾"

Old 11¼"

New Smiley jars are no more than 10-3/4" tall; originals are 11-1/4". Both new and old jars are marked "USA" on the base. The original USA mark is impressed; the USA mark on the reproduction is raised.

Two typical marks that appear on authentic Brush Pottery cookie jars made ca. 1940s-1982. Almost all original Brush Pottery marks are impressed below the surface.

Original Brush Pottery cookie jars are among some of the hobby's most expensive. Its Hillbilly Frog, for example, produced in 1968, is valued at over $4,000. Many other Brush Pottery jars range from $400 to $800. Maybe that's why some manufacturer came up with the idea of marking reproduction cookie jars "Brush McCoy." Although no vintage cookie jars were ever marked that way, the mark began appearing on new jars around the mid-1990s.

At first, the Brush McCoy marks only appeared on reproductions of jars made by Brush Pottery. Now the mark appears on jars by other vintage makers. The original Mugsy jar, for example, was made by Shawnee Pottery but reproduction Mugsy jars are being marked Brush McCoy. Finding Brush McCoy marks on jars known to originate from other potteries is an obvious clue that you're looking at a fake.

Some elements of the new Brush McCoy mark are somewhat similar to original Brush Pottery marks. Perhaps the most confusing is the appearance of the letter W followed by a number. In original Brush Pottery cookie jars, the W indicated jars designed by Ross and Don Winton of Twin Winton Ceramics. The number corresponded to specific designs. The original Brush Pottery "Elephant with Ice Cream Cone," for example, has a W-8 molded in the base. The reproduction Elephant marked Brush McCoy also includes a W-8.

Not all original Brush Pottery cookie jars are marked. If marked, many marks may only include a number or USA and a number. As a general rule, marks found on authentic Brush Pottery cookie jars are impressed below the surface. So far, all the new Brush McCoy pottery marks have been in molded letters raised above the surface. Two typical authentic impressed Brush Pottery marks are shown above.

A new Mugsy cookie jar marked Brush McCoy. The original was made by Shawnee Pottery.

The Brush McCoy mark on the bottom of the new Mugsy cookie jar. The Brush McCoy mark appears on reproductions of jars made by many vintage potteries.

A new Elephant with Ice Cream Cone marked "Brush McCoy." The original Elephant jar was made by Brush Pottery in the early 1950s. Brush McCoy is a fantasy modern mark.

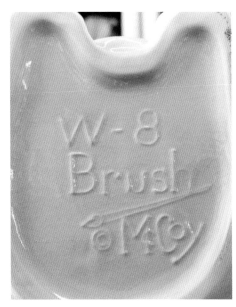

This Brush McCoy mark with paintbrush and W-8 appears on the reproduction Elephant cookie jar. New Brush McCoy marks are raised. The vintage marks of Brush Pottery are impressed below the surface.

Little Red Riding Hood

The most common cookie jar reproduction in the market is Little Red Riding Hood. This jar was among the first cookie jars to be reproduced and has been copied since at least 1996. Collectors need to be aware of two different styles of Little Red Riding Hood cookie jars. One reproduction has a raised McCoy trademark; the other new jar has an incised Hull mark, which includes patent and design information.

A McCoy trademark on a Little Red Riding Hood cookie jar is by itself proof you are looking at a reproduction. Vintage Little Red Riding Hood cookie jars were designed and patented by Hull Pottery, not McCoy Pottery. All Little Red

NEW   OLD

This new Little Red Riding Hood cookie jar, left, has a Hull Pottery mark virtually identical to marks on the vintage jar, right.

The Hull mark on new Little Red Riding Hood cookie jars is virtually identical to the mark on authentic Hull jars. The best test of age is to measure the height of the jars.

NEW

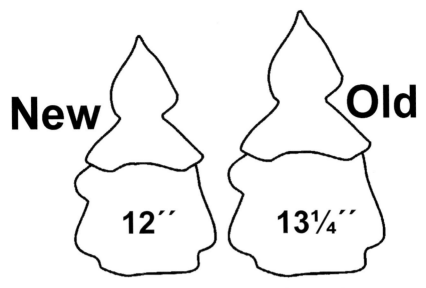

New

Old

12″

13¼″

New Little Red Riding Hood jars are only 12" or less. Original jars are at least 13-1/4".

Riding Hood jars with a McCoy mark are therefore not original but modern fakes. You don't need to consider any other features once you see the McCoy mark.

The second group of new Little Red Riding Hood jars, which are marked almost exactly as vintage Hull originals, require a closer examination. The easiest test of age for any Little Red Riding Hood jars marked Hull is simply measuring the height. Original Hull Little Red Riding Hood jars average right at 13-1/4 inches tall and virtually never less than about 13 inches tall. The reproductions are significantly smaller, averaging only about 12 inches high, and virtually never over about 12-1/4 inches tall.

Here are some other tips and further background on separating vintage Hull Little Red Riding Hood cookie jars from the many fakes in the market:

- Original jars are made of vitrified china; the majority of fakes are generally made of a low-fired soft ceramic clay like that used in china painting and ceramic classes.
- The gold trim on new such as the stars on the apron or gold outlines, show no wear.
- Only reproductions with gold stars on the apron have been seen. Aprons with *gold bows*, a more expensive variation in originals, have not as yet been reproduced.
- Original Hull Little Red Riding Hood jars include baskets of two different shapes, an open basket and a closed basket. So far, reproductions have been made in only the open basket style, shown on P. 86.

Watt Pottery Policeman

Watt Pottery cookie jars have been reproduced since the mid-1990s. During those years, new jars were offered to dealers at a wholesale price of about $60 each.

Like many other fake cookie jars, size is the easiest test of age. Original Policeman jars measure a minimum of 10-1/4 inches top to bottom. Some original jars are slightly taller, but virtually no original jar is much shorter. The fakes are only 9-3/4 inches tall overall. New jars are also about 25 percent lighter than old jars. New jars weigh about 3 pounds; original jars are 4 or more pounds. Original jars have a clear glaze over their entire surface including the base and inside the jar. New jars are not glazed on the base or the inside.

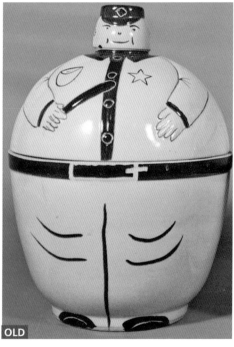

NEW OLD

The original Watt Policeman cookie jar, at right, is at least 10-1/4" tall; the reproduction on the left is about one-half inch smaller at 9-3/4" tall.

Cow Jumped Over the Moon

The original Cow Jumped Over the Moon cookie jar, also called Hi Diddle Diddle, was made by Robinson Ransbottom Pottery of Roseville, Ohio. Robinson Ramsbottom remains in operation today but has discontinued making cookie jars. The company began making cookie jars around 1935 with the heaviest production during the late 1940s through the 1960s. Original Cow Jumped Over the Moon cookie jars have "R.R.P. CO Roseville OHIO NO 317" impressed in the base. These impressed marks are often partially filled with glaze, which may make it difficult to distinguish all the letters.

NEW

This new jar is marked "4546 Brush McCoy Cow Jumped Over the Moon ©."

NEW

This new jar has the mark "©Treasure Craft" impressed in the base. Note that the cat and the fiddle are on the viewer's left side, which is the opposite of the original jar.

OLD

An original Cow Jumped over the Moon cookie jar. All originals were made by Robinson Ransbottom Pottery Co. of Roseville, Ohio. Jars with any other marks are fakes and reproductions.

There are at least two new versions of the Cow Jumped Over the Moon jar. Although these new jars probably wouldn't confuse a cookie jar collector, they might create some problems for buyers who aren't aware of how the original jar should be marked or decorated. The easiest way to separate the jars is by examining the marks on the base. All authentic jars are marked RRP as previously described. One of the reproductions is marked in the mold "© Treasure Craft." The other new jar is marked in the mold "Brush McCoy." Any Cow Jumped Over the Moon jar not marked RRP is a fake.

Hillbilly Frog

The original Hillbilly Frog jar was made by Brush Pottery in 1969. According to company legend, only 100 or fewer of the jars were manufactured. It is one of the most scarce and expensive of all vintage jars and can sell for over $4,000.

With originals bringing such high prices, there have been no shortage of reproductions, copies and fakes.

The first of the new jars were made in 1992. At that time, the original Brush Pottery mold was sold to a private potter who made an estimated 75 to 80 pieces. These 1992 jars, although obviously not vintage pieces, are still valued by collectors as a limited edition which can command $500 to $600 and more. At about the same time, either 1992 or 1992, a fairly crude, low quality mass produced reproduction was also introduced. Now, in 2005-2006, another new version, also purportedly from the original mold, is back in production and selling for $25. Look closely and you'll see one on one of the kitchen sets of the television show, "Desperate Housewives." Matching salt and pepper shakers and a bank are also being made to match the latest cookie jars.

Here is a comparison of the most important features:

Marks—Some, but far from all, original jars are marked "43-D." The reissues made from original molds in 1992 are marked "Reissue Pottery by J.D." The mass-produced low-quality reproductions from the early 1990s are unmarked. The most recently made jars, which are marketed as being made from the original 1969 mold, are marked "American Retro" (for more new jars from this company, see the "American Retro" section in this chapter.) Obviously, any jars marked American Retro or J.D, are not the 1969 originals. But be careful. Some marks on the new jars have been ground away and the altered bottoms have been glazed. Don't assume any unmarked jar is an original. Compare several features before you make a conclusion about age.

Size—Original jars and the American Retro jars are both 13-1/4 inches high; the JD reissue jars, are larger at 13-3/4 inches high. The 1990s reproductions are considerably smaller at only 12-3/4 inches high. Again, don't rely on size alone as your only test. If the mark was removed from the American Retro jar, it would look very similar to an unmarked original.

Colors—Until the American Retro jar appeared, color was a valuable clue to age. On original jars, the body is a light green with a darker green lily pad and hat band. But the Retro jars have the same color scheme. Both the JD reissues and the low quality reproductions use only one color of green for the body, hatband and lily pad.

Glaze—The original Hillbilly Frog has a matte glaze; the American Retro, JD reissue and 1990s reproductions have a shiny glaze.

American Retro also makes a very similar jar with the same frog posed in a Santa Claus hat instead of the country hat on the Hillbilly version.

The low-quality 1990s reproduction, left, is 12-3/4" tall. The original jar, right, is 13-1/4" tall.

The original Brush Pottery Hillbilly Frog cookie jar, decorated with a light green body, a dark green lily pad base and a dark green hat band.

FOLK ART

M any collectors mistakenly think fakes and repro- ductions are only a pro- blem if the original item was mass- produced. While most buyers are at least generally aware of reproductions in cast iron, pressed glass and art pottery, far fewer realize that items originally made one-at-time by hand like folk art are also being copied. Low-cost labor in Asia is now being used to make one-of-kind folk art reproductions by hand. Many folk art reproductions have tool marks, brush marks, and construction details that buyers often mistake as evidence of vintage 19th century handwork.

Besides appearing to be handmade, many new pieces are also direct copies of specific American folk art forms and shapes. This is especially true of patriotic themes, such as Uncle Sam figures, eagles, and other symbols, which have been widely produced since the terror attacks of September 2001. New folk art may appear as trade signs, figures, toys, whirligigs, wall pieces

A new 14" figure in carved and painted wood. This is a direct copy of a 19th century mast carving from the ship *Lottie L. Thomas* featured in *American Folk Sculpture* by Robert Bishop.

and furniture. Since both original and new handmade folk art vary so much, it's difficult to make a definite list of what separates new from old. The best approach is to become familiar with the construction techniques, materials and fasteners found on vintage pieces and to recognize signs of normal logical wear.

There are several "first tests" you can use to eliminate the most obvious folk art reproductions. One of the easiest tests to perform on a suspected piece is to give it a good sniff. Recently made Asian reproductions almost always have a strong odor of fresh paint. Although the odor fades with time, this is still a very reliable test. Strong paint odors can be detected for up to 18 months after manufacture; longer if the item has been enclosed in a shipping box.

Another clue to a fake is the widespread presence of fillers. Fillers are widely used to smooth rough surfaces, fill in manufacturing mistakes and provide a base to create a surface texture. The raised scales of the metal fish on P. 101, for example, at first glance appear to be hand hammered. Look at some of the chipped paint and you'll discover that the scales are formed by a gray-colored resin. The resin is then painted with a red primer, then a top coat of paint. The hand shown at bottom left on P. 95 is also primarily formed of filler. It is easier to shape filler materials than wood so finer details, such as fingers, facial features, ankles, necks and wrists, are often made of filler. These materials are usually exposed by chips in the surface paint. Many modern fillers and primers also fluoresce under long wave black light.

A new carved and painted wood eagle with spread wings, 14" wide, 11" tall. The surfaces are distressed at the factory to suggest age.

Fillers and primers are not consistent with vintage folk art and are clues to a possible fake. Modern fillers should not be confused with gesso, a water and plaster mix used to smooth surfaces. Gesso was used primarily in the commercial production of picture frames, decorative furniture trim and by professional artists for decorative effects. Gesso was rarely used in folk art made by untrained amateurs.

After a thorough examination of the paint, look for modern fasteners. Round head finishing nails and especially Phillips head screws are signs of modern pieces. Early 19th century cut finishing nails are flat in cross section, not round.

Detail of a painted folk art reproduction showing a gray filler (black arrow) and a red primer (white arrow) exposed by a chip in the surface paint. Very few genuine pieces of homemade American folk art were made with primers or fillers.

The white filler in this new piece of folk art is clearly visible in areas where the surface paint is chipped.

Phillips head screws were first used in the 1930s. It would be illogical to find Phillips head screws in folk art represented as having been made in the 19th century.

In this example, there is paint wear in crevices and details below the surrounding raised surfaces. Finding wear in low spots and no wear on surrounding raised surfaces is illogical and almost always a sign of artificial aging.

A detail of the extreme paint wear on the figure shown at right.

A new 12" figure in carved and painted wood with illogical paint wear. The entire figure shows extreme paint wear; the base shows no wear.

Phillips screws were first used in the 1930s to assemble cars. Old glues were made of animal by-products and virtually never fluoresce. Modern adhesives, particularly epoxies and hot glues, almost always fluoresce. Although any of these may be found in repairs of genuinely old pieces, they most often are a warning sign of a modern reproduction.

Once you're satisfied all visible fasteners are old, you can begin to look for signs of normal wear and aging. Virtually all of the new folk art pieces have artificially created wear. Authentic wear marks appear in random directions in various widths and depths. Such wear is produced one mark at a time over many long years. Marks that appear in regular repeated patterns, such as parallel lines or concentric circles or are nearly perfectly uniform in depth and width, are generally made all at the same time by power tools or other deliberate actions. Illogical paint wear is particularly noticeable. Normal paint wear typically begins with the highest points of a surface. It is illogical for recessed areas to show signs of wear while higher surrounding areas are not worn.

Beyond the basic tests just described, you also want to ask yourself, "Is this piece constructed according to its purported use or function?" The blades on the great majority of original whirligigs, for example, are connected by a shaft that runs through the supporting figure. When one blade is in the up position, the opposite blade is down. Blades on many new whirligigs are simply nailed to opposite sides of the supporting figure. The blades are not connected by a single shaft.

Similarly, if an object is represented as a vintage trade sign, it should logically be sturdy enough to withstand exposure to the elements. Hanging loops or brackets or other hardware should be attached to the strongest point of the sign. Most originals are reinforced around the hardware. Pay particular attention to the size. Original trade signs are large enough to be plainly seen at a distance. That was their purpose. Authentic figural signs are generally, at minimum, 24 inches to 36 inches. While some new signs are the appropriate size, many others are too small, especially those copied directly from vintage originals. The majority of original trades signs were designed for display at a right angle to the storefront and were logically double-sided. Many new signs, made as "antiques" and not practical signs, are made to hang on walls and are only one sided.

Another useful examination technique is simply tapping the surface with your fingernail. A surprising number of new pieces of primarily carved wood include one or more pieces of molded plastic. The most frequent use of molded plastic is for heads attached to carved wood bodies. The cast heads are apparently an attempt to provide fine facial detailing without the expense of skilled carvers. Seams where plastic heads are attached to the wood are nearly impossible to detect by visual inspection. I originally discovered the plastic heads when I ordered X-rays of some suspected pieces I was testing for a gallery.

Copies of carved and painted wooden folk art are becoming more common. Many vintage shapes, like this whirligig, are used as models.

New whirligig of carved and painted wood, 14" to top of hat.

The blades are two separate unconnected pieces usually attached with a simple nail.

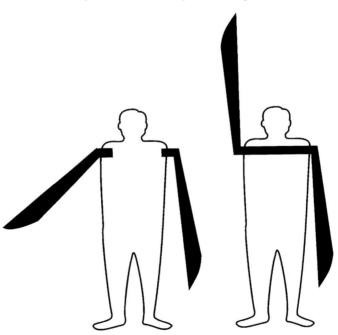

Blades on authentic functional whirligigs are joined by a connecting rod or axle as shown in the figure on the right. Most new blades are two separate pieces, left.

This reproduction slaughterhouse "trade sign" is only 14" across and much too small to be a practical outdoor trade sign.

NEW

An original full-sized 19th century three-dimensional outdoor slaughterhouse sign, about 30" across.

OLD

A new spectacles sign, 11" by 32", three-dimensional sheet metal. Note the small, unreinforced hanging loops. Could these loops logically be expected to support this sign in a strong wind?

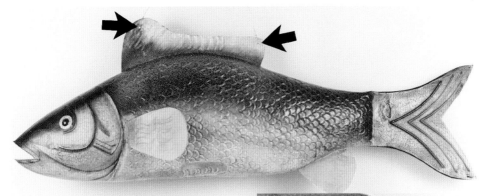

A new three-dimensional fish sign, 38" long. Could this rather large piece logically be supported in a strong wind suspended from the small holes in the unsupported top fin (see arrows)?

A close up of the tiny holes in the fish fin.

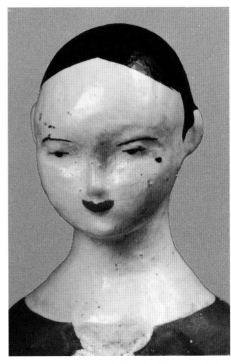

A new 10" figure made with a hand-carved wood body and a cast plastic head. Filler material conceals the body to neck joint giving the appearance of a solid wood figure.

New "mechanical" box, 5" x 4". Pressing the cat's tail raises the lid. The jointed cat's body is cast resin (plastic); the box is wood.

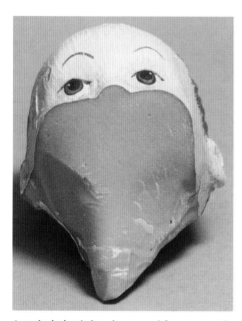

A typical plastic head removed from a wood body. The solid heads are cast from flesh-colored resin.

Flesh-colored resin rather than wood grain shows through any paint chips in the new plastic heads.

Going back over the heads, I did discover they sounded different when tapped with a fingernail. If the sound changes when you tap a surface, it could very well be from a piece of plastic or other modern composition material. One other related clue that can help you detect plastic parts is to look for paint chips in the suspected area. The smooth plastic surface under the paint frequently shows though the chipped areas. (But never deliberately chip a suspected piece.)

Other pieces of new folk art can be detected by asking yourself if the decoration is consistent with the age being represented. Although this will only come with some study and experience, it will be one of your most valuable assets in detecting many fakes. The new 10-inch hand painted wood plate on Page 104, for example, appears to be a genuine example of a mid-19th century style of decoration referred to as "combing" or "trailing." The mustard and black colors are consistent with colors found on authentic examples. So what are the clues to its recent manufacture?

First, the date "1893" is suspiciously late for this style of decoration. The combed and trailed technique was at its height of popularity around the middle of the 19th century, ca. 1835 to 1870. It would be highly unusual for the amateur painter to be using this technique in the 1890s. The other problem is the enormous size of the date. Most pieces of authentic folk art are not dated. When dates are used, they generally appear on some type of commemorative piece such as those made for weddings, birthdays, anniversaries, national holidays and other events. The date is relatively small to the names and other information. Similarly, it is also unusual for a date to appear alone without a commemorative inscription.

There is also a technical problem with how the date and flowers were applied. Look closely and you'll see that the numbers and flowers are very blotchy, not solid, almost as if they were applied with a sponge through a stencil or rubber stamped. Some mid-19th century wares were decorated with stamps and sponges but nothing of with this date. The date and flowers on vintage combed ware should be solid paint applied by hand with a brush. If it truly is vintage folk art, why would anyone make a stencil? Stencils are for quickly producing multiple pieces, not making one-of-a-kind pieces.

Finally, don't assume certain categories of folk art can't or won't be reproduced. Just about every style and form of folk art made in the 19th and first half of the 20th century is being copied; look at the bottle cap photos on P. 105. Special cases like these have to be studied individually. Virtually all pre-1960 American soft-drink bottle caps have cork liners. Present day American bottle caps are lined with only a thin coating of plastic. Cork lined bottle caps are, however, still used in many foreign countries including neighboring Mexico. Check both the liner and lettering on the cap to help determine age and country of origin.

A new wood plate decorated with combed paint. This technique was rarely used after about the 1870s and should raise suspicions on a piece dated 1893.

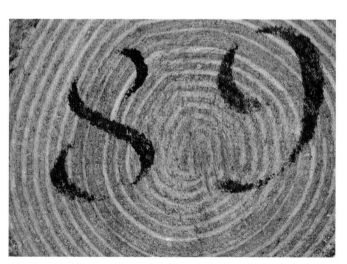

The date and flowers have a blotchy appearance as if sponged through a stencil. They should be brushed on in solid paint.

A new version of an American folk art birdhouse made from modern bottle caps.

NEW

Newer bottle caps are lined with a thin coating of plastic, not cork. Plastic bottles have made metal bottle caps obsolete in America. Metal caps are still being used in some foreign countries including Mexico.

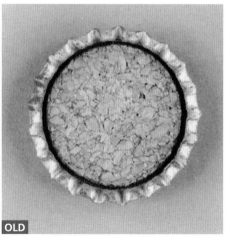

OLD

Older American bottle caps from before the 1960s have cork liners.

FURNITURE

Many reproductions of antique wood furniture like this are made by hand like vintage originals.

Buyers of antiques are confronted with three basic questions when considering furniture: Is a piece a modern reproduction made for contemporary use, a clever fake intentionally made to deceive or an honest copy made many years ago? Around the 1876 Centennial, for example, there was a revived interest in early American furniture. Copies of American Colonial furniture built then, more than 100 years ago, are now frequently confused with pieces originally made in the 1700s. Now adding to the general confusion is furniture of all styles from Asia made with hand tools and joinery similar to vintage antique originals.

A furniture buyer's best defense is to understand basic features of genuinely old furniture. Applying just a handful of simple guidelines will help you detect

A typical workshop in Indonesia where the majority of hand-carved wood reproduction furniture is made.

the majority of modern reproductions and confusing copies in today's market. While reading this chapter may not guarantee you'll catch painstakingly made deliberate forgery $1 million Chippendale tea tables, most buyers aren't finding those pieces in local antique malls and yard sales.

Basic construction

The great majority of reproduction antique furniture in the market since the 1990s has been made in Asia, particularly Indonesia. Many wholesale catalogs of Indonesian furniture factories feature reproductions only; no contemporary designs. All styles of antique furniture are being reproduced. From basic classics such as Chippendale, Louis XV, American Colonial and Victorian designs to exotic forms like Egyptian Revival. Most reproductions are available in a wide range of shapes and forms from simple side chairs and tables to tilt top tables, highboys and massive canopy beds. Reproductions also include child and child- and doll-sized furniture. Most reproductions have stained surfaces but many new pieces are also made in painted country and folk styles. Regardless of style, though, most reproduction furniture can be detected by a simple examination of basic construction.

Primary and secondary woods

The most obvious difference between most reproduction and vintage furniture, particularly the Indonesian reproductions, is the use of wood. In vintage furniture made in cabinet shops and factories, furniture parts hidden from view—drawer bottoms, glue blocks and other structural supports—were made from common inexpensive species of woods. Only the most visible parts of pieces of furniture—drawer fronts, table tops, chair legs, and other focal points—were made of expensive species prized for their unique grain, color or other properties. Woods used in the most visible areas are called primary woods; those in hidden areas are secondary woods.

Eighteenth and 19th century cabinet shops, which only made a profit by efficient use of time and materials, would never use expensive cabinet grade woods for a glue block that no one would ever see. You should logically expect, then, to find more than one species of wood in virtually all old work made as practical furniture. As a general rule, if the piece is represented as being made in a cabinet shop or factory and hidden parts are the same species of wood as the most visible surfaces, the piece is new. The only exception would be some pieces of folk and country furniture (discussed separately.)

With rare exception, Indonesian reproductions are made of a single species of wood. Hidden glue blocks and drawer bottoms are the same species as wood used in table tops and drawer fronts. Virtually all the wood in the Indonesian

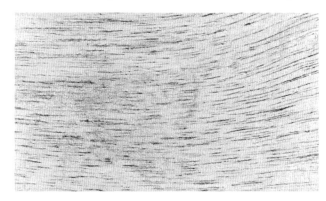

Actual size view of the wood used in the Indonesian reproductions, marketed as mahogany or Philippine mahogany.

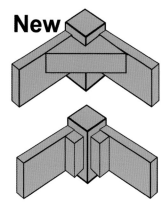
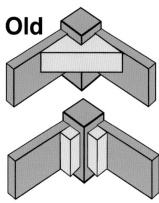

Typical hidden glue blocks in new Indonesian furniture are made from the same wood that is used for the exposed surfaces. Typical hidden glue blocks in old furniture are made of lesser quality secondary wood. Primary wood is used in exposed surfaces only.

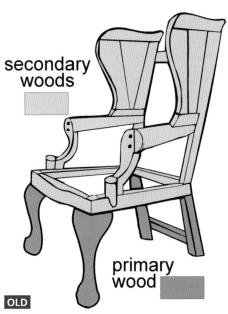

secondary
woods

primary
wood

NEW OLD

The frame of a typical new Indonesian chair with the upholstery removed. The entire frame, including those areas hidden by upholstery, is made of only one species of wood.

Typical old frame with upholstery removed. Only the visible surfaces are made of higher quality primary wood. All areas covered with upholstery are made of less expensive secondary wood.

entire drawer made
from the same species

drawer made from
two or more species

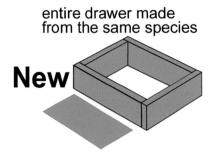

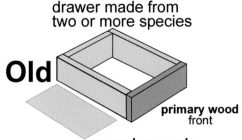

New

Old

primary wood
front

secondary woods
back, sides and bottom

All parts of new Indonesian furniture are made of the same species of wood. Old furniture is made of several species of wood. Exposed wood, or *primary wood*, is used on drawer fronts, table tops, etc. Pieces hidden from view, such as glue blocks, drawer bottoms, etc., are made of less expensive types of wood or *secondary wood*.

reproductions is from the eastern hemisphere species *Shorea, Parashorea,* and Pentacme. All three woods can be and are legally advertised and sold as "mahogany." This is a common practice of unethical sellers, especially the traveling "estate auctioneers." Advertisements from those firms routinely include confusing descriptions such as "genuine mahogany Chippendale-style highboys" or "massive carved mahogany mantel." But this is not the "mahogany" found in fine antique furniture. The cabinet grade mahogany found in fine antique furniture is Swietenia, from Central and South America and Khaya from Africa. Although helpful, it is not necessary for the average buyer to be able to identify the individual species of woods. If all the parts, hidden and visible, are made of a single species, it's almost a guarantee the piece is modern.

Joints

After you have confirmed the presence of primary and secondary woods, the next feature you'll want to consider is how the wood is fastened, or joined, together. Joints in vintage furniture are typically reinforced, especially at natural stress points like chair rungs, drawer fronts and table legs. This might be with pegs and dowels or with specially formed cuts in the wooden members such as mortises and tenons, dovetails and other interlocking patterns. Dovetails in drawers are a particularly good clue to age. Before the mid-1800s, dovetails were hand cut. The earliest form of the hand-cut joint was one large tail with two pins. Additional tails and pins were added up until the mid-1800s. Tails and pins in most pre-1860 dovetails are rarely equal in size. Machine-cut dovetails made after the mid-1800s have tails and pins of equal size. Scalloped dovetails date from late 1800s. Furniture joints should obviously correspond to the age being represented. If a chest of drawers is claimed to be ca. 1780s Sheraton, it should logically have hand cut, not machine cut, dovetails.

Hand-cut dovetails should be accompanied by scribe marks, which are generally a positive sign of age. Scribe marks are thin scratch-like guidelines used to lay out the cuts. Since scribe marks are hidden from view, there was no point in removing them from the finished piece. Be careful, though. Some clever forgers try to fool buyers by putting scribe marks on machine-cut dovetails. Scribe marks on machine-cut dovetails are illogical and cause for suspicion. Similarly, be sure to compare dovetails among a set of drawers. The general layout and proportion of all tails and pins in the same piece of furniture should be nearly identical. Wide variations among tails and pins on a single piece frequently indicate a replacement, substitution or repair.

Many wood-to-wood joints in the Indonesian reproductions are simply hot-glued: no interlocking cuts, no dowels, no nails. As the new furniture dries, the glued joints split leaving obvious gaps in joints. Industrial grade hot glues generally dry white and can usually be seen without difficulty. Many of these modern glues also usually fluoresce under long wave black light. Old hide glues rarely fluoresce. Modern glue may be a sign of a repair to a genuinely old piece, but is most commonly a warning sign of a reproduction.

A new type of joinery, the biscuit joint, is also common in reproductions. This joint was developed to take advantage of the stronger modern glues. Biscuits and glue alone are enough to provide quick production of strong durable edge joints. Biscuit joinery gets its name from a thin oval shaped piece of wood that is called a biscuit. A special tool cuts matching semicircular grooves along the edges of the wood to be joined. Biscuits and grooves are brushed with glue and the two pieces of wood are clamped while the glue sets. Grooves are coated in glue and placed about every 12 inches to 18 inches depending on the strength of the wood and the purpose of the piece being built. Biscuit joinery was developed in Europe about 40 years ago and began has widely been widely used in America for about 20 years.

A modern biscuit joint. The thin oval wooden biscuits fit into grooves cut into the pieces of wood to be joined. Modern glue and biscuits alone are strong enough to make a strong, secure joint. No nails or screws are needed.

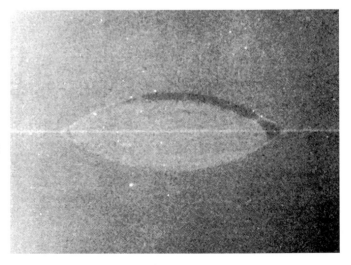

An X-ray of a modern biscuit joint. Biscuits are always about one-eighth of an inch thick; length varies from 2" up to about 2-1/2" long.

Machine cut dovetail joints

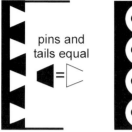

pins and tails equal

since mid 19th century

scalloped dovetails

since late 19th century

Typical hand cut dovetail joints

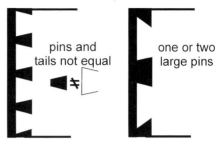

pins and tails not equal

one or two large pins

late 17th to mid 19th century

Typical machine-cut dovetails have pins and tails of identical size. Scalloped, or rounded, dovetails are from the late 19th century. Pins and tails of pre-1850 hand-cut dovetail joints are rarely the same size and should be accompanied by scribe marks.

Modern

Older

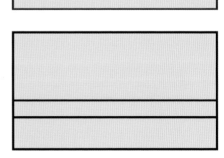

Boards of equal widths evenly divide the surface

Single large boards or boards of random width

Tops of new tables, chests, desks and other larger surfaces, are generally made of evenly spaced boards of equal width. Tops in older pieces are typically a very wide single board or boards of unequal width with irregular spacing.

Unfortunately, biscuit joints are very difficult to detect because they are concealed by the wood. One of the possible clues to the use of biscuit joinery is the absence of any other types of fasteners and unusually smooth tight edge joints. The joint is very obvious, though, in X-rays. Portable X-ray machines may be your last resort for an expensive piece suspected of being new or an older piece suspected of having that undisclosed repairs.

Another joint-related clue to age is the relative proportion and arrangement of boards in tops of tables, chests, desks and in the sides and backs of other large pieces. Generally, such surfaces in reproductions are assembled from multiple boards of identical width evenly spaced across the surface. New boards are usually relatively small, rarely over 10 inches in width and more commonly 6 inches or less. Table tops and other larger surfaces in vintage pre-1860 furniture routinely include boards 20 inches or more in width. The majority of table tops under 36 inches wide in the 18th century were almost always made from a single board. By the middle of the 19th century, the huge old growth trees were gone and boards became narrower. Large surfaces then began to be made from multiple boards of unequal widths randomly spaced across a surface. Although tops made of single large boards don't guarantee a piece is old, it is generally a positive sign of age. Likewise, a top made from multiple boards of identical widths doesn't alone prove a piece is new but is a strong indication of modern manufacture. This is especially true for backs of cupboards and chests.

Painted furniture

For years, the majority of reproduction American antique furniture was made of traditional stained hardwoods. Recent trends, however, have been toward ever increasing amounts of reproduction painted furniture decorated in country and folk art styles. Most of these painted reproductions are imported from India, Indonesia and Mexico. The low wages paid in those countries allow manufacturers to apply extensive hand painting that can be confused with hand work found on antique painted furniture. Most new painted furniture can be separated from old painted furniture based on paint, construction details and determining if wear is natural or artificial. This discussion covers country and folk-style painted furniture originally made at home or in very small rural furniture shops up through the last quarter of the 19th century. It does not include painted formal furniture from master cabinet makers.

Original furniture was painted for very practical reasons. Paint protected and sealed the wood's surface and covered flaws such as knots and streaks in the grain. Paint was also used to cover pieces made from several types of dissimilar species of wood. Practical minded makers of vintage painted furniture—small shop owners or country do-it-yourselfers—did not waste time painting or decorating areas that are not visible. You should not find original paint on the insides of drawers, for instance, or the bottoms of tables. Why waste your time, effort or paint? Painting these hidden areas may make sense though, if you're creating an "antique." About half of all the painted reproductions have paint in hidden areas. If parts and areas hidden from view are painted, it's generally a sign of a reproduction.

The wood used in most authentic American country and folk painted furniture is white pine but can be almost any native American species. Almost all new painted reproduction furniture is made of foreign species of which the most common is the so-called Philippine mahogany (discussed earlier). Although the use of white pine boards is not conclusive proof of age, the use of mahogany in painted country-style furniture is a virtual guarantee of a reproduction. No species of mahogany was ever widely used in original American country and folk painted furniture.

Virtually every piece of reproduction painted furniture has a heavily crazed surface. This finish is deliberately created with a special crackle paint, a paint that shrinks and splits as it dries. The crackle paint is applied as a top coat over a base coat in a contrasting color. As the top coat crackles, or splits, the contrasting base coat below shows through the splits. Such crazing or crackling may or may not be present in original painted surfaces. Crazing, though, by itself is never a guarantee of age.

There are two types of surface crazing that may occur in old original painted surfaces: 1. Crazing of varnish applied to protect the paint; and 2. Crazing within the paint itself. Varnish gets brittle as it ages. As the wood expands and contracts, the hardened varnish can split, bubble and develop fine networks of lines. Most crazed varnish has a definite texture and is easily to feel.

This apparently battered and weathered painted chest of kitchen drawers is new; it's painted mahogany from Indonesia.

Elaborately hand painted new chest of drawers with folk art style nautical scene. Imported from India. Retail price, $900. Part of an extensive line of reproduction painted furniture from that country.

In addition to mass-produced reproductions, new one-of-a-kind pieces are also being made by private artists. This new 48" cabinet is made of solid pine.

New painted mahogany doll cradle with date of 1820. Don't let dates or "artists" names influence your opinion of age.

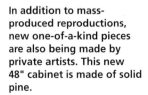

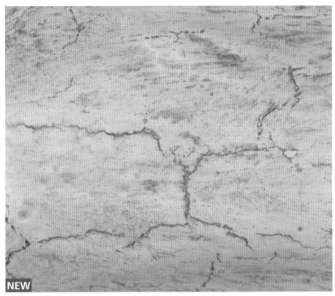

NEW

Close up of the "antique" finish found on the majority of reproduction painted furniture. Such crazing is deliberately created in new paint to suggest age.

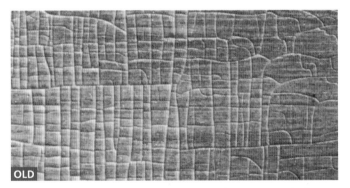

OLD

Crazing in old paints and varnishes doesn't have one particular look. This crazing is a ladder-shaped network of lines.

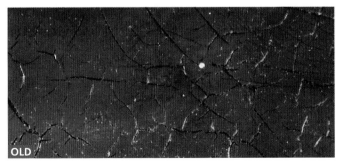

OLD

This old paint is crazed with random lines. All crazing on a single piece should generally be the same.

True crazing in paint is more properly called "alligatoring" or checking. In this condition, the paint surface develops cracks as it ages. Over time, these cracks fill in with dirt and appear as dark lines or veins. Whereas most dark lines in genuinely old paint are actually dirt, dark lines in new "antiqued" paint are simply a contrasting color of paint. In some original surfaces, you may see two layers of crazing, one in the varnish and another in the paint. So far, no crazed varnish has been applied over reproductions, only crazed paint.

The entire surface of original painted furniture is rarely all alligatored or crazed. Such conditions in original paint are usually the result of three highly variable factors: 1) environmental effects such as heat, humidity, ultraviolet (sun light) exposure; 2) accidents like spills, water, fire or smoke damage, and 3) defects in the paint or wood or problems in initial drying and curing. By contrast, painted reproductions have surfaces that are evenly and uniformly crazed. Environmental effects, accidents and defects rarely produced crazing over the entire surface of vintage pieces. If the entire surface is uniformly crazed, it's generally a sign of a reproduction.

Be suspicious of paint in cracks. Cracks that develop in vintage furniture paint will not have any paint in them; dirt maybe, but not paint. Dirt is almost always black; paint is colored. Cracks and other artificial wear are intentionally created in reproductions. If paint is down inside a crack, the crack existed before the paint was applied. It is possible a paint-filled crack might mean an old piece has been repainted, but it's much more likely that paint inside a crack means a reproduction.

Here are some guidelines to help you judge the age of paint. First, old paint is generally very hard. It is brittle and breaks or shatters into irregularly shaped chips or powders when scraped with a knife. Old paint is almost impossible to dent with a fingernail. New paint comes off in curls with a knife and dents with a fingernail. Newly painted pieces very often have a strong new paint odor especially in confined spaces like drawers. Don't be afraid to put your nose to the surface and take a whiff. Original paint used on country and folk pieces varied widely from oil bases to milk. Virtually without exception all the new painted furniture is decorated with water-based acrylic paint. Acrylics weren't invented until the 1940s and not generally available until the early 1950s.

One last warning: Many painted reproductions include dates, geographical place names and maker's signatures. A date of 1820 applied in acrylic paint to a piece made with machine-cut dovetails assembled with Phillips screws would obviously be a fake. Painted dates and names should always be thoroughly inspected. They are commonly added to genuinely old pieces as well as being found on reproductions.

Natural or artificial wear?

The absence of normal wear or the presence of artificial wear are among the most important clues to age. Authentic wear is always logical and consistent with the original function of the piece examined. In other words, does the paint wear match how the piece was supposedly used? Put your hand on a drawer pull, open a cupboard door, sit in a chair. Do moving parts match the pattern of paint wear? Does wear occur where hands and feet make contact?

Look, for example, at the glass door cupboard on P. 120. Note that the paint is completely "worn" from the middle of the door (arrows). What caused the paint to wear in these areas? Hands wouldn't touch these areas as the door opened and closed. There is no moving part to swing against the surfaces. This is illogical wear that can't be explained by normal everyday use. Any wear that can't be explained is a warning sign of a reproduction.

You also need to pay particular attention to how the paint and surface is worn. Gouges and dents, for example, should generally expose bare wood. If there is paint in or over a dent or gouge, that means the paint has been applied after the gouges and dents were made. This could mean a genuinely old piece has been repainted but is much more likely to indicate a new piece has been "distressed" before new paint was applied.

Be particularly suspicious of any wear that appears in a regular uniform pattern. The surface in the photo on P. 120, for example, is a close up view of a typical distressed wood surface in a reproduction. A powered wire brush has left a series of fine parallel valleys and ridges. Parallel lines, concentric circles and most other uniform, regularly repeating patterns are almost always the result of artificial wear. Natural wear, produced one scratch or dent at a time, occurs over many years and should generally appear in random widths, directions and depths. Also note that the paint is applied over the wear. Unless an item has been repainted, wear should go through paint, not be covered by paint.

New
no wear on bottom edge

Old
bottom edge shows wear

Drawers represented as being 100-150 years old should show wear along their runners. Pull the drawer out and compare its runner to a straight edge or any flat surface.

Side view of drawers

Why is the paint worn at the arrows on this new glass door cabinet? These areas are not gripped to open the door or exposed to general walk-by traffic. Neither are the areas exposed to wear as the door moves. This is obviously artificial wear.

Regular patterns, like these repeating parallel lines, are almost always a sign of artificially applied wear. Authentic wear is random, virtually never uniform in direction and width.

Look closely at cracks, dents and gouges. If paint is inside cracks (A) or covers holes and dents, the paint has been applied after the cracks and dents have been made. Dents and gouges produced through normal wear go through the original paint and expose the wood below (B).

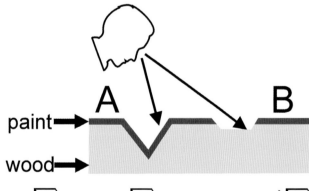

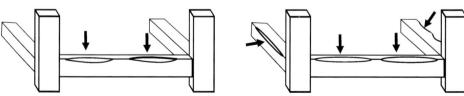

The lowest front rung of chairs, left, should show the most wear because that is where feet naturally fall. Side rungs may show some natural wear but should not show the same degree of wear as the front. If wear on all the rungs—front, back and sides—is about equal, right, the wear has likely been artificially created.

Inside of vintage chest with a drawer removed. As a drawer moves in and out of the frame, it produces wear in at least two places: along the side (inset upper right) and the bottom edge (inset lower right). Wear points on the drawers should match wear points in the frame.

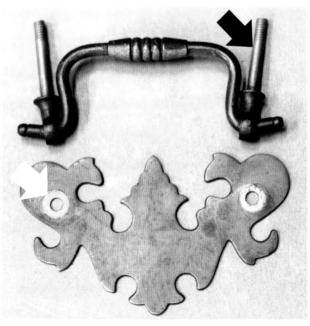

Genuinely old ca. 1880 brass drawer pull. When the pull is removed from the back plate, the protected areas under the posts are lighter in color (white arrow). The parts of the posts which pass through the wood are also protected and are lighter in color (black arrow).

The front of a genuinely old brass pull with a natural dark patina. For the back side, see photo below.

The back side of the old pull shown above is a lighter color. Patina does not have a chance to develop where hands are continually touching the pull to open the drawer.

Authentic cast brass pull on vintage chest, ca. 1880-1900. The original finish surrounding the pull is so darkened the wood species is almost unrecognizable.

The pull above is removed to expose the original finish underneath. The lighter shadow is a perfect match for the outline of the hardware.

Genuinely old pieces are frequently repainted to increase the selling price. You can generally catch most of these alterations with a simple checklist of questions:

1. Does the entire surface *feel* the same to the touch? If the painted surface is all original, the finish should feel the same all over. If one area or one color feels different, investigate further.
2. If there is crazing, does all the crazing look the same? Mismatched crazing is a warning sign that different materials from the original have been used.
3. Does the surface look the same under black light? New materials rarely fluoresce the same as old materials. Any differences would indicate a disturbance in the original surface.

One of the clues furniture experts use to authenticate furniture is the presence of appropriate "shadows." When discussing antique furniture, "shadow" refers to differences in finish and color produced by natural aging. Shadow in this sense does not mean dark or black. It refers to a relative difference between surfaces exposed to wear and surfaces protected from wear. In many cases, a furniture shadow is lighter, not darker, than a surrounding surface, but it is still referred to as a shadow.

The part of a drawer covered by a handle or pull, for example, is not exposed to the wood smoke, grime and abrasion as exposed parts of the drawer. If the original hardware has been on the furniture for 100 years and the piece has not been refinished, the protected surface under the hardware should logically look different than surrounding unprotected surfaces. The bottom of the lowest drawer in a chest of drawers, for example, should be darker than the bottom of higher drawers in the same chest.

Hardware also shows wear shadows. Those parts of a handle, for example, hidden under wood will appear different than the parts of the handle exposed to wear. Likewise, parts of hardware that are constantly touched or moved, like a door knob, will have a different pattern of wear than parts that merely support the knob but are not touched in normal daily use.

Drawers are one of the best places to check for shadows because they include both hardware and movement. Whether inspecting an entire chest of drawers or a single drawer in a desk, drawers can often tip you off as to whether the entire piece is right or wrong. The bottom edges of drawers and the sides of drawers, for example, should have matching shadows where these points slide against the chest frame (see the photos on P. 124). These typical wear patterns of vintage pieces are missing from the reproductions.

The exact time it takes to produce a shadow depends on the original finish, how the piece has been used or stored and the conditions to which a piece is

Authentic brass pull on vintage American oak chest, ca. 1890 to 1920s with original finish The pull is removed, below.

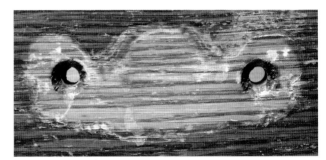

A hardware shadow produced by normal wear and aging. Note that the holes are darkened from contact with the metal.

Does this genuinely old walnut knob belong on this genuinely old maple drawer? Compare the base of the pull to the shape of the shadow, shown below.

Obviously this is not the original knob that created the shadow. This pull is distinctly smaller than the shadow in the finish.

exposed such as coal or wood smoke, cooking fumes, sunlight, humidity and other variables. Generally, drawers in the original finish made before ca. 1930 should show at least some evidence of hardware shadows and movement shadows. Usually, but not always, the older a piece the more obvious the shadows.

Trim and ornaments

It's not unusual to find genuinely old pieces of furniture that have been "enhanced" to increase their value. Gluing lion heads to plain headboards or massive claws to simple feet can dramatically increase the selling price. The new pieces used for these enhancements are cast of resin, or plastic, in molds taken from vintage counterparts. The grain, surface texture, small cracks, puddles of old varnish and tool marks on the originals are all reproduced in the copies.

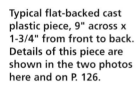
Typical flat-backed cast plastic piece, 9" across x 1-3/4" from front to back. Details of this piece are shown in the two photos here and on P. 126.

Detail of new trim piece in head. Every feature of the original is captured in the new piece including chisel marks, grain pitting. Shown about actual size.

The back side of the piece on P. 125. The reverse side of the new piece is a plain plastic surface. No sign of wood grain or hand carving. Shown about actual size.

Anything in the wooden original is included in the plastic copy. This is a bottom view of the new trim piece on P. 125. Note that the new one-piece plastic reproduction shows a seam line as if made from two pieces of wood. The seam line was copied when a mold was made from the two-piece original.

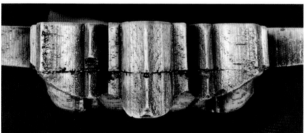

Close up of the grain pattern in the plastic reproduction. It is an exact copy of the grain in the oak original. The finish has been removed to show the pits and waves in the grain. Shown about 5 times actual size.

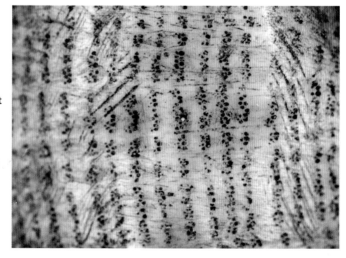

New plastic heads with oak finish. Each about 3" high.
Copied from carved solid wood originals.

A new plastic foot, 8" x 10" x 3".
It weighs nearly four pounds.
Copied from an oak original.

Not all the reproductions copy wood originals. The
new cherub medallion above copies an original made
with glue and sawdust. The surface of such originals
is slightly rough and pitted.

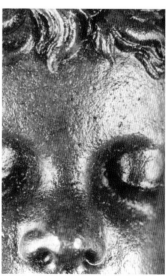

New reproductions of sawdust
and glue originals perfectly
duplicate that textured surface.
as this closeup shows.

New plastic trim includes just about every style, type of wood and purpose imaginable, from Gothic Revival oak legs to Classical medallions in cherry; from shallow appliqués to full three-dimensional figures. Most new trim pieces are sold already finished. Golden oak is the most common color followed by Victorian black walnut, English oak and natural cherry. Using water-based stains, it's fairly easy to blend in new trim on old pieces of furniture. New pieces are not just found on furniture but on shelves, mirrors, picture frames, pedestals, doors and interior woodwork such as fireplace mantels.

If possible, begin your examination of a suspected piece by looking at the back side. Nearly all new backs are smooth with no grain pattern or texture. As a general rule, an authentic piece of carved wood trim would show the same pattern of grain on the back as the front. If there is no grain on the back surfaces, the piece is a new piece of cast plastic. Another easy test is to look for nails or some other fasteners. The great majority of new plastic trim is simply glued onto the surface. Genuine wood trim, even quite small pieces, is generally nailed. Putting a nail into the new plastic requires drilling a hole. Although nails don't guarantee a piece of trim is old, absence of nails or other fasteners should be considered a warning sign of new plastic trim.

You can also try pressing your thumbnail into the suspected surface. Most furniture woods-oak, walnut, cherry, mahogany-can be dented with a thumbnail. Most new plastic trim cannot be dented with a thumbnail. The advantage of this test is that you can perform the test quickly and inconspicuously. The disadvantage is that some people don't have the necessary strength. Your thumbnail also needs to be short or you will split it. Do not use pointed metal objects such as keys, nails, knives and similar objects because they can slip and scratch the finish.

Scraping an exposed edge with a sharp blade is also an effective test. Shallow cuts in real wood almost always produce a curled shaving or single sliver. The surface under the cut will have a uniformly dull appearance and should have the same grain pattern as the surrounding surface. When the brittle plastic trim is cut, it generally chips off in random bits and chunks. Below the cut, there is no grain pattern in plastic trim.

As a last resort you could also carefully swab acetone or fingernail polish remover on the suspected piece. Acetone removes the colored finish on most new pieces exposing the plastic body. Use this test with extreme caution, though, because acetone is highly flammable and very caustic. Acetone will very probably damage or at least produce spots in original finishes unless very carefully applied.

Not all genuinely old trim is carved wood. Some vintage Victorian trim, for example, was made by pouring a mixture of sawdust and glue into molds.

There are also new plastic copies of sawdust and glue trim. Tests for detecting copies of sawdust and glue originals, though, are different than those used for detecting copies of solid wood trim. Vintage sawdust and glue trim, for example, does not have a grain like solid wood trim so grain is not a reliable test of age.

One of the clues to a plastic copy of molded sawdust and glue trim is color. As a general rule, vintage glue and sawdust trim is almost always made from the same species of wood as the furniture to which they are applied. That is to say sawdust and glue trim on walnut furniture would logically be made from walnut sawdust, which is dark brown. If the body color of a piece of trim on walnut furniture is any other color than dark brown, that could be a clue that a cast plastic substitute has been used.

Another test to separate most new and old glue and sawdust trim is whether the suspect piece is solid or hollow. Plastic trim is cast in two-piece molds and is almost always solid in cross section. Large pieces of vintage glue and sawdust trim were generally made in one-piece press molds and are hollow in cross section, not solid. Clusters of vintage fruit, for example, have concave backs, which follow the design. A plastic copy would have a solid flat back.

Never perform any test without the seller's permission. Acetone and small scrapes are potentially destructive if not carefully conducted.

Phillips head screws are modern fasteners first introduced in the 1930s.

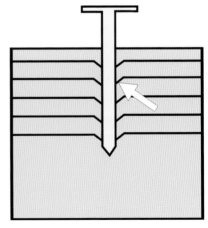

Driving nails splits wood cells. As the nails pass, cells spring back (arrow) putting great pressure on the nail shank. Cellular pressure holds the nail in place and makes it difficult to withdraw.

Fasteners

Certain types of fasteners virtually eliminate the possibility of a piece being old. Staples and Phillips head screws, for example, are obvious signs of a reproduction. One or two might be accepted as a legitimate repair, but more than several almost always indicate a reproduction. All bright shiny hardware with no evidence of patina or normal wear should also raise suspicion.

Nails are the most common fastener used in making furniture. Nails are effective fasteners due to the cellular structure of wood. As a nail is driven into wood, the tip of the nail pushes apart or crushes wood cells in its path. When the tip of the nail passes, the cells spring back and try to resume their former position. This applies pressure to the nail shank in the opposite direction of the nail path and creates resistance that holds the nail in place.

The wood surrounding nail heads can provide clues about age. Nails before about 1930 generally have a much lower carbon content than later nails. As a low carbon nail rusts, it generally leaves a black stain in and around the nail hole. Newer nails with higher carbon generally leave red or reddish-brown rust stains in the wood.

Be sure that the condition of the nail matches the surrounding wood. It is a common practice for forgers to combine old wood and old hardware, including nails, from several genuinely old but derelict pieces to make one "right" piece. If the wood around a nail head is blackened, then the nail should be blackened, too. You would never expect to find a rusty nail in wood that has no rust stains in and around the nail hole.

An unusually large filled-in nail head on a typical piece of Indonesian reproduction furniture. Actual size of filling is over 1/4" diameter.

Scraping away the filling reveals a common nail with a large flat head, not a finishing nail. A removed common nail shown on left.

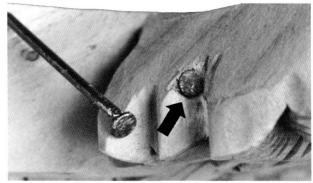

Top view of nail hole. Large arrow shows black stain created by original vintage nail. Small arrows point to more recent reddish-brown rust left by modern nail placed in the same nail hole.

Cross section of the nail hole shown in the photo above, created by splitting the wood. The blackened top of the hole was formed by the original nail. The reddish-brown rust was formed by a modern nail.

GLASS

Art glass is a frequent target of reproductions, especially fake and forged marks and signatures, due to its high value. When evaluating a suspect piece, you should consider many factors including: 1. Shapes known to be original; 2. Glass quality and finishing; and 3. Any markings and signatures and how they were applied.

Shape

Shapes and patterns of major companies like Steuben, Lalique and others are fairly easy to document in original catalog drawings. Steuben shapes obviously should not have Tiffany signatures. As you'll see in the following pages, though, original shapes are being copied, so shape alone should not be used as your only test of age.

Many original pieces, particularly Steuben, include shape numbers in original markings. If a shape number is present, it should agree with the original catalog shape of the same number. But again, this is a general rule; some forged marks on copied shapes do include the correct shape number. However, many forgers are careless and make up shape numbers at random when applying fake marks.

Glass quality and finishing

The vast majority of all authentic 19th and early 20th century art glass has a polished or ground out pontil (see photos on P. 136). Pontils on the reproductions are rarely ground out or polished. If you encounter a piece marked or signed with the name of a well-known art glass maker, such as Tiffany, Steuben, etc., and the piece does not have a ground pontil, it is almost certain to be a forgery.

On the other hand, a ground pontil is not a guarantee of age. Forgers now are polishing out rough pontils on reproductions. It has also become common to buy new studio glass made in an Art Nouveau style, such as Orient and Flume, Lundberg Studios or others, polish out those legitimate marks, and add forged marks of old companies like Tiffany, Steuben, or Loetz (see illustration on Page 135). Even though pontils can be added, it is still a good idea to check for a polished pontil. With rare exceptions, if a piece doesn't have a ground pontil, you really don't need to bother with any other tests.

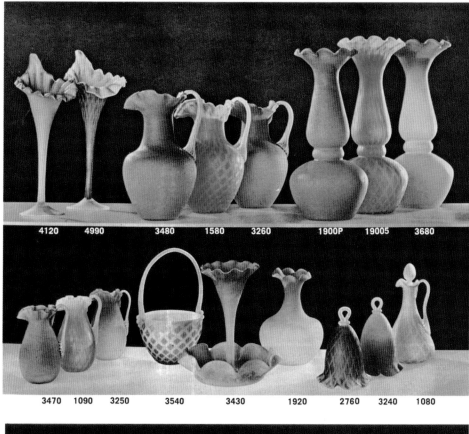

Antique and collectible glass has been widely reproduced for many years. Collectors need to avoid not only current reproductions, but also copies from previous years like the art glass shown here in a 1970s' reproduction wholesale catalog.

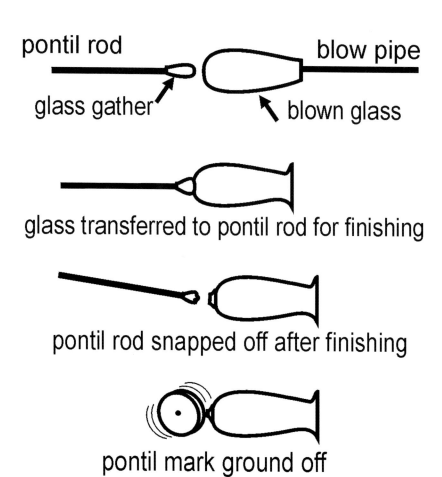

pontil rod   blow pipe

glass gather   blown glass

glass transferred to pontil rod for finishing

pontil rod snapped off after finishing

pontil mark ground off

The majority of blown art glass is removed from the blow pipe with a pontil rod. The rod has a small dab of hot glass on the end, which is joined to the blown glass. Then, the blown glass is sheared off the blow pipe. Now, held on the pontil rod, the blown glass receives its final shape and decoration. After decorating, the pontil rod is snapped or "cracked" off, leaving a pontil mark or "scar" where the rod was attached. On good quality pieces, the pontil mark is ground out and polished.

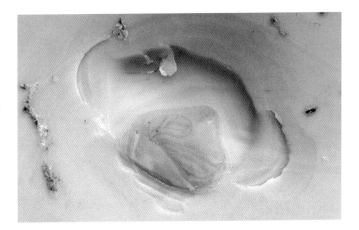

Typical rough pontil; also called open, cracked, or scarred pontil.

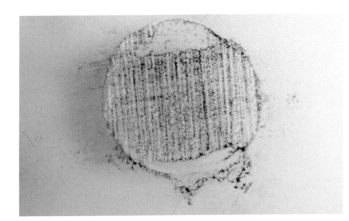

Roughly ground pontil. Grind marks are highlighted by pencil rubbing.

Close-up view of a typical vintage polished pontil.

Markings

Fake marks are now so common they should never be used as a single test of age or authenticity. It has become more important than ever to know and understand what original marks are appropriate for the pieces to which they are applied and how original marks and signatures were made. In other words, learn which marks were used during what years and which marks should be acid-etched, which were wheel-engraved, and which appear only as paper labels.

Some lines of art glass, for example, were never marked. Original Burmese by Mt. Washington Glass Co., for example, were never permanently marked. The only documented mark applied to those wares are rarely found paper labels. Any form of permanent mark, such as an acid stamp or engraved mark, is a forgery.

Many new engraved marks are applied with modern diamond or carbide tipped tools. These modern tools create letters and numbers with very smooth outlines. Most, but not all, vintage marks produced by engraving have ragged broken outlines, not continuously smooth outlines.

Be especially wary of all acid etched marks. Rubber stamps can be made from all kinds of artwork such as logos, trademarks, letterheads and patent applications that appear in reference books on antiques. These rubber stamps are then used to apply liquid acid to new glass, as well as genuine old glass that was never originally marked. Frequent targets of acid-etched forgeries include Tiffany, Loetz, and Gallé. None of those firms ever used acid stamps to apply original marks. Knowing how original marks were applied is one of the best ways to protect yourself against forgeries.

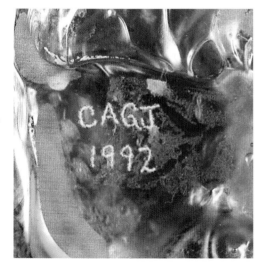

The mark on a new piece of iridescent studio glass, which resembles vintage pieces of Loetz and Tiffany. Legitimate marks are often removed so fake marks can be added.

The legitimate mark shown in the photo on P. 137 has been removed. The next step is to apply a forged signature.

A forged mark of a vintage maker, Loetz, has been applied on the new piece of art glass. Authentic Loetz marks are wheel-cut, not engraved.

Typical recently applied engraving made by a modern carbide or diamond tipped tool leaving smooth-sided outlines.

Detail of typical vintage engraved mark. Letters and numbers in most, but not all, old marks have a ragged interrupted outline.

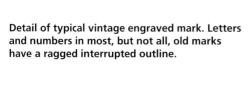

Burmese

Original Burmese was made by the Mt. Washington Glass Co. beginning in 1885. It was later made under license in England by Thomas Webb and Sons. Burmese shades from a yellow body to a salmon pink toward the edges and rims.

Authentic Burmese and other internally shaded 19th century art glass, such as amberina, peachblow and others, are made from heat sensitive glass formulas. Burmese, for example, after being blown and worked, was entirely yellow. The pink shading was produced only by exposing selected areas to a higher temperature. The key ingredient to any heat-sensitive glass is gold, which causes the glass to turn red, or a shade of red, when reheated. The soft yellow color of Burmese was produced by uranium oxide. The gold caused the yellow to turn pink when reheated.

Keep these guidelines in mind when evaluating a piece of Burmese:

1) All authentic 19th century Burmese has a smooth polished pontil, although it will be satinized on acid finished Burmese. The great majority of reproduction pontils are not polished. Although some reproduction pontils have been just recently ground out, this is still a good first test.

2) The majority of the Italian reproduction Burmese has narrow ridges on handles and feet. Most original handles and feet are smooth. When old handles and feet are ridged, the ridges are very broad and wide (see photos on P. 140).

3) Swirled streaks in the glass body are a sign of a reproduction. Original Burmese is one homogeneous body that comes from the furnace all yellow. Only when it is reheated do some areas change into pink. New Burmese glass is often, but not always, mixed from two separate colors, pink and yellow. This often produces streaks and swirls in the body glass that are never found in original Burmese.

4) The very edge of rims on most Italian reproductions of Burmese are nearly transparent (clear glass). Sight along the rim and you'll see a line of what appears to be clear frosted glass.

5) Most original Burmese has softer texture due to acid finishing. The majority of reproductions have a coarser texture from sandblasting.

6) Original Burmese, which contains uranium, will fluoresce under long wave black light. However, some of the Italian reproductions also fluoresce because they also contain uranium. Black light is helpful to eliminate the more obvious fakes but is not a positive guarantee of age.

It is also becoming more important to carefully inspect decorated Burmese pieces. Genuinely old but originally undecorated pieces are now being painted to bring higher prices. All original decorations are fired on; many recent paintings are not. Black light may be helpful in spotting recently applied decorations.

A group of Murano reproductions of Victorian art glass is shown in the catalog on Page 134.

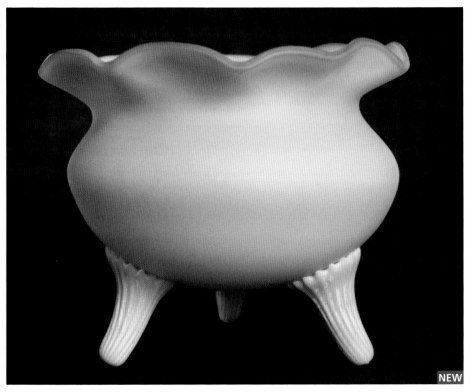

NEW

This reproduction Burmese bowl was made in Italy. The shape is a very close copy of the original Mt. Washington Burmese shape #129.

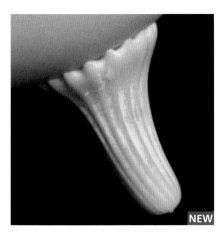

NEW

Most applied handles and feet on the Italian reproductions have narrow ridges like this example. These narrow ridges are not found in original Burmese.

OLD

Ridges were rarely used on vintage pieces. Any ridges on vintage feet and handles are very broadly spaced as in this example.

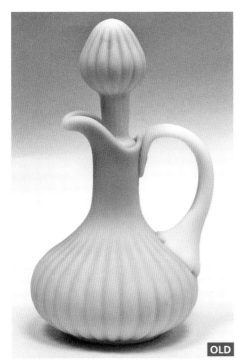

OLD

NEW

The only authentic Mt. Washington Burmese cruet shape is this ribbed example. Smooth applied handle and matching ribbed mushroom-shaped stopper.

Imitation Burmese cruet with painted decoration. The cruet was made in Murano, Italy ca. late 1970s through the mid-1980s.

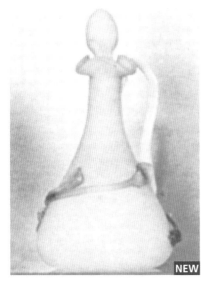

NEW

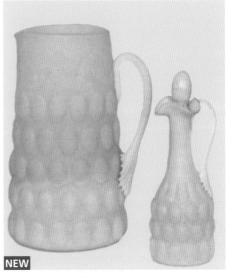

NEW

Imitation Burmese cruet with applied leaf and vine decoration. Very thin applied ridged handle. Made in Murano Italy, ca. late 1970s through the mid-1980s.

Reproduction 10" pitcher and 7" cruet made in Italy ca. 1970-1980s. The only genuine Mt. Washington Burmese cruet shape is shown in the photo at top left.

Lalique

Rene Lalique (1860 to 1945) was one of the most successful artists/designers of all time. Lalique began commercial production of his own glass around 1905, which continued until his death in 1945. The glass business was carried on by his son, Marc, who died in 1977, and then his granddaughter, Marie-Claude Lalique. The business still operates today as Cristal Lalique. Many of the original pre-1945 designs remain in production.

There are several considerations when evaluating Lalique. There are genuine Lalique pieces made after 1945 with forged pre-1945 marks; new frosted glass (especially from the Czech Republic) with forged marks; and pre-1945 glass by other manufacturers with forged Lalique marks.

Virtually all authentic Lalique glass is marked. Authentic marks can be molded, engraved, sandblasted through a stencil or wheelcut (see examples in on P. 144). Pieces made before Lalique's death in 1945 were marked "R. Lalique," usually followed by the word "France." After 1945, the "R" was dropped and the mark was simply "Lalique, France." The single letter "R" is commonly forged on post-1945 Lalique to suggest a piece was made before 1945. Since 1980, Lalique engraved marks have also included the ® symbol, which was never used before 1980. If the initial "R" appeared with that symbol, it would automatically be a forgery.

Acid marks were not generally used on Lalique until after 1945. Any acid mark including "R. Lalique" represented as pre-1945 is almost certainly a forgery. No authentic pre-1945 Lalique has a mark that includes "Made in France." No authentic pre-1945 Lalique marks include "Rene" spelled out, only the initial "R."

New Art Deco-styled glass made today in the Czech Republic is frequently represented as "unmarked" Lalique or sold with forged Lalique marks. Most is inferior in quality to Lalique. One quick test of quality is to look for mold seams. Mold seams are almost impossible to find in genuine Lalique. Seams on the inexpensive copycat pieces are usually very obvious. Most original Lalique has at least some polishing, either on the base or top rim. The look-alike pieces are generally frosted all over.

Glass made before 1945 by other manufacturers are also found with forged Lalique marks. Forged marks on look-alike glass made before 1945 have the same general problems as other typical forgeries just discussed. Most pre-1945 look-alikes are simply not the quality of Lalique. Some types of glass never made by Lalique, such as cameo glass, are also appearing with fake Lalique marks.

If there is confusion about the authenticity of a mark, consider using a black light. The formula for clear colorless glass changed after 1945. Pre-1945 clear colorless Lalique fluoresces a soft yellow-green to yellow under long-wave black light. Clear colorless Lalique made after 1945 does not fluoresce. The only exceptions to this rule are a handful of pre-1945 pieces that fluoresce a peachy-yellow color, which is also a reliable test of age.

Car mascots

Among the rarest and most expensive vintage pieces of Lalique are the car mascots, or hood ornaments. Lalique made 29 mascots during the 1920s and 1930s. Eight of the originals are still in current production and frequently cause confusion, especially if the legitimate marks are altered.

The eight mascots which have been reproduced are: peacock head, St. Christopher, Chrysis (nude), eagle head, small cock, boar, perch, and cock's head. With only one exception, Lalique reproduction mascots are marked on the bottom of the base with "Lalique France" engraved in script. The exception is the St. Christopher, which was made with molded R. Lalique marks up until the late 1980s. Since then the mold has been reworked and the St. Christopher, too, is issued only with engraved marks. No other reproduction mascots have molded marks and no other marks on new mascots include "R" before "Lalique."

Marks on original mascots vary from style to style so there is no one single rule for authentication. Buyers interested in mascots should study and learn how specific mascots were marked. Some original marks are molded raised letters while others are molded below the surface (intaglio) and still other original marks are sandblasted or etched.

Buyers also need to be aware of close copies of Lalique mascots by other manufacturers. Copies were made during the 1920s as well as in recent years. Two of the most confusing current Lalique look-alikes are a frosted glass horse's head and an Art Deco woman made in the Czech Republic from vintage 1920s molds.

Fake marks

Acid-etched forgery, "R. Lalique FRANCE." No authentic pre-1945 Lalique mark was acid-etched. Authentic post-1945 acid-etched Lalique marks are all uppercase sans-serif style, not cursive and not a mixture of upper and lowercase letters.

Forged intaglio mark below the surface. Authentic marks are in molded letters raised above the surrounding surface, not below.

Molded raised glass forgery, "R. LALIQUE," on the foot of a vase. Letters are almost 1/2" tall. Original molded letters are under 1/4" high. Original marks are in inconspicuous locations, never in such prominent positions.

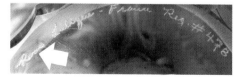

Engraved forgery "Rene Lalique-France." Original marks were marked with the single letter "R," not "Rene" spelled out.

Authentic marks

Authentic pre-1945 molded mark. Virtually all authentic Lalique molded marks appear as raised letters. Note the simple sans serif block-style letters.

Authentic pre-1945 engraved mark. Engraved marks were usually applied to mold-blown, not pressed pieces. Although there is considerable variation among genuine engraved marks, almost all have the same general appearance as this example. Note the unique shape of the "R."

Authentic pre-1945 engrave mark. Genuine marks may or may not include an order, catalog or merchant number. The presence or absence of a number is not a test of age or authenticity. Note again the distinctive shape of the "R."

Authentic wheel cut mark. Wheel cut marks were made with the edge of a small grinding wheel. Letters made with grinding wheels appear as short straight lines as seen in this typical example.

Genuine R. Lalique France mark etched through a stencil. Note the gaps in the letters left by the stencil.

A close copy of Deux Flours with obvious mold seams made in Taiwan. Watch out for new Taiwan stoppers in Lalique bottles.

NEW

Lalique's Deux Flours (Two Flowers) was introduced ca. 1935 as an empty dressing table bottle and is still in production. Note the shape of the stopper.

OLD

A look-alike Lalique bowl sold by a reproduction wholesale firm during the 1970s. Marked in molded raised letters "Made in France."

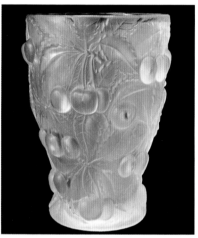

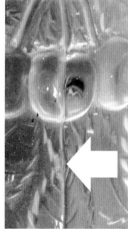

Most new pieces of frosted glass have prominent mold seams like the example shown in cherries. Molds seams are barely noticeable in pre-1945 Lalique.

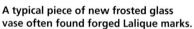

A typical piece of new frosted glass vase often found forged Lalique marks.

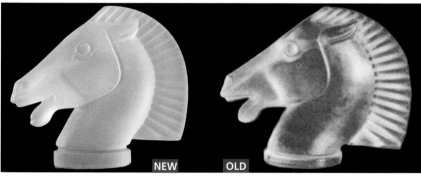

Frosted clear glass horse head made today in Czech Republic, left. The original ca. 1929 Lalique "Longchamps" car mascot, right. The new piece is gray and chalky with obvious mold seams.

Fake engraved Lalique mark applied to the new vase in cameo.

New 10" cameo vase with purple overlay on clear frosted body. Marked with the factory engraved Lalique signature shown above.

Look-alike mascot figure made in the Czech Republic since the mid-1990s from old 1920s molds. Frosted clear glass, 10" across. No permanent mark.

NEW

Genuine Lalique Victoire made ca. 1920s-1930s. About 10" across, permanently marked with molded letters "R. LALIQUE FRANCE." Mold seams virtually invisible.

OLD

Loetz

Johann Lötz never owned a glass business. The iridescent glass known by his name was made at a glass factory started by his widow, Susanna, in 1851. She named the business "Johann Lötz Witwe" (the widow of Johann Lötz). The business began making common objects but turned to art glass in 1879 when Johann's grandson Maximilian Von Spaun II took control of the business. Around the turn of the 19th century, spelling of the business name was changed from Lötz to Loetz. Pieces made for export, if marked, usually read "Loetz, Austria."

Far more iridescent Loetz was originally unmarked than iridescent glass made by Tiffany or Steuben. Before Loetz prices began rising in the 1990s, many originally unmarked pieces of Loetz carried forged signatures of other makers like Tiffany or Steuben. Now that Loetz prices equal or exceed those of other makers, earlier Tiffany and Steuben forgeries are being ground off and faked Loetz marks applied. A number of relatively low-value pieces by other makers have even had their authentic original marks removed and faked Loetz marks added. Similarly, many vintage pieces of Loetz that were originally unsigned, are now being found with recently applied forged marks.

There are a couple of simple rules to keep in mind when examining suspected Loetz marks. First, all acid-stamped marks with "Loetz" or "Lötz" Lötz are forgeries. No original Loetz mark which included "Loetz" or "Lötz" was acid stamped. Similarly, any mark applied with a diamond-tip pen or electric pen is almost certainly a forgery. All original engraved marks with "Loetz" or "Lötz" are wheel engraved. Permanent marks of any kind are virtually unknown on authentic standard production Loetz iridescent glass shades. Any mark with "Lötz" or "Lötz" on an iridescent shade should be considered a forgery unless the seller can provide convincing documentation to prove otherwise.

Vintage Loetz was of the very highest quality. Virtually all vintage Loetz has fire-polished rims and ground and polished pontils. Many iridescent look-alikes, both old and modern, with forged marks have sheared top rims and rough pontils.

A typical new 10" iridescent glass vase made in China, frequently found with forged Loetz marks.

New art glass 5" vase, $55, frequently offered as vintage Loetz with forged marks.

An authentic wheel engraved mark with "Lötz" and arrows in circle.

An authentic wheel engraved mark with "Spaun" and arrows in circle. Spaun, the nephew of Lötz, ran the glass factory.

This authentic mark was used as a paper label only, never engraved. Known to be forged as an acid stamped mark.

All original marks that include "Loetz" or "Lötz" are wheel engraved, not acid-stamped or diamond-tip pen.

Moser

Ludwig Moser founded several glass decorating studios in the middle of the 19th century and a glass factory in the early 1890s. From the 1860s to 1893, the Moser firm decorated blanks from other glass houses. Moser began making its own glass in 1893, when Ludwig Moser's four sons were brought into the business. The business went bankrupt during the 1930s and production was severely limited until the end of WW II in 1946. After the war, the company resumed production and remains in production today.

The Moser specialty was enameling, but the company also worked with cutting and engraving. The company also produced cameo and various acid-etched products. Moser designs have spanned many different styles including Art Nouveau, Art Deco, and Modernism.

Forgeries of Moser marks are frequently applied to new glass as well as genuinely old but unmarked wares of other makers. The most common targets of forged marks are enamel-decorated pieces and cut tablewares. Modern Czech glass is frequently found with forgeries of vintage Moser marks. As a general rule, Moser glass will have ground and polished pontils and polished top rims. Since many pieces of new Moser are very similar to vintage pieces, new marks are often removed and replaced with forgeries of old marks.

New malachite glass like this vase from the Czech Republic is frequently found with forgeries of vintage Moser marks.

Many forged marks include "Austria." No authentic mark of Moser, either old or modern, includes "Austria." Any mark with Austria is a fake.

This new American-made malachite glass figural piece has a faked Moser acid mark.

A fantasy acid-etched mark with only the outline of letters. The person using this mark sells primarily through online auctions. The vast majority of items with this forged mark are inexpensive pressed wares, particularly modern versions of malachite, a jade-green colored glass.

A fantasy forgery usually acid etched, but sometimes applied with a diamond-tip pen.

A fantasy acid-etched mark. "Austria" never appears in any registered Moser mark, either vintage or modern.

Fantasy acid-etched mark with cursive lettering.

An authentic early cursive mark from the late 1880s, usually engraved.

An authentic engraved mark used throughout the 20th century from the 1920s through the 1980s. Earlier forms were acid-stamped or enamel. More recent marks are engraved.

This authentic mark was used from about 1911 through the late 1930s. It is a standard mark, which may be in gold, colored enamel, raised glass or acid stamped. This mark is probably the most widely forged and imitated Moser mark.

Mother of Pearl

Mother of Pearl (MOP) is so named because of its lustered or "pearlized" surface. It is generally made of three layers of glass: 1. A clear outer layer; 2. A middle colored layer; and 3. An inner casing, usually white. MOP was made by blowing or placing a gather of glass into a mold to give the gather a raised pattern. This was then dipped into or rolled over the clear glass. The clear layer runs across the top of the raised pattern, trapping air in the gaps below. These trapped pockets of air reflect and spread light back through the outer surface to give MOP its glowing pearl-like luster. Some variations of MOP also used heat sensitive glass for special effects. The MOP process was patented in America and England by different companies but the technique was used widely throughout the glass industry in the USA and abroad.

Different molds created different patterns of air-trapped designs. MOP is generally named for these designs such as Diamond Quilted and Rain Drop. Some of the other pattern names include Herringbone, Zipper, Peacock Eye, Flower and Acorn, Federzeichnung and Swirl. Original MOP is usually a pastel color such as blue, pink and apricot but can be found in a wide range of other colors. Rainbow MOP refers to pieces with three or more separate colors that usually appear as bands or stripes.

MOP has been reproduced since the mid-1970s. Some pieces are quite crude; others, particularly pieces made in Italy, are quite good and very commonly mistaken for Victorian originals. One of the best tests to separate old from new MOP is to examine the pontil. Virtually all reproduction MOP has open, rough pontils. The great majority of Victorian MOP has ground pontils.

The most widely reproduced MOP pattern is Diamond Quilted followed by Rain Drop and then Herringbone. New pink and blue MOP pieces are nearly an identical color match to the old pink and blue. Colors in the new Rainbow MOP are also very similar to originals. The new apricot color is the least like the original color and often looks brown or appears a muddy bronze.

Many pieces of reproduction MOP are made in new shapes with no Victorian counterparts. An electric lamp in new rainbow MOP from Italy, for example, was never made in any vintage MOP pattern. Other new shapes never seen in old MOP are two bells: one is a smoke bell, the other a hand bell. Both bells are in the Diamond Quilted pattern and were sold in several colors. A new MOP three-trumpet epergne is another new shape never made in Victorian MOP.

Some pieces of new Italian MOP can be identified by a unique crimping in the top rim. Viewed from above, the crimping has the appearance of semicircles. It appears on toothpick holders, rosebowls, baskets and other shapes. No Victorian MOP has any similar crimping. Any piece with this rim is a modern product from Italy.

Another general clue to age is the overall quality of the piece. Many new applied handles, for examples, are attached without being properly centered.

Other new handles are noticeably much too thin and spindly to be practical. Remember, all original pitchers, cruets and other serving pieces were meant for daily use at the dinner table. Does the handle look strong enough to lift the pitcher if it were filled with water?

Once you confirm a MOP piece is genuine, be sure to give it a thorough examination for damage. The air bubbles that give Victorian MOP its unique appearance are often trapped near the surface during manufacturing. The glass is very thin around bubbles near the surface and can break very easily. This leaves jagged holes and pits, which can seriously lower the value.

(RAINBOW MOTHER-OF-PEARL)

New Rainbow MOP from a wholesale catalog.

Pitcher	Rose Bowl	Trumpet Vase
1617/109	1617/106	1617/110

A ca. mid-1970s catalog page of new Rainbow MOP offered by Koscherak Bros, a New York-based gift importer.

re glass—satined herring se mother-of-pearl with nbow stripes.

top left
i/537—VASE, 7" high $13.75 ea.
i/543—BOTTLE VASE, 7½" high $12.50 ea.
i/538—PITCHER, 9" high $17.50 ea.
i/553—CRUET, 7½" high $10.75 ea.
i/550—BELL, 4½" high $11.75 ea.
i/539—ROSE BOWL, 3" high $ 7.50 ea.
i/536—TUMBLER, 4" high $ 7.50 ea.
i/554—ROSE BOWL, 6" high $15.00 ea.

All prices are wholesale and subject to change.

KOSCHERAK BROS., INC.

Estab. 1887   SUITE 211-219 · 225 FIFTH AVENUE · NEW YORK, N. Y. 10010

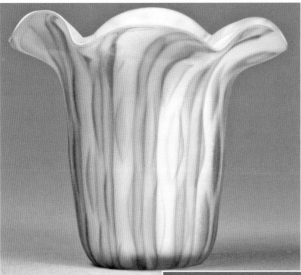

This new toothpick and many other new MOP pieces from Italy have the distinctive semicircles crimped in the top rim. This crimping appears only in modern Italian glass, not in vintage MOP.

The toothpick and most all other new MOP does not have a ground pontil. The base of this example is slightly concave because of its shape, but it's definitely not ground; the pontil rod has been snapped off.

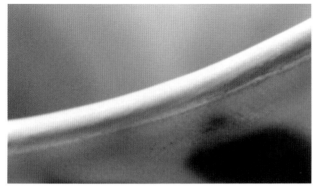

The casing, or lining, of some new MOP is bright white and often spills over onto the colored outside layer. This new example shows the casing actually forming a lip around the entire top rim of a vase.

New Diamond Quilted MOP in a wholesale catalog. The smoke bell shapes were never made in vintage MOP.

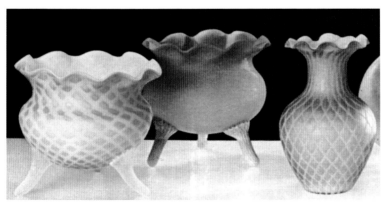

New Diamond Quilted MOP from a wholesale catalog.

Steuben

Steuben Glass Works was founded in 1903 in Corning, New York. Led by Frederick Carder, the firm began making iridescent glass in the Art Nouveau styles similar to Tiffany. Steuben continued to make high quality colored art glass until 1932. In 1932, colored glass was discontinued and Steuben turned to producing clear crystal only, which remains the glass it makes today. Reproductions are getting more sophisticated and are now frequently made in original shapes. Forged Steuben marks are also improving and often include model numbers that correspond to the original shape.

Generally, original iridescent Steuben Aurene should feel silky smooth over the entire surface. Many reproductions have rough, pitted or wavy surfaces. Original iridescence is consistent over the entire surface. That means the underside of the base looks about the same as the sides. Many reproductions will not have iridescence on the undersides of bases.

Virtually all original Steuben pontils are polished. Most reproductions with forged marks have rough pontils. It is not unusual, though, for unethical sellers to polish out new rough pontils to create an imitation of an original piece. Marks on legitimate new studio glass in Art Nouveau styles—like Orient and Flume, Lundberg Studios, and others—are also frequently ground out before applying forged marks.

Be sure to hold up all pieces to a light. The great majority of reproductions have internal flaws in the glass. In ordinary light, these flaws are hidden under iridescence or other surface decorations. Held to the light, bubbles, streaks, and folds are easily seen. These types of flaws are virtually never found in original art glass.

Steuben's line of iridescent art glass, named Aurene, was made from 1904 to 1932. Most, but not all, Aurene is marked either "Aurene" or "Steuben Aurene" and usually located around ground pontils. No authentic iridescent Aurene is marked "Steuben" only. Authentic marks are always engraved and tend to be irregular and slightly wavy in appearance. Original engraved marks are usually, but not always, followed by a catalog shape number. Authentic marks vary considerably in size of letters, style and technique.

Original fleur-de-lis marks were used between 1903 and 1932 on non-iridized colored art glass including art glass shades. An authentic acid-stamped fleur-de-lis is only about three-eighths-inch tall. Forged marks are almost always much larger; many up to an inch tall. Many faked marks are made up of areas filled in acid with only the letters left clear. In the original mark, only the outline of the fleur-de-lis and the letters are in frosted acid. The fleur-de-lis also appears as a raised mark on some acid cut back pieces made from 1915 to 1932. Acid fleur-de-lis marks never appear on authentic clear colorless Steuben made after 1932.

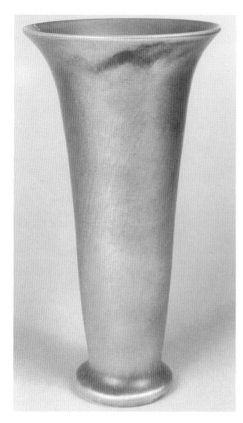

This new 11" vase, with gold iridescent finish over an opal glass body, is similar to original Aurene and Calcite. The new vase is a copy of the original 2564 shape.

Forged signature "Aurene," followed by model number "2564." Note the large broken pontil mark. The forged model number is correct for this shape.

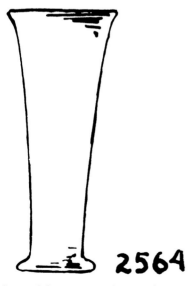

The shape of the new vase is a nearly identical copy of the original #2564 shape vase as shown in the 1903-1932 Steuben shape book.

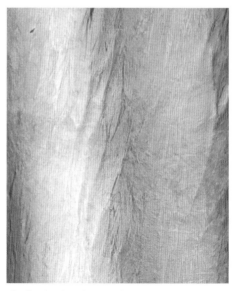

The body glass below the iridescent surface is wavy and rough. Area shown about actual size. This rough surface is typical of many reproductions with an iridized surface.

Original fleur-de-lis marks on Steuben art glass lamp shades are found primarily on shades with two and one-quarter inch fitter rims. Many of those marks included a powdered metal added to the acid to produce a fleur-de-lis silvery in color rather than colorless matte acid. The great majority of original fleur-de-lis marks on shades appear on the inside of the fitter rim. Most, but not all, original marks on shades were applied with the tip of the fleur-de-lis pointing towards the inside of the shade.

An authentic fleur-de-lis mark is formed by the lines and letters only etched in acid. Original marks are quite small, about 3/8" tall. Used ca. 1904-1932 on wide variety of colored art glass but never on any iridescent glass.

Authentic silvery Steuben fleur-de-lis marks on fitter rims generally point toward the inside of the shade. Unlike the original acid version, which is generally quite sharp, original silver fleur-de-lis may be slightly blurred. If the mark is so filled in with silver as to be illegible, it's a forgery.

Typical forged acid stamped fleur-de-lis mark. Very ragged and blurry; the fleur-de-lis is filled in with acid.

Many forged fleur-de-lis marks are reversed from the original mark. Only the letters and outline of the fleur-de-lis should be frosted.

Tiffany

Louis Comfort Tiffany (b.1848 to d.1933) was a leading designer of the Art Nouveau period. He is perhaps best known for his art glass and table lamps, but worked with jewelry, metalwork, textiles, pottery, and complete interiors.

Tiffany was a designer and company owner; he did not personally shape any glass or assemble any lamps. All work was performed by highly skilled artisans according to Tiffany's designs. The facsimile signature "L.C. Tiffany," like similar signatures of Emile Gallé and Rene Lalique, is simply a company mark, not a personal signature.

Before 1890, most objects were custom-made for special commissions in Tiffany's interior design business. After 1890, more goods were made for the general public and those are the majority of pieces in the market today. All production of Tiffany products ended in 1938. Tiffany's companies operated under various names over the years, and these are reflected in the marks. There are so many Tiffany marks that it is particularly important to understand which marks were originally used on the various materials. Some original marks appear only on metal, others only on glass. Some of today's forgeries are trademarks that only appeared on legal documents and were never used as marks on products.

The most common forgeries of Tiffany marks are found on iridescent art glass. Original engraved marks appear on Tiffany blown glass made from 1893 to 1928. There are many differences found among original engraved marks. Some are illegible; others are in beautiful flowing script. Marks on original iridescent pieces are almost always rotary-engraved. Some pieces were marked with only a diamond-tip stylus but these are mostly the later pastel pieces. Most, but not all, original engraved marks include model numbers or date codes. Keep in mind, however, that clever forgers know all about date and shape codes and will include those codes in faked marks. Original engraved marks are quite small with most letters virtually never over one-quarter inch tall.

Large, poorly spaced, badly proportioned or awkwardly located marks are always suspect. Original engraved marks are usually only three sixteenths to one quarter-inch tall on even the largest pieces. Any acid-etched Tiffany mark is a fake. No original Tiffany glass was ever marked with acid. Many of the acid fakes are copied from trademarks and logos that were originally used in stationery, patent applications and advertising only, never as a mark on glass.

Faked paper labels have been increasing in recent years. It's a relatively simple matter to make paper labels on home computers with image editing software and high quality printers. The majority of new paper labels fluoresce under black light. Many marks used on the new paper labels were never used on original paper labels.

Like other types of art glass, the construction and quality of the glass is a better clue to age than marks. Iridescence should be smooth and even across the entire surface. No internal flaws should be observed when held to a light. Virtually all authentic Tiffany blown art glass will have ground pontils and fire polished top rims.

Genuine engraved marks, like this example, were made with a variety of tools including small wheels, ball-shaped bits and a diamond-tip stylus. Original marks vary widely in appearance. Most genuine engraved marks, other than those made with a diamond tip, have a jagged appearance. Most authentic signatures are placed in or around ground pontils.

Forged mark on new iridescent art glass vase. Marked "LC Tiffany Favrile 3343B." Note large open pontil mark.

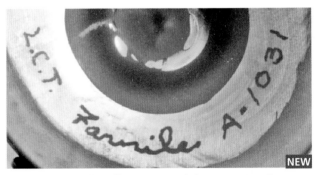

New 11" iridescent art glass vase with forged Tiffany mark. Complete forged mark shown in base. When held to the light, there are numerous internal flaws and swirls in the glass body.

Typical forgery of a Tiffany engraved signature. Very large half-inch tall letters extend halfway around the base. Letters in the great majority of original engraved marks are rarely over one-quarter inch tall, most closer to one-eighth inch. This fake includes a date mark, A-1031, for the year 1894.

Forged Tiffany TGDCO paper label. Very poorly formed letters, black letters on white paper. Irregular wavy edge from hand cutting; about five-eighths inch diameter.

Forged LCT monogram paper label. Black lettering on white paper. Hand cut wavy edge on label; about three-quarter inch diameter.

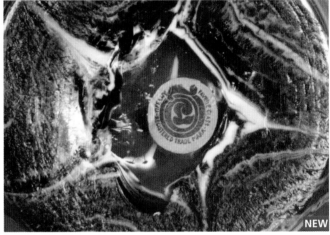

Authentic LCT monogram paper label. Embossed gold printing on green background on white paper. Original labels are only about three-quarter inch diameter. Shown here on polished pontil with authentic engraved mark. Note the small size of original engraved letters. Authentic labels rarely appear alone; most labels appear in addition to an engraved signature.

Cameo glass

The most recent cameo glass reproductions are becoming more like vintage originals. While copies of old signatures and marks have been used since the early 1990s, recent reproductions intentionally duplicate vintage designs and decorative techniques.

One of the vintage techniques new pieces try to copy is "mold blown," also known as "blown out." Typical vintage cameo glass was formed by blowing the shape in a mold, and the design was created in glass overlays cut away with acid. The manufacture of mold-blown cameo was more complicated and costly. Shape molds used in blown out cameo production were deeply cut with the design. As glass was blown into the shape mold, glass was forced into the designs cut into the mold. This produced a final shape with a highly raised design molded in the surface, much higher than designs produced by acid cuttings alone. The raised design was usually wheel polished to further increase the contrast between the design and background.

Virtually all pre-1930 mold-blown cameo glass was made by the Gallé factory. Gallé introduced its mold-blown wares around 1924 in preparation for the 1925 Exposition Universelle. Most subjects of mold blown Gallé were fruits and vegetables such as apples, pears, lemons and oranges, which appeared on a variety of vases, lamps and ceiling fixtures. Some of the more unusual pieces in Gallé's mold-blown series include exotic animals such as elephants and polar bears.

There are two ways to catch the majority of new cameo glass that imitates the mold-blown originals. The raised designs on original Gallé mold blown ware is hollow on the inside and perfectly smooth. Raised designs on the great majority of "mold blown" reproductions are originally solid glass. The area behind the raised design has been hollowed out by grinding, not pushed out by blowing. Depending on the size of the mouth, you can look down inside many new mold-blown pieces and see the grinding. If the mouth is large enough, you can reach inside with your fingers and feel the rough grinding. The majority of original mold blown raised designs were wheel polished and have a shiny finish. Raised designs on almost all the new pieces are not polished. The new raised designs are frosted, not shiny.

Although Gallé pioneered the mold-blown technique and made virtually all vintage mold-blown cameo, many reproductions of mold blown-style cameo are often marked with names of other vintage makers. Mold-blown style cameo marked with any name other than Gallé should be examined very carefully. Other than a well known Daum vase with a forest scene, there are only a handful of documented mold-blown originals by other vintage makers.

"Hammering" is another technique copied on recent reproductions. Also known as Martelé, the French word for hammered, this effect was produced by going over the glass surface with a rounded grinding stone or burr. Lightly touching the burr tangentially against the glass produced a shallow concave depression similar to "dents" or pebbling produced by hitting metal with a hammer. The best original examples were made by Gallé and Daum, but the technique was used on at least some pieces by a variety of vintage makers.

Generally, hammering in reproductions is much cruder than original treatments. Most original hammering was either over the entire surface or gradually faded in and out of selected backgrounds In most new examples, hammering is strictly confined to very limited areas with very rigid well defined borders. Old hammering "dents" are rarely over one-quarter inch across; anything larger should be inspected closely. Vintage hammered surfaces are typically quite subtle, often disappearing from view with changing light. Old hammering has a soft rounded appearance from acid polishing or wheel polishing after it was ground. New hammered surfaces are generally sharp and distinct because they are not finished with acid or further polishing. The reproduction shown on P. 166 happens to be marked Daum but other new hammered pieces have forged marks of other vintage makers.

Signatures and marks are the most unreliable tests of age. Marks of virtually every vintage maker are being reproduced on new cameo glass. Most new marks are virtually identical copies of vintage marks including well known variations especially of Gallé. Even marks of relatively obscure and small manufacturers have been copied.

Marks

There are only a handful of marks that conclusively prove a piece of cameo glass is a reproduction. One of the most obvious is the mark T-I-P. These three letters in raised glass appear on reproduction Gallé made in Romania. The exact style and size of the letters vary in appearance. The location of TIP relative to the location of the Gallé mark can also vary considerably. Sometimes the two marks are almost touching but can be separated by as much as eight or more inches. Some sellers attempt to explain the TIP mark as an "apprentice" to Gallé or as an "export" mark. Neither, of course, is true. Any piece with the TIP is new.

Attempts are frequently made to remove TIP marks by grinding them away. Whether this is successful depends on the skill with which it's done. Unskilled do-it-yourself work with a small grinding tool is generally easy to spot. Glass repair shops, however, can remove the marks virtually without a trace. Of course, such professional work only adds to the cost of the reproduction. Most people who sell reproductions usually don't waste the time having such work done. Just be aware that the letters can be removed.

Other marks immediately suspect are those that cannot be found in any reference books on vintage cameo glass. Be logical. What are the chances of the mark of a legitimate pre-1930 manufacturer not being recorded? If a seller claims a previously unreported mark is from an authentic vintage maker, let them prove it. Ask them for some kind of documentation. If a mark isn't listed in an auction catalog, a reference book on cameo glass or a book of glass marks, you have every right to be skeptical. Some of the unusual names you'll find on new cameo glass are Cristo, Ramski, Tudor, Pierre and Statescu.

Pontils

For many years, one of the most reliable and easiest general tests for dating most cameo glass was to check the base for a ground pontil. French cameo glass made before 1930, almost without exception, has ground pontils. Until recently, virtually no reproduction cameo glass included a pontil.

That changed in early 2005 when new cameo marked Gallé began appearing with ground pontils. Pontils in new pieces were very similar to pontils found in pre-1930 Gallé. The new cameo with pontils is also similar to vintage pieces in other ways. Top rims, for example, are now properly finished and rounded

NEW

Reproduction "blown-out" elephant vase with raised glass Gallé signature at top. The new pattern is a close copy of the original pattern at right.

OLD

Authentic ca. 1924 Gallé blown-out elephant vase. Most original blown-out elephant vases in this shape are signed at the bottom. There are various original color combinations.

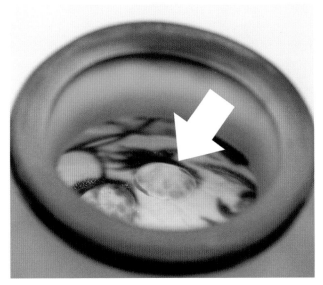

A view down inside a new blown-out style piece of cameo glass. The areas behind the raised pattern is ground out on the inside of the vase. There is no grinding on the insides of authentic vintage cameo.

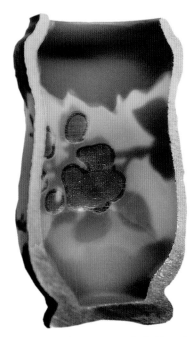

New cameo glass vase with pears in blown-out style. This piece is marked Gallé in raised glass lettering.

A new cameo glass vase cut in half to show the grinding behind the pattern. The insides of vintage pieces are smooth, not ground.

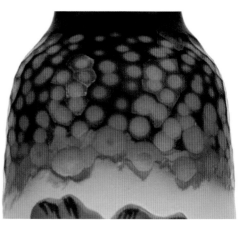

NEW

OLD

Reproduction polar vase. The bears in the new vases are fairly crude raised outlines. The top rim is not polished, the Gallé mark is in raised glass with letters arranged horizontally.

Original 15" polar bear Gallé vase from the mid-1920s. Virtually all original polar bear pieces have a sapphire blue, almost electric blue, body glass. All top rims on authentic polar bear pieces are rounded over by grinding and all originals have ground pontils. Nearly Gallé marks on the polar bear series are below the surface, not raised above the surface.

This new vase marked "Daum Nancy" attempts to duplicate the "hammered metal" effect found on some original cameo glass. The effect was originally made by carving the surface with a small grinding wheel. New hammering shown at right is fairly close in appearance to the original effect, but overall not as finely finished.

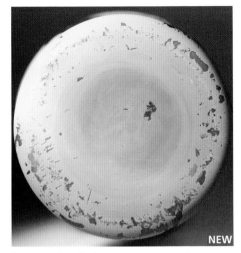

NEW

Bottom of typical new cameo vase. Some new bottoms may be concave or slightly depressed, but they are almost never ground.

NEW

A very rough base found on many typical cameo glass reproductions. Even rough surfaces should have ground pontils.

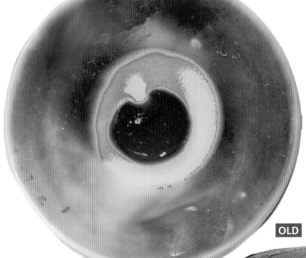

OLD

Ground pontil on a typical authentic French cameo vase showing concentric rings of different colors. Some original ground pontils may be too shallow to expose all the overlays but should show a minimum of two colors. This example shows three colors.

Another typical ground pontil in the base of an original piece of cameo glass.

OLD

This new vase is marked "TIP" (see arrow) and "Gallé" in raised glass lettering. All Gallé marked "TIP" are new (see photo at top right). No vintage Gallé mark includes TIP. The appearance of the letters T-I-P varies; several common styles are shown above. The relative position of the Tip mark to the Gallé mark also varies. Sometimes the two marks almost touch. In other pieces, the marks may be widely separated by up to 8" to 10".

New cameo glass with Art Nouveau-styled mushrooms is similar to original designs by both Gallé and Daum. This has naturalistic earth-tone colors.

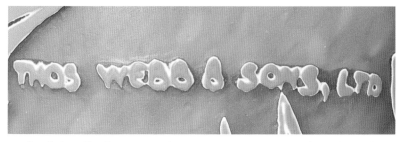

Some of the unusual names you'll find on new cameo glass are:
Cristo, Ramski, Pierre, Tudor and Statescu.

Marks of virtually all vintage makers appear on new cameo glass. Shown here
are fake marks of Schneider, Legras, Richard and Webb.

New 5-1/2" cameo vase, above, is marked with a Gallé signature. It is one of a series of new Gallé pieces made with ground pontils, right.

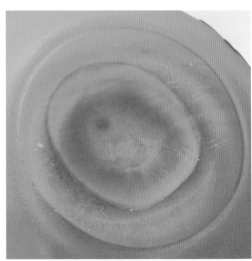

over like most originals. Previous cameo reproductions typically had top rims, which were sheared flat, not rounded over or ground. The surface finish is also more like originals. On new pieces with ground pontils, the raised designs are highly polished while the backgrounds are frosted. On the great majority of reproduction cameo produced up until now, both the raised designs as well as the background have a frosted matte surface.

New pieces with pontils are more difficult to detect then previous reproductions. New pontils are often slightly rougher than many vintage pontils, but there is considerable variation among old pontils so that is not a positive test of age. Many reproductions with pontils have obvious flaws that would never be found in originals. New necks and top rims, for example, are often noticeably out-of-round or lean to one side. The color range of new pieces with pontils also appears to be rather limited, usually dull green designs on dull yellow-brown bodies. So far, only pieces marked "Gallé" have been found with the factory-ground pontils.

Buyers should still inspect suspected pieces for pontils. Virtually no cameo reproductions made from the late 1980s through 2004 have ground pontils. The absence of a ground pontil is still a strong warning sign of a modern piece. While a ground pontil does not a guarantee a piece is old, ground pontils are still a positive indication of age. Never depend on any single test to determine age or authenticity. Look at many different features and use a variety of tests when forming an opinion on age.

Daum enamel

One of the more sought after vintage products of Daum Nancy's glass shops is a series of pieces decorated with crows. Although this may seem a strange subject, it was part of the widespread interest in nature which characterized the Art Nouveau period. Daum's original crow-decorated pieces, like their more famous "seasons" series, rely on enamel and vitrified powders for color rather than contrasting glass overlays. The decoration is often linked with cameo glass, though, because the surface is manipulated and decorated with acid cuttings.

The acid cuttings serve two purposes: to dull the naturally slick surface so enamels and powders can fuse to the glass more efficiently, and secondly, to raise or outline the design by cutting back the surrounding background. Applying enamels and powders to the raised designs gave artists the ability to create the illusion of great three-dimensional depth to such pieces with light and colors.

An additional technique used on the seasons pieces and on many of the better crow pieces was adding colored powders to the surface or in between the body of the glass and a clear overlay. This gives a soft misty effect suggesting rain, fog, mist or snow.

The new crow pieces, of course, have none of this skilled work. Birds in flight are little more than crude squashed V-shapes. The snow on the trees is garish layer of white glass. Nor do the new pieces have ground pontils found on virtually all originals. New pieces are signed Daum Nancy in raised glass with a nearly identical copy of an original signature. New pieces are being made in a range of different sized vases and several different lamps.

Cut glass

New cut glass has been widely reproduced since the 1950s. It is so widespread at shows, auctions, shops and malls that even experienced dealers and longtime collectors may have trouble telling new from old.

Reproduction cut glass is most frequently represented as being made during the American Brilliant Period, a span of years from about 1880 to shortly before World War I. During this time, American cut glass was the finest in the world. It was made of the highest quality glass and cut with the finest and most imaginative patterns. Nearly the entire surface was cut or decorated. New patterns and polishing techniques gave the glass never before seen sparkle and reflections, which came to be called "brilliant." Unless specifically stated otherwise, all references in this chapter to authentic cut glass will mean cut glass of the American Brilliant Period (ABP).

The focus of this discussion is on mass-produced reproductions made to imitate genuine cut glass in the $50 to $1,000 range. Individually made elaborate forgeries of rare and expensive cut glass valued at more than $5,000 are not included, although some of the same guidelines apply. The new mass-produced cut glass can generally be detected by tool marks, composition of the glass (detected by black light), certain basic shapes, cutting techniques and evidence of normal wear.

Wheel marks

Rough cuts on authentic ABP glass were made with *steel* or *iron* wheels with abrasives dripping down from a hopper above the cutting frame. These cuts were then smoothed at *stone* wheels and finely polished with wood and cork wheels. Eight inch bowls in relatively simple patterns might take a total of 10 to 20 hours of labor.

New cut glass, by contrast, is mass produced with high-speed *diamond* wheels. Embedded with industrial diamonds, these wheels cut 10 to 20 times faster than the old iron and steel wheels that used dripping abrasives. In tests and demonstrations sponsored by the American Cut Glass Association, even elaborate ABP patterns were produced in only a couple hours time using diamond wheels. Most new glass cut with diamond wheels goes directly to polishing and finishing after its first cutting. The smoothing step used in ABP pieces is generally eliminated in present day reproductions.

Diamond wheels cut so quickly and easily that modern cutters can generally make even long cuts in one pass. This produces virtually continuous unbroken parallel ridges and grooves the length of the cut. The areas between the ridges also frequently have a *pebbled or textured* appearance. In the vast majority of new cut glass, these marks are never polished out and remain in the finished piece when it is offered for sale. These marks can be seen by the unaided eye but are easier to study with the aid of a magnifying glass or 10X loupe.

Old ABP glass cut with iron and steel wheels, on the other hand, may show some faint cutting lines but not the prominent ridges left by modern diamond wheels. Virtually all traces of tool marks have been polished out of ABP glass. If there are some faint lines present in ABP, they tend to be short and broken because they are the result of *multiple passes* with the old wheels, not long continuous passes as with diamond wheels.

Diamond wheels were not in existence until World War II when they were developed to speed up production of war goods. Any piece cut with a diamond wheel could not possibly be from the ABP and must logically have been made in the second half of the 20th century. While it is possible to polish out ridges left by diamond wheels, the added labor expense generally takes away any profit gained from selling the piece as genuine ABP. Besides, there are several additional guidelines to help detect new cut glass besides marks left by cutting tools.

Teeth

Although we now admire ABP cut glass for its decorative value, we often forget its original function was to serve lemonade, hold sugar for your coffee or carry fruit salad. Authentic ABP cut glass logically had to withstand reasonable amounts of handling, washing and storage. In contrast, almost all reproductions are made as decorative objects; after all, they're antiques, right? Their new construction and design are almost always illogical with the function or purpose of the original antique they seek to imitate. This is most obvious with the teeth in cut glass reproductions.

Whether tall, wide, short or deep, virtually all new teeth come to very sharp points. This style is a characteristic of new eastern European cut glass and was never used on ABP cut glass. Authentic ABP teeth are rounded or squared off. The edges of some ABP teeth are even beveled, tooth by tooth. Teeth on original ABP are blunted for two very practical reasons: safety and appearance. Sharp points on teeth would knock off at the slightest touch with a ladle or serving spoon, sending chips of glass into the strawberries or ice cream. After a couple of dinners, the chipped and missing points would look a sorry sight indeed. Designers of original cut glass prevented those problems by eliminating sharp teeth. Even those original teeth that appear pointed are seen to be blunted when viewed under magnification.

Details of quality

Other clues to a reproduction are found in the small details related to overall quality. Pinhead size and larger bubbles, for example, are rarely found in ABP cut glass, but are fairly common in new cut glass. Large bubbles in old blanks caused the piece to be discarded, or the pattern was deliberately cut over the bubble to hide it.

Patterns should also remain within logical boundaries. It's common in new cut glass to find overlaps in patterns where elements of one design intersect, overcut, or run over elements of another design. In many pieces, entire segments of the pattern are eliminated because they run off the edge of a blank due to poor planning. Such poor work wouldn't have been tolerated in the ABP. Grossly out-of-round circles, stars with wobbly irregular points, unbalanced patterns, and crossover cuttings are all signs of new work.

Signs of normal wear

Another feature of genuine ABP cut glass hard to duplicate in new cut glass is normal wear. In other words, if a piece of glass is represented as being 100 years old, it should logically show some evidence of that age. Decanters, cruets, jars, etc., should show wear where the stoppers and lids rest on the body. Serving pieces such as bowls, trays, relishes, etc. should show wear on *inside bottoms* as well as on their bases or feet. Even essentially stationary pieces such as vases and candlesticks had to be cleaned or dusted and should show some wear on the base or feet.

Normal wear appears as lines of *random* width, direction, depth, and length. Normal wear occurs over many years with each bump, knock or jiggle, an entirely separate event producing unique individual marks (a scratch, chip, scuff, etc.). The only source of repeated wear should be at a point of constant contact, such as a foot or a high spot on the bottom of a bowl, for example. Areas of repeated wear in genuinely old pieces tend to show up as frosted patches or spots. Under a 10X loupe, you can see that even these areas are formed by many (tiny) random scratches.

Artificial wear, because it is generally applied all at one time, almost always shows a definite *pattern*. Moving an object back and forth over a rough surface, for example, produces a pattern of parallel lines. Twisting an object produces a pattern of concentric circles. Tools, such as a wire brush or rough grinding wheel, will also leave a definite repeated pattern. If the majority of scratches seem to run the same direction, are about the same depth and run about the same length, it is almost a sure sign of artificial aging. Although it is theoretically possible to find a genuinely old piece that has been never used and shows no wear, it is not likely.

Shapes

Genuine ABP cut glass was made in literally thousands of shapes. Rather than try to learn authentic shapes, you would be better off learning to recognize a few shapes that are almost a virtual guarantee of a reproduction. Probably the easiest shape to recognize as new is the so-called "helmet-shaped" one-piece basket. This is a European shape virtually unknown during the ABP. It is, however, almost the only basket shape shown in antique reproduction wholesale catalogs since the late-1940s. Authentic ABP baskets were made of *two pieces* of glass with a *separate* handle *applied* to the body. Only a handful of authentic ABP baskets are known to exist in the helmet shape; they are exceedingly rare, costing thousands of dollars. As a general guideline, *all helmet-shaped* cut glass baskets should be considered new.

Another shape that must be on the wholesalers' bestseller list is the so-called "biscuit jar." Like the helmet basket, this veteran has appeared unchanged in the catalogs since the late 1940s. It is basically a straight-sided cylinder 8 to 10 inches high with a flat lid. The lid is fitted with a solid glass knob; an inner rim fits down into the base. This shape is a modern design; no similar shape in these large dimensions was ever used during the ABP. The closest similar shape in genuine ABP cut glass was the *cigar jar*. Although these old jars are also straight-sided cylinders, their knobs are *wide* and *hollow,* not round and solid like the new biscuit jar. In addition to clear, the new jars are widely available with colored overlays such as ruby, green, and cobalt.

Blanks

In general, blanks of new cut glass show much more variation in thickness within a single piece than old blanks. Bases will be thicker than side walls, one side of a plate will be thicker than the opposite side, etc. This is especially noticeable in plates, tumblers, and some bowls; the smaller the size, the more noticeable the differences.

Many bottoms of new tumblers and plates are frequently twice the thickness as old blanks of similar shape. The center of the new thicker blanks also frequently, but not always, forms a high spot. There is some debate as to exactly why this occurs. Some persons believe the extra thickness is a deliberate attempt to make new glass more closely resemble the weight of old. Others believe irregular thickness is only another sign of the poor quality typical of the new cut glass.

Marks

Never base your judgment of age or quality on marks. Fake and forged acid signatures and marks are widespread in cut glass and applied to both new and genuinely old but originally unmarked pieces. Fake marks on new cut glass can usually be caught by applying the guidelines on quality and construction details listed above. Catching new marks on genuinely old ABP cut glass is somewhat tougher.

One way to catch many forged marks on old but originally unmarked ABP glass is to examine the mark with a 10X loupe. If a piece is truly old, it will have some signs of wear. Many careless forgers place their new marks over normal wear. When acid is applied over an old scratch, the acid tends to flow through the scratch and fills the scratch. In other words, you'll have a frosted scratch (see illustrations on P. 181).

Black light tests

Virtually all authentic ABP cut glass fluoresces green with some yellow under long-wave black light. Small lights of low wattage may only fluoresce rims and bottoms; larger more powerful lights will fluoresce larger areas. The darker the room, the more obvious the fluorescence. Nineteenth and early 20th century cut glass from other countries may or may not fluoresce. Until the mid-1990s, many cut glass reproductions fluoresced pink, purple, or white or appeared to have no reaction. Cut glass made in Turkey since the mid-1990s fluoresces yellow sometimes with a slight greenish cast. Although black light is an important test, it should not be your only test. Be sure to look at the shape, signs of wear, and overall quality before making a judgment of age.

New 14-inch cut glass pitcher from Turkey. Price: $45 from antique reproduction wholesaler.

The potentially confusing fluorescence of the Turkish glass proves that buyers must *never rely on only one test* to determine age. As many tests as possible should be used before making a judgment as to age.

The most important clues to a possible reproduction are: 1) grooves left by a diamond wheel; 2) lack of normal wear; 3) dagger-like teeth; 4) shapes that were never made during the ABP; 5) blanks with illogically thick areas; 6) obvious flaws in the blank and irregularities in patterns; and 7) incorrect fluorescence.

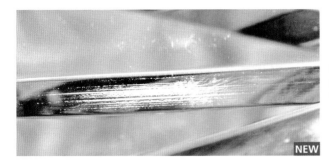

Close-up of grooves and rough surface made by diamond wheel.

Close-up of grooves and rough surface made by diamond wheel.

Close up of smooth cut in old glass made with iron or steel wheel.

Teeth on most new cut glass are cut to a dagger-like point.

Pointed teeth on new cut glass platter, shown about twice actual size.

Typical ground, or blunted, teeth found on vintage cut glass; shown about twice actual size.

Beveled edges of deliberately blunted teeth on vintage cut glass. Beveled edges are a sign of extra work found on some but not all ABP.

Poorly planned typical new cutting with pattern running out beyond rim.

Another example of a poorly cut pattern in a piece of new cut glass. The rays of the center star overlap rays from other stars.

Large frequent obvious bubbles are common in new cut glass but rarely found in vintage cut glass.

"Artificial Wear"

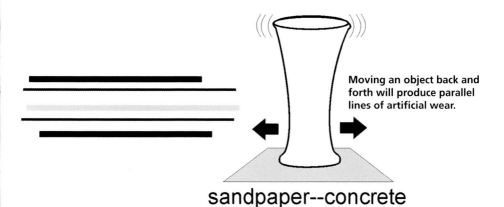

Moving an object back and forth will produce parallel lines of artificial wear.

sandpaper--concrete

Twisting an object back and forth on a rough surface will produce lines of artificial wear in concentric circles.

sandpaper--concrete

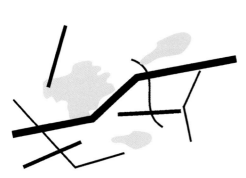

random direction & depth

Lines of normal wear are random in direction, width and depth.

Close up view of typical normal wear found on vintage cut glass. Random lines of unequal width; areas of heavy wear appears as frosted white patches.

NEW

OLD

One-piece helmet-shaped baskets are almost exclusively a European shape. Only a handful of original ABP baskets are known in this shape. Any basket in this shape is virtually guaranteed to be a reproduction.

Virtually without exception, ABP baskets are made of two pieces: a body and a separate applied handle.

NEW

NEW

The only remotely similar old jar shape is the cigar jar. However, all the vintage jars have wide hollow knobs, not solid knobs.

There are no old ABP counterparts to the new straight-sided 8" to 10" "biscuit" jars with solid glass knobs.

Typical new cut glass tumbler with extreme differences in side walls and base. Sides are about one-eighth inch thick; base is about one-half inch.

Rubber stamps, left, are used to apply etching fluid to forge marks on new and old cut glass. Many forged acid marks are generally blurred, smudged and ragged looking like this Libbey example.

A genuine acid mark applied at the time of manufacture has logically been subjected to the same wear as the piece to which it was applied. Scratches from normal authentic wear pass through the frosted mark leaving a scratch in the mark and the glass, left. Any scratch passing through genuine marks should not be frosted. Many forged marks are applied to old but originally unmarked pieces. If a new acid stamp is applied over a scratch already on the old piece, the acid frequently flows into the scratch, right.

Depression glass

Depression glass has been widely reproduced since the 1970s. Reproductions include rare patterns and colors such as Royal Lace in cobalt blue, as well as everyday standards such as pink Cherry Blossom.

The most reliable way to catch the reproductions is to compare details in the molded pattern. Unfortunately, there is no one single test that can be used across all the patterns, colors, and shapes. Eliminating the fakes is pretty much a piece-by-piece process, requiring comparisons to the originals you'll find in the following pages.

That said, here are some very broad rules of thumb about Depression glass reproductions:

- Almost all new pieces feel slick or greasy to the touch due to a high sodium content in the glass formula that attracts moisture and dust.
- Many pieces will not function for the purpose they were supposedly created. New spouts often don't pour correctly. Knobs and handles, like those on pitchers and butter dish lids, can be difficult to grasp.
- Color alone is not a good test of age. Colors change with the glass batch. The best test is to compare molded details.
- Some new glass has a strong vinegar-like odor.

It is very important to apply guidelines to only the particular piece of a pattern piece being discussed. Don't assume the test for tumblers, for example, is the same test you would use for shakers. Don't assume a particular test described for a piece in one pattern can be used for a similarly shaped piece in any other pattern.

There are many more reproductions than those listed in these pages. Pieces for this section were chosen because they are either so widespread almost everyone will encounter them or are very similar to originals and harder to detect. Patterns are listed alphabetically with the various shapes listed separately under the pattern name.

Cherry Blossom

Original: Jeanette Glass Co., 1930s.

Reproductions: Reproductions have been on the market since 1973. The majority of new pieces have been made in Japan, Taiwan and China. New colors include pink, green, red, transparent blue, Delphite, cobalt blue and a variety of iridized (carnival) finishes.

Reproduction Cherry Blossom has been made or is being made in the following known shapes:

Berry bowls, 8-1/2" and 4-3/4"

Butter dish, covered

Cake plate (on three feet)

Cereal bowl, 5-3/4"

Child/toy sizes in cup, saucer, butter, sugar and creamer
Cup and saucer
Pitcher, 36-oz all over pattern (AOP), scalloped foot
Plate, 9" dinner
Shakers
Platter, 13", divided
Tray, 10-1/2", two-handled, sandwich
Tumbler, all over pattern (AOP), scalloped foot

As a general rule, most Cherry Blossom reproductions can be identified by crudely shaped cherries and leaves. Old leaves have a realistic appearance with serrated (sawtooth) edges and veins that vary in length and thickness. New leaves commonly have perfectly straight and uniformly even veins that form V-shaped grooves. Original cherries usually give an illusion of a rounded three-dimensional ball-shaped figure; many new cherries appear to be only a flat circle. Differences between old and new patterns are generally greater in earlier 1970s reproductions than in more recent reproductions.

Most original Cherry Blossom in green glass fluoresces under long wave black light. This is not a positive test for age, though, because several green reproductions also fluoresce. This includes a new butter dish, new tumbler, new cup, and several other shapes. While a black light is useful, don't rely on it as your only test of age.

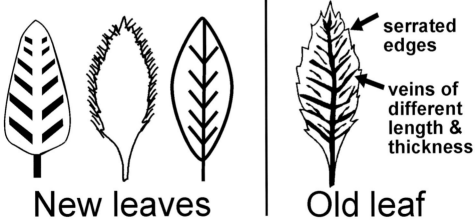

serrated edges

veins of different length & thickness

New leaves | Old leaf

Original lid has two lines around bottom rim of lid. Original base has realistic cherries and leaves; the branch touches both sides of the rim.

First reproduction base has unrealistic flat cherries and fishbone-type veins in leaves.

Second reproduction base has improved pattern, but note that the branch stops short of the rim.

Original Cherry Blossom leaves look real. They have irregular sawtooth edges and both large and small veins. Reproduction leaves usually have smooth or feathery edges. New veins are generally straight-sided V-shaped grooves or regularly spaced lines.

Butter dish (covered)

Child/toy size: This is a fantasy item; no original child's butter dish was ever made. All pieces now on the market are new.

Full size: There are at least two styles of reproductions. The 1970s reproduction has a very crude pattern in the base. A later reproduction has an improved pattern in the base, but the branch stops short of the rim. The original base has realistic leaves and cherries with a branch that extends from rim to rim. All reproduction lids made so far have a smooth band separated from the rest of the lid by a single line. On old lids, the band is separated by two lines.

Cups

The pattern in old cups is very realistic. Each old twig ends in a blossom with the twig touching the blossom. In new cups, there is an obvious gap between the blossom and the twig. In old cups, the pattern fills almost the entire bottom; in new cups, the pattern is faint and weak. Leaves on old cups look like leaves; leaves on the new cups look like arrowheads or barbs.

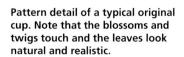

Pattern detail of a typical new cup. The blossoms don't touch the ends of the twigs and the leaves do not appear natural.

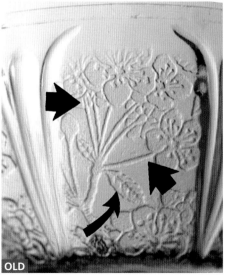

Pattern detail of a typical original cup. Note that the blossoms and twigs touch and the leaves look natural and realistic.

Pitchers and tumblers

The allover pattern (AOP) scallop foot pitcher and tumbler have been reproduced since the 1970s. The easiest way to tell old from new pitchers is to turn the pitcher over and look at the design on the bottom. Now, count the cherries. Old pitchers have nine cherries; new pitchers have only seven cherries. The arrangement of leaves and cherries on the bases of new pitchers is poorly designed with lots of open space in the pattern. Leaves and cherries on the bases of original pitchers are realistic and the pattern covers almost the entire bottom.

NEW

OLD

The base of new AOP pitchers have crude leaves with unnatural V-shaped veins in leaves. There are only seven cherries visible in the base of new pitchers.

There are nine cherries visible in the pattern on bases of original AOP pitchers. Leaves and cherries are well molded and natural in appearance.

New and old tumblers can also be separated by examining the pattern on the base. The pattern of cherries and leaves in the bases of original tumblers is sharp and well defined. The pattern nearly fills the entire concave space of original tumblers. There are least two different reproductions of AOP tumblers. Both have very poorly molded details in their bases with the unrealistic cherries and leaves. In both new tumblers, the pattern is primarily in the center of the concave center with lots of open space between the pattern and the flat rim. You can also separate

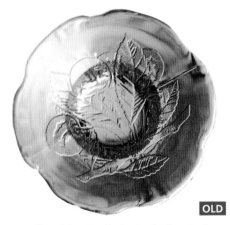

OLD

Original Tumbler The design in the foot is sharp and almost fills the entire base; the leaves and cherries are natural and realistic.

old and new tumblers by examining the molded horizontal lines running around the smooth band in the top rim. Old tumblers have three horizontal lines; new tumblers only one. The three molded lines on original tumblers are sharp and strong.

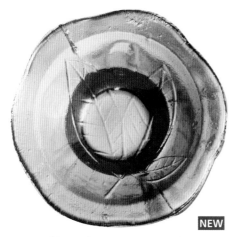

New tumbler, Style A, introduced mid-1970s, continued to be made through 1990s. The design in the foot has the typical new leaves and cherries. The pattern in the foot is mostly in the center with lots of open space around the edge of the foot.

New tumbler, Style B. The design on the foot is also very weak and usually found in the very center only. This style was made in pink, green, and Delphite Blue. New Style B was made around 1980 and was reported when it first came out by H.M. Weatherman in *Price Trends 1981*.

Floral (Poinsettia)

Original: Jeannette Glass Co., 1931 to 1935. Original colors include amber, crystal, delphite, green, pink, red, and yellow.

Reproductions: New shakers are appearing in cobalt blue, dark green, pink and red. Shakers in cobalt blue, dark green and red are obvious reproductions because those colors were never used in original production. The new pink shakers, however, are very close in color and pattern to the originals.

Shakers

The quickest test for separating new and old shakers is to examine the molded glass threads. In old shakers, there is a 1/4" horizontal gap between the raised threads along the mold seam. No thread goes over the mold seam on old shakers. In the new shakers, threads are continuous and there is no gap at the mold seam. New shakers also tend to have more glass at the bottom, but this can be hard to measure and may vary slightly. Checking the threads is a more reliable way to identify the new pieces.

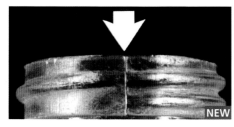

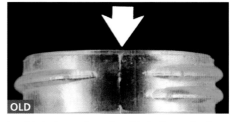

In new shakers, the threads run in an unbroken continuous line across the mold seam.

In old shakers, there is a 1/4-inch gap in the threads as they cross the mold seam.

The center of the bases in new Florentine #2 tumblers, left, is plain without a pattern. The pattern is included in the bases of old tumblers, right.

Florentine #2 (Poppy #2)

Original: Hazel Atlas Glass Co., 1932 to 1935.

Reproductions: Cone-footed 7-1/2" pitcher and 4" footed tumbler. New colors include a blue that is often mistaken for the rarest original color, which is ice blue.

Iris (Iris and Herringbone)

Original: Jeanette Glass Co. The original factory name was Iris, but now commonly called Iris and Herringbone. First made in clear crystal 1928 to 1932. A limited number of shapes were made in crystal in the 1950s and vases were produced into the 1970s.

Reproductions: Include beaded edge 4-1/2" berry bowl, coaster, 6-1/2" footed tumblers, candy dish and 10" dinner plate.

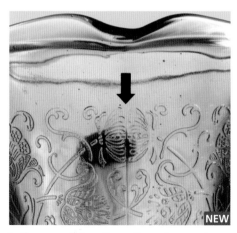

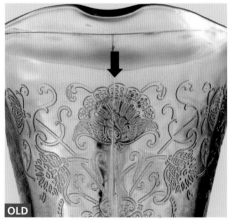

In the new pitcher, the pattern stops and starts at the mold seam under the pour spout.

In the old pitcher, the pattern is split by the mold seam under the pour spout.

The new candy dish is easy to spot because there is no rayed pattern in the bottom of the piece. Vases were reissued in the 1970s and are identical to vases produced in earlier years. Generally, molding on originals is much sharper and crisper. This means pieces of original Iris catch more light and generally sparkle more and appear brighter than the reproductions.

Berry bowl, 4-1/2"

The surface of the flowers on the new bowl are pitted and coarse with a dark gray frosted appearance.

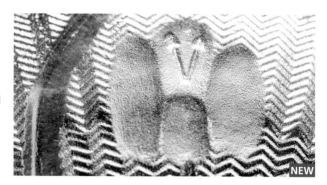

The surface of the flowers on original bowls is perfectly smooth and transparent with no appearance of frosting.

Coaster

The pattern in new coasters is weak overall but fades away almost completely in the lower left of this example.

The herringbone design in all old coasters has a sharply molded border for a full 360 degrees around the iris in the center.

Tumbler, 6-1/2" footed

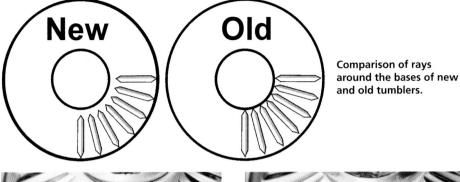

Comparison of rays around the bases of new and old tumblers.

In new tumblers, there is a distinct gap between the end of the ray and the molded ring running around the stem. New rays are also much sharper to the touch than old rays.

In the old tumbler, the rays nearly the molded touch ring around the stem.

The pattern in new tumblers is different from front to back. The reverse side of the pattern in new tumblers does not have the pointed leaf found in the original tumblers.

The pattern in original tumblers is identical on both the front and back. The pointed leaf behind the tall flower bud appears on both sides of original tumblers.

Madrid

Original: Federal Glass Co., 1932 to 1939.

Reproductions: There are two groups of modern Madrid. In 1976, Federal changed the pattern name to Recollection and began making new pieces. The first new pieces of Recollection were easily identified because pieces were dated in the mold with the year "1976." But then, Federal Glass went bankrupt, and the rights to the design were acquired by Indiana Glass. Indiana Glass discontinued dating the glass and that has caused problems for collectors. So far, new pieces have been made in five colors: amber, blue, clear, pink, and teal. Teal, a greenish-blue almost aqua color, is the only new color not originally made. The other four colors—amber, pink, blue and clear—were all used for the 1930s Madrid.

The situation is further confused because Indiana Glass has also introduced many shapes never originally made, such as the cake stand, goblet, covered candy dish and others. Don't mistake these items for rare or unlisted pieces just because you can't find them in a book.

Known shapes reproduced to date include: covered butter dish, dinner plate, grill plate, luncheon plate, creamer, open sugar, shaker, cup, saucer, goblet*, vase*, hurricane lamp*, pedestal covered candy dish*, footed cake stand*, footed fruit stand/dish*, 9-1/2" bowl, 10" oval vegetable bowl, 7" soup/cereal bowl, and candle holder. Items marked with an asterisk* are shapes never made in original 1930s Madrid.

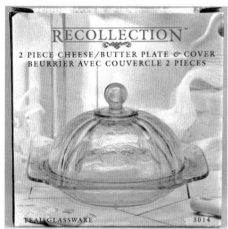

The original Madrid pattern was renamed "Recollection" and marketed by Indiana Glass Co. Many new shapes are similar to the original 1930s Madrid, including the butter dish shown here in the new Recollection's box.

New covered candy dish, left; footed goblet, right. Neither shape was made in the original 1930s Madrid.

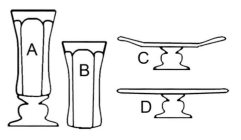

New shapes not made in original 1930s Madrid: A. "hurricane lamp" made by attaching candle holder to tumbler; B. tumbler; C. fruit stand made by joining candle holder joined to dinner plate; D. cake stand, same as C. but with flat edges.

Butter dish

The mold seam in the knob on the new butter dish lid has a vertical mold seam.

The mold seam on the old butter dish knob is horizontal.

Shakers

The new shaker is a squat barrel-shape. There are two styles of old shakers. Both old shakers are slender, vertical shapes: one is footed, the other with a flat bottom.

New **Old**

Creamer

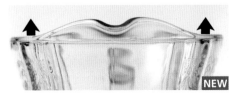

Spouts on new creamers rise above the top rim.

Spouts on old creamers dip below the top rim.

Cup and sugar bowl

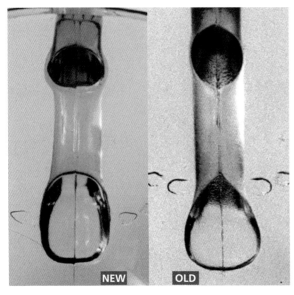

NEW   OLD

The easiest way to detect new cups and new sugars is to examine how their handles join the bodies. Looking at the inside of a sugar bowl or cup, the lower part of old handles, right, forms a tear drop shape. The same area in new handles form an oval, left.

Royal Lace

Original: Hazel Atlas, 1934 to 1941.

Reproductions: Cookie jar, 9-oz tumbler, and 5-oz juice glass. The majority of new tumblers are cobalt blue. Cookie jars are in a variety of colors.

New Royal Lace cookie jar.

Cookie jar

Pay particular attention to lids, as they are the most valuable part of the cookie jar. Genuine old jars are easier to find than old lids, so be alert for new lids on old jars. All old lids have a single mold seam that splits the lid in half. There is no mold seam on the new lids.

The bottom of the base of the new cookie jar is smooth and plain.

The bottom of the base of the old cookie jar has a molded circular plunger mark.

Tumblers

The glass in the sides and bottoms of both sizes of new tumblers is generally about two to three times as thick as originals.

Bottoms of new 5 oz. juice glasses are plain with no pattern, left. Old 5 oz. juice glasses have a geometric design molded in the bottom, right.

Sharon (Cabbage Rose)

Original: Federal Glass Co., 1935 to 1939.

Reproductions: Includes covered butter dish, candy jar, cheese dish, shakers, and sugar and creamer.

Butter dish

The best test for lids is to examine the knob. On old lids there is only about 1/4" between the bottom of the old knob and the top of the lid. It's very hard to get your fingers under the knob of an original lid. The gap under the knobs on new lids is about 1/4".

An original Sharon butter dish. New and old can be separated by the knob on the lid.

OLD

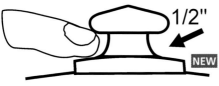

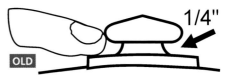

There is a much larger gap under the knobs of new lids. The gap under the knob in new lids is about 1/2". The space under the old knob is 1/4".

Candy jar

The new Sharon candy jar, left, is very similar to the original, right.

The foot on the new base, left, is only about 2-7/8" diameter. The foot on the original base, right, is 3-1/4" in diameter.

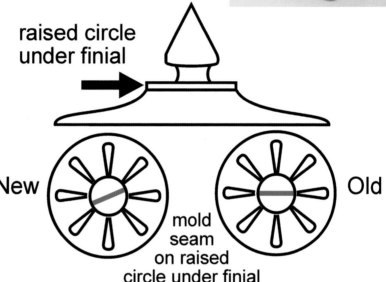

raised circle under finial

New

Old

mold seam on raised circle under finial

You can separate new and old lids by the location of the mold seam, shown in red, on the raised disc under the finial. When you look down at the circle from above, the mold seam on old lids is aligned with two raised ribs. The mold seam in the new lid appears between two raised ribs.

Sugar and creamers

If you look inside the bowls of sugars and creamers, you'll see a difference between how handles join the body. In new sugars and creamers, the area where handles join the body form a circle or very rounded oval, above left. The same area in the original sugar and creamer forms a pointed oval or teardrop shape.

O or O

how handles join sugar and creamer bowls as seen from inside

Jadite

In this book, "jadite" is used as a generic term to mean any opaque green glass made by many manufacturers. "Jade-ite" with a capital "J" and a hyphen, is the registered brand name of opaque green glass made by Anchor Hocking. Jadite reproductions of jadite have been mass-produced in both China and the United States since the late 1990s. Some new pieces are of shapes never made originally, or fantasy items, and are fairly easy to spot. But other new pieces are very similar to vintage shapes made by original makers such as McKee, Jeanette, Anchor Hocking and others. The great majority of vintage American jadite was made from the 1930s up through the 1950s. Although most original jadite was made for home kitchens, such as shakers, bowls, storage jars, and other shapes, original table settings were also made for home use, as well as institutional use in hotels and restaurants.

Most, but not all, new jadite is being produced in new molds. Although many new pieces from these new molds appear similar to originals, molded details can be used to separate new pieces from originals. No known new pieces have yet been made from original Jeanette molds. The only known original McKee mold in production is the double-ringed rolling pin, made by Fenton.

Perhaps more confusing is new jadite made in genuinely old molds originally owned by Imperial, Westmoreland, Cambridge and others. Although those companies never made jadite glass ca. 1930-50s, new jadite coming from their molds often has the original company mark molded in such as Westmoreland. Some of these old molds date back to the 19th century and are for distinctly Victorian-era shapes such as figural animal covered dishes, cake stands, salt dips, mustard pots and others. Such early shapes were never associated with original jadite produced in the mid-20th century, ca. 1930-50s.

One of the largest retailers of new jadite has been the Martha Stewart mail order catalogs and online shopping sites. Almost all of the Stewart jadite was made by the L.E. Smith Glass Co. Some, but not all, of the Stewart pieces are permanently marked in the mold. Typical markings are "Martha by Mail" or "MBM" in raised letters or the raised capital letter "S" in block letters or a raised molded capital letter "S" in cursive, or script. This letter does not stand for Stewart, but L.E. Smith, which makes new jadite for Stewart. Fenton also makes jadite for Stewart. Photos of these new marks are shown in the following pages. Currently, there are no jadite or opaque blue reproductions with exact copies of old marks. But that doesn't mean marks are a guarantee of age. Marks on both new and old jadite can be so faint as to be practically invisible, especially on the new Rosso and old McKee.

Another large distributor of new jadite is Rosso Glass. Many, but far from all, of its new jadite pieces carry a molded trademark of the letter "R" in a keystone. Much of Rosso's jadite is made in genuinely old molds. These include Westmoreland reamer shapes and animal covered dishes, Imperial Candlewick tableware and a wide variety of kitchen styled glass including mortar and pestles, toothpicks, shakers and other early shapes. Rosso also developed and is the leading distributor of new jadite with new decals.

There is no one single test to reliably separate new jadite and new opaque blue from vintage pieces. Your best tests of age are a close examination of glass quality, inspecting mold details of originals, and knowing what shapes were originally made in jadite or opaque blue. Generally, many new pieces in both colors have a slick, greasy feeling. Embossed detail is often poor and mold seams can be obvious. Pits and broken bubbles can also be a sign of the low quality glass commonly used to make new jadite. These flaws are more obvious in reproductions from China. New jadite by American makers such as Fenton tend to be quite good quality.

New jadite ball pitcher is very similar to old pitchers in Pillar Optic pattern by Anchor Hocking. This sample was on sale for $19.95 at the local Target department store. New pitchers have been selling on eBay for up to $200 and more. Made in China.

5 3/4"   New

6"   Old

New Pillar Optic pitchers, left, are smaller than originals measuring 5-3/4" from the base to the lip. Original Pillar Optic pitchers, right, are 6" from base to lip.

Raised mold seam on handle of new Jadite ball pitchers made in China. It is almost 1/8" tall.

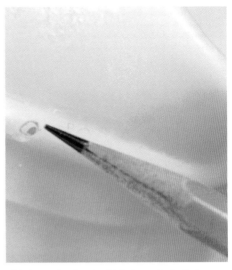

This large broken bubble is typical of the many flaws found in most new jadite pitchers. Other common flaws are obvious swirling in the glass surface, inconsistent finish going from shiny to dull and obvious mold seams.

New jadite batter bowl in Swirl pattern. No old Swirl pattern batter bowl in jadite is known. New batter bowl weighs in at slightly over 4 pounds and is 8" dia; 5" tall.

New swirl batter bowl, left, with original Anchor Hocking plain-sided Fire-King Jade-ite batter bowl on right. There is no vintage swirl pattern batter bowl.

These new jadite canisters, from 7" to 9", copy the original Hazel Atlas Crisscross pattern. No vintage Crisscross was made in jadite.

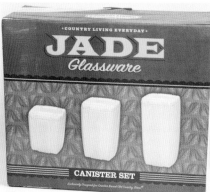

This is the box for the new canisters shown in the photo above. The new set was $30 retail.

New 6" jadite canister marked "TEA." A matching new canister is marked "COFFEE."

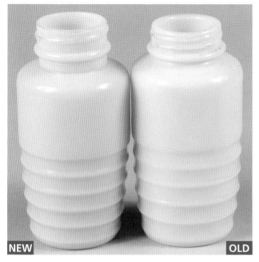

A new jadite round shaker, left, is a close copy of original jadeite 6-oz shaker by Jeannette, right. Sizes are virtually identical, about 4-1/4".

The top of the new shaker has a distinct neck between the shaker body and the beginning of the threads. Original Jeanette shaker has virtually no neck between threads and body. New shakers, $8 pair, retail.

New flat-sided jadite bodies by Mosser Glass sold by Rosso Glass. Various names appear applied in black decals on the sides. Metal shaker tops are typical but a syrup top is also available. Bodies are very faintly marked with the Rosso trademark in reverse on bottoms.

NEW **OLD**

Rosso shakers have a distinct neck between the shaker body and threads. McKee originals do not have a neck.

Comparison of a new Rosso shaker to an old McKee* and Jeanette square shakers. Top opening in Jeanette is only 1-1/4" dia., which makes it easy to separate from the other two shakers which have top openings of 1-5/8" dia. The new square shaker is closest in appearance to McKee original. Although many old McKee shakers are marked, many original marks are faint and hard to see. The best test for age is to look at the bases and necks.

McKee shaker shown is custard, but the same mold was used for jadite.

Original McKee has a horizontal mold seam near the base; there is no similar seam on Rosso shaker. Rosso shakers have a stepped raised base; McKee base is concave, domed inward.

New jadite 3-3/4" shaker set by Mosser Glass, distributed by Rosso Glass. No permanent mark. This shaker body is also made as a spice set with various names such as Nutmeg, Flour, Oregano, Paprika and others.

New flat-sided jadite bodies by Rosso Glass. Available with various decals and names of condiments. Syrup tops also available. Shaker bodies are faintly marked with the Rosso trademark on bottom.

New eight-sided jadite shakers, 4-1/4" high. No vintage eight-sided shakers are known in jadite.

New eight-sided jadite shakers, 4-1/4" high. The great majority of vintage jadite kitchen shakers are either four-sided or cylindrical, not eight-sided (see McKee and Jeanette catalog pages on P. 204).

New eight-sided jadite shakers, 4-1/4" high. With rare exceptions, Old English-style lettering was almost never used to label vintage Jadite kitchen glass.

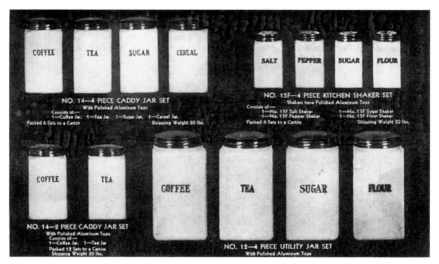

Original McKee Glass Jadite shakers with lettering, ca.1930s.

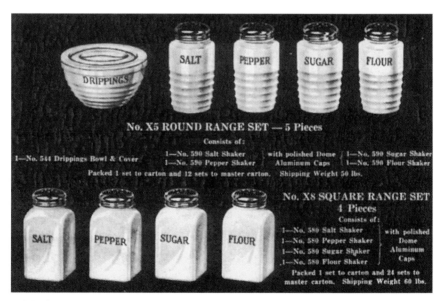

Original Jeanette Glass Jadite shakers with lettering, ca. late 1930s.

New jadite covered butter in Crisscross pattern. No vintage jadite covered butter dish in Crisscross pattern was ever made. This is sold by Cracker Barrel for $10.

Top of new Crisscross butter with "BUTTER" in center panel. This has very crude lettering with some letters incomplete.

Surfaces of the new eight-sided shakers have irregular swirls in the glass. Such surfaces are virtually never found on vintage jadite shakers.

New jadite 4-1/2" butter dish; black decal "Butter" on side. Molded "M" in base for Mosser Glass.

New Cracker Barrel jadite 4-1/2" tumbler; $5 retail. No old jadite tumblers like this are known.

New jadite covered butter dish. No old counterpart to this shape is known in jadite. No mark.

New jadite 10" cake stand. It's marked "Martha by Mail" in small letters along bottom rim.

NEW

Molded mark on the bottom of new D-handle mug: "Anchor Hocking" is above the anchor trademark; "Fire King" script mark is in the center; the date "2000" is at the bottom.

OLD

The original molded mark that appears on most, but not all, vintage Anchor Hocking Fire-King Jade-ite.

New and old orange reamers in jadite. The original reamer, on the right, was made by Jeanette Glass.

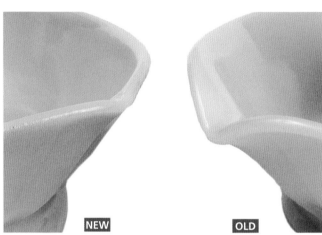

Spouts on the reproduction Jeanette reamers are barely more than a slight bend or dent in the rim, left. Spouts on original Jeanette reamers have a much deeper crease and extend well beyond the rim, right.

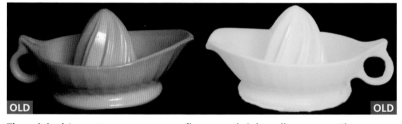

The original Jeanette orange reamer fluoresces bright yellow-green. The reproduction does not fluoresce.

You can test the glass in ordinary room lighting by holding a keychain-size black light directly against the glass.

Original Jeanette Jadite tab-handled measuring cups fluoresce bright yellow-green under longwave black light. The new tab-handled measuring cups do not fluoresce.

OLD

NEW

This new set of tab-handled jadite measuring cups is virtually identical to sets made by Jeanette Glass Co. New sets average around $20 retail.

An original set of tab-handled Jadite measuring cups made by Jeanette Glass Co during the late 1930s. Original sets can sell for $124 to $175 or more. Sizes of both new and old sets are marked 1-, 1/2-, 1/3- and 1/4-cup.

OLD

New

Old

Virtually all original tab-handles are perpendicular to the cups forming a nearly perfect right angle. Many of the new handles sag and droop.

Two-piece new jadite reamer made in an old Westmoreland mold. An orange is molded on one side; a lemon is molded on the reverse. The original reamer was made only in transparent pink, transparent green and clear crystal. Jadite and all other colors are reproductions.

NEW

New jadite rolling pin by Fenton from original McKee mold. Sold through Martha Stewart mail order catalog.

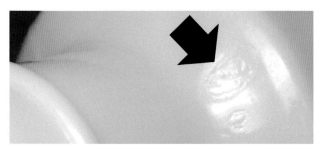

New Fenton rolling pins are marked (arrow) but marks are very faint and hard to find. Most new Fenton pins have obvious raised mold seams not found on the original McKee jadite pins.

New jadite 13-3/4" rolling pin with "BAKERS CHOICE" in raised molded letters. No pre-1950 jadite rolling pin has ever been found with raised molded advertising.

New jadite 14" rolling pin with black lettering "Kardov, Famous Self-Rising Flour." The only authentic pre-1965 jadite rolling pins are those made by McKee Glass.

New jadite kerosene lamp in Princess Feather pattern. This is a reproduction of an old pattern, but no old Princess Feather pattern lamp was ever made in jadite.

Aladdin Mantle Lamp Co. sells three new lamps in jadite. A full-size Lincoln Drape, shown here, and a smooth-sided fount like those used in bracket and hanging lamps. The Lincoln Drape pattern is also sold as a fount only without the base. New Aladdin lamps are marked as shown below.

New Aladdin jadite lamps are clearly marked in raised molded letters including the year.

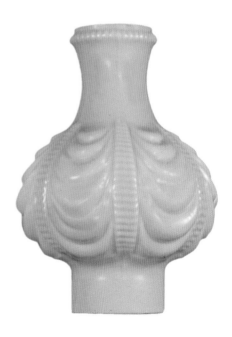

Reproduction jadite Coolidge Drape pattern-molded chimney for #2 and #3 burners with a 3" fitter. The new chimney is heavy and nearly one-quarter inch thick at the base. The original jadite colored chimney is thinner, and not much over 1/8" thick.

New 3" cup and saucer made from original Imperial Candlewick molds. Original Candlewick was never made in jadite.

New 4-1/2" mayonnaise or sauce boat from Candlewick mold. There is no old counterpart.

New 9-1/4" oyster plate. No vintage counterpart known. Very thick and heavy glass, weighs slightly over two pounds.

Pair of new 7-3/4" candlesticks. Eight-sided panel design.

New jadite sold as a miniature water set. The pitcher is a 4" creamer; the "tumbler" is a 2-1/4" toothpick holder. Made from original Thousand Eye Westmoreland molds. Both new pieces have a molded Westmoreland mark and the molded mark of Rosso Wholesale Glass, the letter R in a keystone. These two shapes were never produced in vintage pre-1960 jadite.

New jadite Ball and Swirl water pitcher and 5" tumbler. This pitcher and tumbler were unknown in jadite until this set was made. Has molded mark of Rosso Glass.

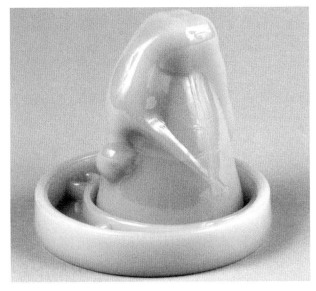

New jadite Bottoms Up tumbler and matching coaster. The original was introduced by McKee in jadite and other colors in the 1930s. Original tumblers are marked in raised molded characters "PAT 77725" above the nude's heels. The new tumbler is not marked. The new coaster is marked with the Rosso trademark.

New 7" jadite covered dish in Ring and Petal pattern. This piece is made in an original Westmoreland mold and both top and bottom are marked with the Westmoreland WG. The only opaque green glass used by Westmoreland in Ring and Petal was Mint Green, which wasn't introduced until 1979. No vintage jadite was ever made in this pattern.

New jadite "Chickenserver" made by Fenton for Martha Stewart. Most, but not all pieces are marked with the molded Fenton oval and decade number. The original "Chickenserver" was made by Fenton between 1953 and 1956. Originals were never available in jadite. The 1950s colors were all milk glass (#5189) or milk glass with the heads in various colors such as purple and green (#5188). The 1950s Fenton pieces are not marked.

New jadite covered turkey made by L.E. Smith for Martha Stewart. The bases are marked with a molded letter "S" for Smith. Many marks are very faint and difficult to find. Lids are not marked. No L.E. Smith turkeys were made in vintage jadite.

New jadite lion covered dish. Made from mold originally owned by Westmoreland Glass. Westmoreland never produced this covered dish in vintage jadite.

New jadite rabbit covered dish. Manufactured by L.E. Smith for Martha Stewart. The inside of the base is marked in the mold with "S" for Smith. No vintage jadite covered dishes were made.

Molded R in keystone mark of Rosso Glass, a present-day glass wholesaler.

One of the molded marks on new jadite made by L.E. Smith. A large "S" with a small "G" within the top curve and small "C" in the bottom curve. SCG, Smith Glass Co.

This cursive "S" is another molded mark found on new jadite made by L.E. Smith. This mark was first used in 1997.

Molded mark "MARTHA BY MAIL" on some pieces of new jadite.

New Jade-ite from Anchor Hocking

Anchor Hocking, which made vintage opaque green glass under the trade name Jade-ite, has brought back the color in a new line of kitchen glass. Fortunately, the new pieces are permanently marked and shouldn't pose a problem to collectors of the vintage pieces. The new mark includes the date "2000," the first year the new pieces were introduced, and the Anchor Hocking trademark formed with the letter "H" and an anchor. Marks on some new Jade-ite also include "microwave and dishwasher safe" which never appeared in marks on vintage pieces. Another important difference between old and new marks is the absence of "Made in USA" in new marks. New Anchor Hocking Jade-ite is made in China, not the USA. Marks on vintage Jade-ite include "Made in USA."

NEW

Molded mark on new Jade-ite includes "2000®" and the Anchor Hocking trademark, an "H" and anchor.

OLD

Molded mark on vintage Jade-ite by Anchor Hocking includes "Made in the USA" which is missing in new 2000 marks.

New Anchor Hocking Jade-ite 2-quart casserole.

New Anchor Hocking Jade-ite 9" x 13" baking dish.

Blue Opaque Glass (Delphite)

Blue opaque glass was made about the same time as the green jadite. The major makers of vintage opaque blue glass were the same companies that produced vintage jadite: Anchor Hocking, McKee and Jeanette. McKee's blue opaque was sold under the trade name "Chaline" while Jeanette called its blue glass "Delfite." Anchor Hocking made a line of blue glass dinnerware it named "Turquoise Blue," which collectors today frequently use to refer to all opaque blue by Anchor Hocking.

At the time this book was written in late 2006, there were far fewer reproductions in blue opaque glass than in jadite. However, you need to be aware that blue glass is also being widely reproduced and many more shapes could appear at any time.

New opaque blue batter bowl. Very similar to a vintage Anchor Hocking batter bowl. All originals are marked "Fire-King." The new piece is not marked.

New opaque blue ribbed bowl, 12" x 5", weighs over 6 pounds. No exact old counterpart, but this is very similar to the Manhattan and Park Avenue patterns.

New opaque blue serving plate, 13" dia.

New opaque blue mortar with black lettering "Spices." No vintage blue glass is known in this shape.

NEW OLD

A new measuring cup with reamer top, left, made in an old Gillespie mold. The only top sold with the original cup was a measuring-style lid, right. This new cup with a reamer lid has been extensively reproduced in a variety of colors including opaque blue, shown here, and jadite.

Milk glass

Unusual pieces of milk glass always bring premium prices. The steady demand for rarities is a tempting market for manufactures of reproductions. Recent years have seen a number of milk glass reproductions never before attempted. Many of these pieces are hard to identify because little is known about the scarce originals. This chapter highlights some of the more unusual harder to trace milk glass reproductions currently in the market.

Pumpkin lanterns

Battery operated lanterns with novelty figural milk glass globes were first made from the mid-1940s through the 1950s. Reproductions of a lantern with a pumpkin globe began to appear in 2003. From a photo, you'd think new and old are virtually identical. A closer examination will show that the new lanterns have a cord that plugs into a 120-volt wall outlet. The originals operate on batteries in the lantern's base. Original globes are painted milk glass; new globes are made of clear glass, not milk glass.

New figural pumpkin lanterns with painted glass globes are made in two sizes: 5-1/2" dia. glass shade, left; 3-1/4" shade, right.

A new lantern showing the 120-volt power cord and plug. Original lanterns are battery operated.

Log Cabin Lamp

The original Log Cabin milk glass lamp was made by Thomas Atterbury Glass and Lamp Co., ca. 1876. Atterbury's original Log Cabin lamp was made in a complex four-piece mold which produced the body and handle as a single piece of glass. In contrast, the body and handle of new Log Cabin lamps are made from two pieces of glass-the handle is made separately and applied to the font, not cast as one piece with the fonts.

There has been considerable confusion surrounding the Log Cabin lamp due to a slight error in one of the most widely used reference books, *Miniature Lamps*, by Frank and Ruth Smith (Book I). Although the Smiths picture an old Log Cabin lamp, the caption describes the lamp with an "applied handle." Several other lamp books can also be confusing because they show genuinely old versions at an angle, which hides the handle. If you are bidding on a lamp

NEW

A new Log Cabin figural lamp in milk glass. Marked "Very Rare" by the seller and priced at $675. The new lamp is made from two separate pieces of glass.

OLD

Original Atterbury Log Cabin lamp. Handle and lamp body are molded as one continuous piece of glass. Shown here in clear glass but the same mold was used to make milk glass versions.

Close up view of new lamp with applied handle. Note curling tail on lower handle.

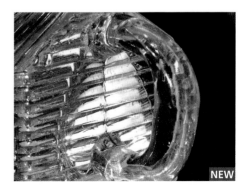

NEW

you haven't personally inspected or have viewed only pictures that do not show the handle, be sure to ask very specific questions about how the handle is joined to the font.

Miniature owl lamp

The original miniature milk glass owl lamp is one of the more expensive small lamps. Old lamps can sell for $1,500 and up. Look-alike reproductions began appearing in 2004 for $20 each. Although not exact copies, the new lamps have frequently been confused with or represented as the vintage original.

Look at the rims of the shade. New lamps are made of clear glass cased with a paper thin layer of white glass. Original miniature owl milk glass lamps are made of a single layer of solid milk glass. Vintage lamps were also cold painted but many have considerable wear to paint is not a reliable test of age.

The new miniature owl lamp is made of two layers of glass: clear glass cased with white glass.

Original lamps are made of a single thickness of solid white glass.

McKee marks faked

New milk glass with a molded McKee script mark first started appearing in 1998. It's thought that at least 12 different shapes were made with the fake marks but only four are confirmed: double-humped camel covered dish, buffalo paperweight, the so-called "wavy base" duck covered dish and a humpback rabbit covered dish. All the new pieces marked McKee were made by Summit Glass. Since none of the McKee items were ever listed in Summit's general price lists, it's assumed but not known, that the McKee pieces were private mold work.

None of the confirmed shapes with fake marks were originally made by McKee. The camel was a Westmoreland product; the buffalo by Indiana Tumbler and Goblet Works (Greentown); the duck by Challinor-Taylor and the rabbit by an unknown maker but definitely not McKee.

New raised molded McKee script mark on reproductions. Note that leg of the letter "K" ends in large semicircular curve. The legs of the letter "M" are of equal length.

NEW

Original raised molded McKee script mark. Note how the leg of the letter "K" loops back towards the letter "E". The first leg of the letter "M" is longer than the other leg.

OLD

New molded McKee script marks end in a rounded curve. The original script McKee mark hooks back towards the full word (see photos on the previous page). Original McKee animals and covered dishes with authentic script marks are among the rarest and most expensive pieces of milk glass. Depending on subjects, some pieces sell for over $2,000. An original Greentown milk glass buffalo sells for $300-$500.

New figural buffalo paperweight with fake McKee script. The original buffalo paperweight was made by Indiana Glass & Tumbler (Greentown), not McKee.

The original buffalo paperweight. The original has an opening between the leg and head (arrow). New paperweights are solid glass in this area.

Jefferson Davis-Robert E. Lee flask

A milk glass piece with Confederate States President Jefferson Davis is often thought to have been made in the 19th century. The piece appears both as a flask, with a sheared mouth, and also as a vase with fluted mouth shown here. Confederate General Robert E. Lee is on the reverse. The mold was designed to give the finished piece a "whittled" look similar to early flasks made in wood molds. A swirl on the base resembles a pontil mark.

The piece is identified in *American Bottles & Flasks and Their Ancestry* by H. McKearin and K. Wilson as a souvenir of the 1961 Civil War centennial. It was first sold at celebrations in Gettysburg, PA and then at other sites.

The maker is unknown but presumed to be from the United States and is possibly Clevenger Bros.

This flask shape with Jefferson Davis was issued around the 1961 Civil War centennial celebration. General Robert E. Lee is on the reverse side.

Egg server

In 2003, L.E. Smith reissued a classic shape in milk glass the company first made in the 1950s. The large 12-inch piece has a covered chicken in the center of a platter with scallops for 12 eggs. Smith introduced this shape in the mid-1950s but original colors are unknown. Neither new or old Smith versions are marked.

This Smith version, new and old, is sometimes confused with a similar egg server made by Fenton in the 1950s. The Smith tray, viewed from above, is distinctly egg-shaped with one narrow end. The Fenton tray is a simple oval with both ends equal. There is also a chick molded under the hen's wing in the Smith piece.

Reproduction milk glass egg server by L.E. Smith. The original was made during the 1950s.

HALLOWEEN

Halloween-related objects continue to be one of the fasting growing categories of reproductions. While Halloween reproductions of the early 1990s were rather crude lanterns and candy containers, recent pieces are often very well-made creations which are very close copies of vintage originals. The shapes and forms of reproductions have also expanded to include wall and ceiling hangings, three-dimensional figures (other than lanterns and candy containers) and a wide range of paper items. Separating new from old has become more difficult because the reproductions are made by hand in much the same manner as vintage originals. Many new pieces from China, India and the Philippines have the random hand-made irregularities and flaws collectors previously used to authenticate genuine pieces.

NEW

The reproduction cat in moon, above, is a direct copy of the original, right, made in Germany in the 1920s. The reproduction is made of a ceramic glazed resin and is double sided. The original is die-cut cardboard; only one side is finished, the reverse is raw cardboard. *Image of original courtesy of Mark Ledenbach, Vintage Halloween Collectibles, Krause Publications, 2003.*

OLD

The growing number of shapes and forms of items being reproduced makes it difficult to offer a list of hard and fast rules for detecting Halloween reproductions. So many new and improved reproductions keep coming into the market, and what's true today may be incorrect next week. The following suggestions are some of the general guidelines to help you detect a good majority, but certainly far from all, of the reproductions currently in the market.

Paint—The dull flat paint on the latest reproductions is nearly identical to that found on vintage pieces. Many new colors are close matches for vintage colors. Long wave black light will fluoresce some, but far from all, new paint, particularly reds and most white. One of the best tests of age for paint is simply to smell the surface. Many reproductions still have a strong paint odor for a year or more after manufacture. If the paint stinks, so does the seller if they're offering the item as old.

Surface—The great majority of vintage pre-1940 paper mâché and composition lanterns and candy containers have a relatively smooth dull exterior surface. A rough exterior surface is often a sign of a reproduction. Many of the latest reproductions are coated with a factory-applied deeply crackled surface. This surface appears on many new lanterns, candy containers and other three-dimensional pieces. As a general rule, any piece with this deeply crackled surface is suspicious and is almost certainly new. Another paint-related clue of a potential reproduction is the presence of clean white chips in the surface. Many new pieces of paper mâché, like the originals, are coated with gesso, which is a mixture of water and plaster. Gesso is applied to paper mâché to smooth the surface before painting. If the paint is chipped, the gesso shows through. Chips in vintage pieces made 50 to 80 years ago have darkened with age from absorbing dust and dirt. If the surface under a chip is bright white, it is likely a sign of a recently made piece.

Paper—Lantern paper, the paper behind the eyes, nose and mouth in lanterns, can provide important clues to age. Recently made lantern papers are very often produced on printing presses or digitally driven laser and inkjet printers. Laser and inkjet printers almost always create distinct patterns visible under 10X magnification. Inkjets, for example, form fields of color made up of randomly shaped blobs, or drops, of colored ink. Both lasers and inkjet printers deposit inks and toners in relatively narrow horizontal rows, one row at a time. If the rows become slightly misaligned it can produce "banding," a horizontal striping obvious to the unaided eye (see chart on P. 231). New lantern papers made on home inkjet printers are particularly common as replacement papers on genuinely old lanterns.

Some mass-produced lantern papers are printed on traditional printing presses. These are identified by solid colors broken into a regular repeated network of similar sized dots, or screen pattern. The human brain fuses the separate dots together to create the illusion of a solid mass of color. The typical dot pattern can usually be detected with a 10X loupe; some coarse patterns may even be observed with the unaided eye (see chart on P. 231).

Nearly all original lantern paper is translucent. A number of reproductions and modern replacements are made from ordinary office-quality white opaque paper. This is especially true of replacement papers made on home inkjet printers. Inkjet papers are specially designed to be opaque in order to prevent bleed-through of the inkjet droplets of color. Most new lantern papers, especially inkjet and laser papers, will fluoresce under long wave black light. Original papers rarely, if ever, fluoresce. Modern synthetic glues used to attach new papers to new lanterns generally fluoresce. Most old glues made of natural

New 6" paper mâché lantern with new paper behind the eyes and mouth and deeply crackled surface.

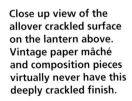

Close up view of the allover crackled surface on the lantern above. Vintage paper mâché and composition pieces virtually never have this deeply crackled finish.

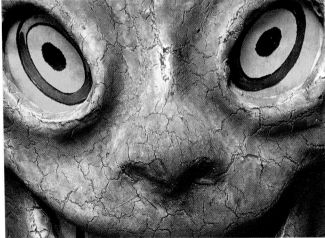

materials do not fluoresce. Of course, you might find a repair where a genuinely old paper has been reattached to an old lantern with new glue.

When you examine a suspected piece, don't rely on a single test for determining age. Examine as many features as possible. If you're looking at a lantern, be sure to inspect how ink was applied to the paper and the paper itself. Is there an odor of new paint? Does new glue fluoresce under long wave black light? Using the general guidelines already discussed, you will be able to catch many of the reproductions in the market. But keep up to date with changes; new reproductions are constantly appearing.

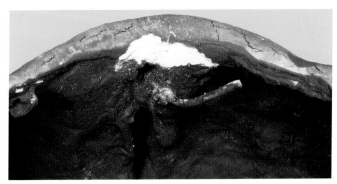

Typical bright white plaster coating, or gesso, showing through a paint chip on a reproduction lantern. Chips on vintage pieces would logically be darkened from normal wear and age.

This reproduction lantern paper has been factory stained on the front to suggest age.

The clean, spotless reverse side of the same paper proves the "stain" is actually only a surface coating on the front.

Lantern paper

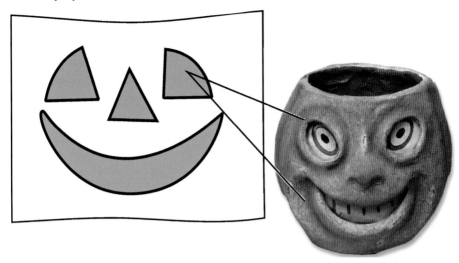

Printing on lantern papers

The colored features on the great majority of old lantern papers appear as smooth continuous fields of solid color.

Colored features applied by laser and inkjet printers are characterized by randomly spaced fuzzy dots of various colors. May include misaligned bands of color.

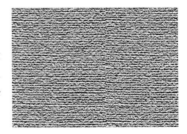

Colored features produced on a printing press are arranged in a consistent repeating pattern of similarly sized dots.

New 10" paper mâché black cat combination lantern and candy container. Scuff marks were applied at the factory to suggest wear and age.

New cone-shaped cardboard 6" hanging vase. Metal band around the top rim is embossed with cats and pumpkins.

New devil paper mâché lantern, about 6-1/2" tall.

A new 5" chauffeur combination lantern and candy container copied from a vintage original. The figure has carrot arms with green carrot tops hands and squash for legs.

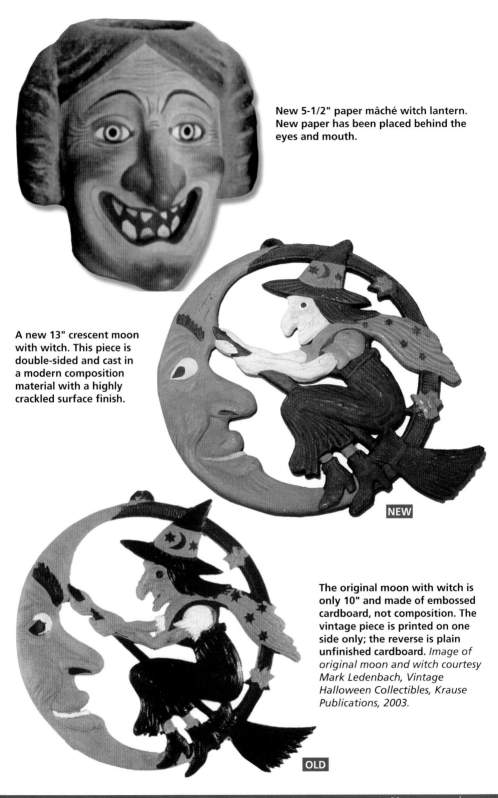

New 5-1/2" paper mâché witch lantern. New paper has been placed behind the eyes and mouth.

A new 13" crescent moon with witch. This piece is double-sided and cast in a modern composition material with a highly crackled surface finish.

NEW

The original moon with witch is only 10" and made of embossed cardboard, not composition. The vintage piece is printed on one side only; the reverse is plain unfinished cardboard. *Image of original moon and witch courtesy Mark Ledenbach, Vintage Halloween Collectibles, Krause Publications, 2003.*

OLD

JEWELRY

Reproductions of classic costume jewelry have become widespread. Many fakes are made from new molds taken from vintage originals. Most reproductions have forged marks of all the vintage makers including Eisenberg, Trifari, Boucher, Hobé and others so marks alone are no guarantee of age. The best test of age is a careful examination of how a suspect piece is constructed, how any marks are applied and whether a mark is appropriate for the piece on which it appears.

Never make a judgment of age base on any one single test. Conduct as many tests as possible. Also keep in mind that small unknown companies often copied popular designs from the larger makers. You could find a cheap copy that was made in the 1930s as well as a deliberately faked copy made in the past year. Copies and knockoffs made 60 to 30 years ago or yesterday can generally both be detected using the tests and guidelines discussed in this chapter.

General construction

Most differences between reproductions and originals exist because originals were essentially handmade and reproductions are mass-produced as rapidly as possible. The clearest evidence of these differences is in the construction of the mountings and settings. The mounting is the entire metal portion in which the stones are displayed; a setting is the specific portion of the mounting, which actually holds the stone.

Mountings of inexpensive costume jewelry reproductions are usually molded, or cast, as one single piece. The majority of vintage original pre-1940s mountings generally made of multiple separate pieces carefully soldered together. On the back sides of new mountings, metal appears to flow in wide flat continuous channels from setting to setting. There is little space between settings; the mounting has little depth from front to back. About 90 percent of all reproduction mountings are single piece castings.

Typically, settings in old mountings are individually soldered to the mounting, not cast as a single piece with the mounting. From the back side, each setting is distinct from other settings, they do not appear to be joined by a channel of flowing metal. Since each setting can be individually placed, the depth of old mountings front to back is usually greater than new mountings. The distinct space between settings also generally gives vintage mountings a lighter, airier look. About 95 percent of vintage mountings pieces are assembled from multiple pieces soldered together.

Prongs—slender tabs of metal in a setting which grip the stone—also generally differ between new and old mountings. Prongs on many reproductions are

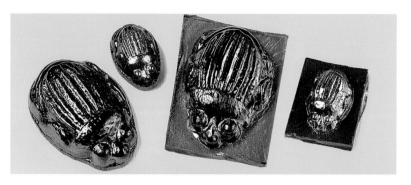

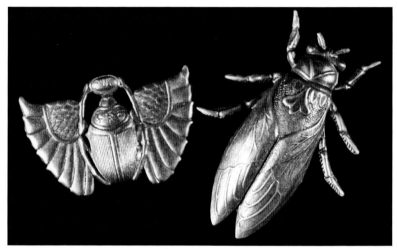

In addition to factory made reproductions of jewelry, buyers have to be increasingly aware of do-it-yourself copies assembled from old appearing bits and pieces. All the components here have been assembled into various pieces of jewelry: imitation Tiffany scarabs (top photo), new metal castings (above), plastic copies of cameos (bottom left), and vintage clothing buttons converted into brooches and
hatpins (bottom right).

wider, thicker and longer than prongs on vintage costume jewelry. New prongs are cast as a part of the entire one-piece mounting and must be made larger to survive being removed from the mold. The longer new prongs frequently come up over the girdle, or horizontal center, of the stone and extend into the table, or flat surface at the top of the stone. Prongs in original settings are generally only long enough to secure the stone to the mounting. Old prongs rarely extend much beyond the girdle. Long prongs are illogical because they hide the stone. The entire purpose of the mounting is to display stones, not hide them.

Upright, unbent prongs also indicate a new mounting. Bending all the prongs in all the settings takes too long for mass production. It's quicker to simply glue the stones in the settings. Stones in any reasonably well-made vintage mounting will be held by bent prongs, not glue.

Another frequent warning sign of new construction is size. Many reproductions are made in new molds and are substantially larger than originals. The fake Trifari lyre bird brooch in the photo on P. 240, for example, is almost twice the size of

NEW

OLD

The back side of a typical new one-piece molded mounting. Little space between settings; settings appear to be joined by a flowing channel of metal.

The back of a typical vintage mounting assembled from many separate pieces. Settings are individually soldered to the mounting; each setting is distinctly visible from other settings.

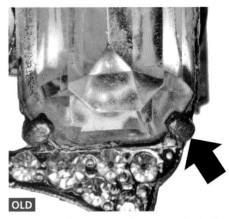

NEW

Many prongs on reproduction costume jewelry are wider, thicker and longer than original prongs. The new prongs shown above extend almost to the top of the stone. Compare these to the original prongs shown at right.

OLD

Prongs on vintage jewelry are typically just long enough to hold the stones in place. Exact proportions will vary, but generally the longer, wider and thicker the prongs, the more likely the piece is a modern copy or fake.

the vintage Trifari. The fake is marked "Trifari" and could easily be confused for old without checking the measurements of the original. Size can also be helpful in separating legitimate modern legitimately made costume jewelry from vintage counterparts. Christmas tree pins made prior to the 1940s, for example, are relatively large, usually 3 inches to 4 inches. The majority of Christmas tree pins on the market today have been made since 1950 and are half that size. The Christmas trees made by Eisenberg in the 1980s, for example, are each under 2 inches. With the authentic mark of a legitimate maker, these trees are frequently represented as examples from the 1930s. The small size, and considering Eisenberg never made Christmas trees before the 1980s, proves the trees are modern.

Unlike general construction techniques, which can be broadly applied, size is specific to each piece. You'll need to refer to a reference book to make individual comparisons.

These authentic Eisenberg Christmas trees made in the 1980s are frequently represented as 1930s jewelry. These modern examples are under 2" tall. Vintage trees made prior to World War II are 3" to 4" tall.

A reproduction Coro pin with fake Coro Craft mark. The rim of the fins have gapes and are not continuous. The fake is base metal, not sterling.

The original Coro pin. Note how the rim of the fins form a single continuous unbroken edge. Original pin is made of sterling.

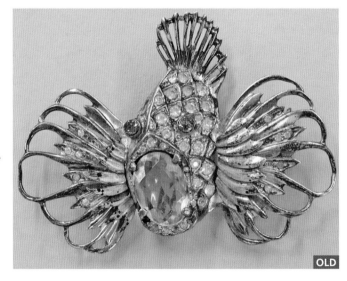

Forged Coro Craft mark applied on an irregularly shaped tag has very poor detail.

Authentic Coro Craft mark on a well-shaped tag, good detail in lettering. Mark on the original fish pin includes "sterling."

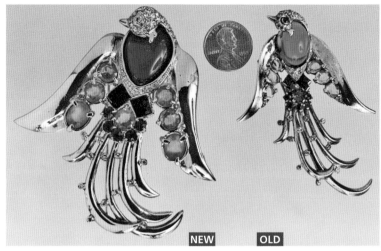

Size is often a clue to a recent copy. The reproduction marked Trifari, left, is nearly twice the size of the Trifari original on the right.

New and old marks

Many manufacturers whose costume jewelry lines began in the 1920s have used a variety of marks on their work. Through the years, these marks often changed to correspond with style trends or the introduction of new lines. It is very important to learn which marks are appropriate for which years and lines.

Generally, authentic marks in vintage costume jewelry are die stamped. The great majority of fake marks are molded, not stamped. Molded marks are never as clean and sharp as stamped marks. Many new molded marks appear in a recessed bar or block. Vintage die stamped marks are never found in similar recessed blocks. Some forged marks, as well as authentic marks, are applied as raised tags. Marks in raised tags may or may not be old; marks in the recessed blocks are virtually always new. Consult a reference book to verify whether any questionable mark was in fact applied in the form represented by the seller. Reviewing the construction of a piece is a much more reliable test of age than marks which are widely forged.

Trifari marks are among the most widely seen forgeries. An authentic Trifari mark is virtually never the single word "Trifari." Authentic marks typically include at least one or more of the following: a © copyright symbol, a patent notice or number, a crown above the "T" and, if the piece is sterling, the word "STERLING."

Any mark set into a recessed bar or block is virtually guaranteed to be a fake. These marks are molded; vintage marks are die stamped.

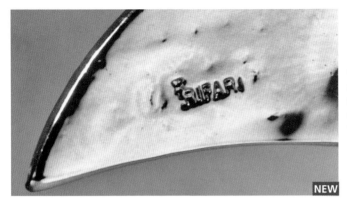

Typical forged Trifari; cast in the mold, not die stamped. "Trifari" appears alone with no other words or symbols.

NEW

Marks on an authentic Trifari piece. All marks are die stamped; patent number and "sterling" appear with "Trifari."

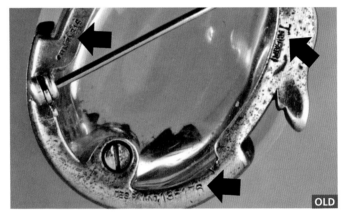

OLD

Eisenberg designs are probably the most widely imitated pieces of costume jewelry. Many of the fakes are marked with a separate applied oval plate that may or may not include "sterling." Generally, authentic Eisenberg marks are stamped into the metal, not applied. Another positive sign of an authentic Eisenberg mark is a model number, which may be a single letter or number, in addition to the company name. The only exceptions to these general rules would be the newer pieces of Eisenberg such as Eisenberg Ice, which don't carry a model code like earlier pieces. While those pieces are genuine Eisenberg, though, they are modern pieces and not vintage examples. You may also find authentic signature plates on some very small early authentic Eisenberg when stamping wasn't practical due to size.

In addition to forgeries of marks on copies of well known vintage designs, many designs from previously unknown makers are being made with desirable marks added. Coro and Coro Craft marks, for example, are showing up on designs never attributed to that company. "Boucher" has appeared on designs originally made by Trifari and Coro. Any jelly belly (discussed on P. 243) pieces signed Boucher or Hobe is automatically a fake. Those two companies never manufactured a line of Lucite jelly belly pieces.

Although this Eisenberg mark is stamped, it's a fake because it is on an applied plate. Except for a handful of exceptions, authentic Eisenberg marks are not on applied plates.

A typical authentic Eisenberg mark is generally stamped directly into the metal like this example, not a separate applied plate.

A fake 2-3/4" pin marked "Eisenberg Original" on a raised plate. The settings are made of colored plastic.

This mark is on the fake pin above.

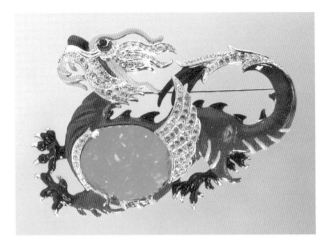

New dragon 4" pin marked Boucher. The vintage original was made by Trifari, not Boucher.

New 1-1/2" x 2-1/2" jelly belly crab marked Boucher. Boucher never made Lucite jelly belly pieces. The original was made Trifari, not Boucher.

New 2" jelly belly parrot marked Boucher. The vintage original was made by Coro Craft, not Boucher.

A new 3" sterling swordfish marked Hobé. The mounting is base metal, not sterling.

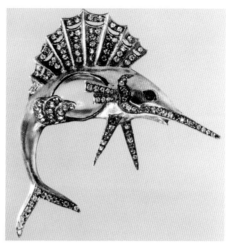

A new 4" sterling dragonfly marked Hobé. The mounting is base metal, not sterling.

A new 2-3/4" sterling basket with plastic stones; stones in the vintage piece mounting were glass. Faked Coro mark is in block letters.

Enamel

The new pins shown here and on P. 246 were sold as "enameled" in an estate sale. It is relatively easy to identify these pieces as modern fakes with a simple 10X loupe. The telltale clue is the obvious brush strokes in the surface. True enamel is begins as a powder. It is then fired at high temperature which melts the powder into a smooth glass-like, or vitreous, material permanently fused to the metal surface. No brush marks are ever found in true fired enamel. The fakes represented as enamel are simply coated with ordinary paints and a brush. Another clue to new "enamel" may be found with a close inspection of any chips and scratches. True enamels were applied over a dark dull primer. The dark primer almost always shows through chips in true enamel. The new "enamels" do not have the dark undercoating. Chips or scratches in the new painted surfaces reveal shiny metal below, not a dark primer.

New jester head pin with imitation enamel; marked "Staret" in recessed panel.

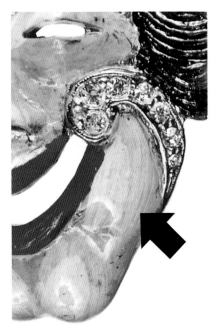

The "enamel" on the jester pin has obvious brush marks. True enamel is created by firing powders in a kiln, not paint. Brush strokes never appear in genuine enamel.

New bird pin with brush marks in the "enamel." Fake mark "Coro" is molded in back.

New prongs in the bird pin are not bent over the stones. The new stones are glued. Straight, unbent prongs are one sign of a reproduction mounting.

Bakelite

There are several problems that buyers face when considering Bakelite. First, is the material truly Bakelite? Many sellers, either through ignorance or deliberate intent, call all plastic jewelry "Bakelite." Next, are all the parts original to the object being sold? There has been a steady increase in reworked and "married" pieces, items made by joining bits and parts of several pieces into a complete object. Finally, if the material is true Bakelite, when was it made into jewelry? There are currently many pieces in the market recently made from vintage raw stock. Fortunately, a few simple tests are all that's necessary to separate genuine Bakelite from plastic and detect the fakes and reproductions.

Bakelite is a trade name derived from its inventor, Leo Baekeland, who invented Bakelite in 1907. Bakelite is made from carbolic acid (phenol) and formaldehyde. It is referred to as a phenolic resin. Bakelite was first used as an insulator against heat and electricity. As ways were found to manufacture Bakelite in bright colors, it began to be used for all sorts of decorative objects, especially jewelry.

Although Bakelite was the trade name of the first thermosetting phenolic resin, it was not the only one. Other important trade or brand names include Catalin, Marblette, Prystal, Phenolia and a number of others. Since brand names rarely appear on the products, collectors generally use "Bakelite" to refer to all phenolic resins, not just the Bakelite brand. And that's how I'll use the term. In this discussion, "Bakelite" will refer to all phenolic resin pieces regardless of their original brand name.

A 1930s catalog page of stock Bakelite shapes. This photo from a catalog issued by Catalin, a manufacturer of Bakelite.

One of the keys to identifying original Bakelite is to understand how it was manufactured. Modern hard plastics are generally produced by injecting a liquid resin into a mold. In other words, to get a pin shaped like a dog, you'd pour molten plastic into a dog-shaped mold. All the details of the finished product, fur, eyes, collar, hanging loop, were created in the mold. When the mold was opened, the final piece was essentially ready for sale.

By contrast, the majority of vintage Bakelite jewelry was not individually molded. The majority of pieces were assembled by hand from simple stock shapes such as cylinders, tubes, sheets, blocks and cubes. If you wanted to make a bracelet, for example, you'd typically begin with a pre-formed tube. Workers then sliced off sections, which could be carved, set with stones or laminated with other pieces.

Because finishing and assembly of Bakelite was done by hand, special designs and small custom orders could easily be made without the overhead of expensive molds required by hard plastics. Anyone could buy the raw Bakelite material. Small studios, workshops and amateurs could all afford to experiment with their own colors and designs.

Unlike plastic, authentic Bakelite oxidizes over the years developing a patina, which changes the surface color. Normal oxidation provides a valuable clue whether a suspected piece is true Bakelite (phenolic resin) or a look-alike material. All true Bakelite, regardless of surface color, will leave an ivory or pale yellow smear on a cotton swab wetted with one of several common products: the cleaning fluids 409 and Scrubbing Bubbles and the paste-form Simichrome Polish. Look-alike materials, such as modern hard plastics, will not leave any color on the swab or will leave a smear in the same the color as the plastic (blue plastic will leave a blue smear, etc.). All the testing products cause eye and skin irritation and should be used carefully. Use rubber gloves and wash your hands thoroughly when you're done.

Use only a tiny amount of any of the testing materials on a cotton swab. Apply to a small, hidden area such as the back side of a pin or inside of a bracelet. Scrubbing Bubbles can dull the original finish; Simichrome will leave the tested area with a higher shine; 409 leaves the surface virtually unchanged and is the best choice. Most non-Bakelite products are not affected by the products, but you should always be careful and carefully wash and wipe dry all tested areas to prevent any possible long-term changes. The swab test is effective on virtually all Bakelite. The most common exceptions are pieces of genuine Bakelite that have recently been completely polished or cleaned and the original patina has been removed. Certain colors, particularly black and some reds, can also occasionally give confusing results.

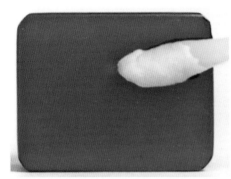

Test swabs of genuine Bakelite will be ivory or pale yellow regardless of the color of the Bakelite.

When testing with hot water, heat only the edge of an article. Run the water over the thinnest edge for best results.

The three most widely available materials to test Bakelite are 409 household cleaner, Scrubbing Bubbles bathroom cleaner and Simichrome Polish.

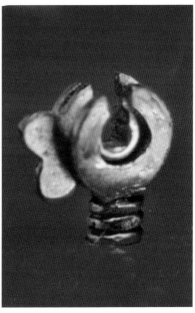

Examples of original applied findings in vintage Bakelite. Left: typical hinge fastened with tiny nails. Right: a vintage clasp screwed into the Bakelite.

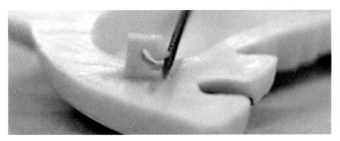

All findings on vintage Bakelite are applied, not molded. Later plastics, like this piece, often have pin catches, barrels of hinges and other features cast as one piece with the jewelry.

A new pin has been glued on a genuine Bakelite clothing button to make a more expensive Bakelite "brooch." Metal findings like pins, clasps and hinges, are never glued to vintage Bakelite.

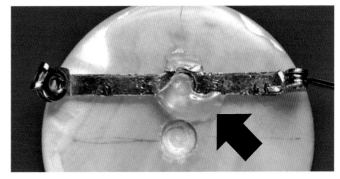

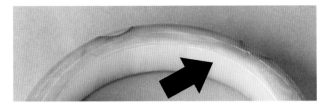

Exposed surfaces of vintage Bakelite are almost always darker than protected surfaces. The inside of this vintage bracelet is lighter than the outside surface.

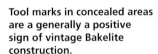

Tool marks in concealed areas are a generally a positive sign of vintage Bakelite construction.

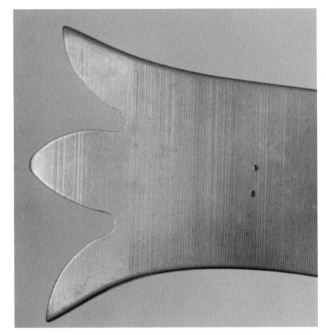

Another simple test is to place a suspected piece under hot water from your household faucet. Hold the piece so an edge is in the middle of the flow. After 20 to 30 seconds, most genuine Bakelite gives off a strong phenol odor, which is similar to paint remover or varnish. Modern plastics and other look-alikes do not generally produce any odor when held under hot water produced by the average household hot water heater.

Once you determine a piece is made from genuine Bakelite, it doesn't mean you have proved the piece is necessarily old. There is a surprising amount of original unfinished Bakelite stock that has survived. This old but never-used stock can be carved today and offered as vintage Bakelite. Genuine vintage jewelry that is plain and low value, is frequently recarved into more desirable and higher priced designs. Old stock and recarved pieces will both pass the swab and hot water tests because the pieces are genuine Bakelite (phenolic resin).

One way to confirm age is to carefully examine the findings, or hardware, such as pins, hinges, etc. Findings on genuine vintage Bakelite jewelry are generally attached with mechanical fasteners such as tiny screws, pins and nails. Findings in modern plastic are typically formed in the mold or glued on later; original metal findings almost always show some tarnish or even rust. Be wary of shiny hardware with no sign of normal age or wear.

Glued hardware is also a sign of modern pieces, or at the very least, a repair. New pins are commonly glued to inexpensive Bakelite clothing buttons to make a piece of "jewelry." Remember, even if a piece passes the cotton swab test, it doesn't mean the hardware is original. New hardware is frequently glued to odd, broken and mismatched bits and pieces of low value old Bakelite, which is then offered as more expensive "jewelry."

Since genuine Bakelite produces a patina, outer surfaces on truly vintage pieces should normally be darker than protected inner surfaces. Insides of bracelets, for example, are generally lighter in than the exposed outer surfaces. Backs of pins and earrings should also be lighter than exposed outer surfaces.

Nearly all vintage Bakelite jewelry was hand worked, sawed and carved and generally has some signs of tool marks. Vintage tool marks are, however, at the very least, tumbled and rounded off, never jagged or sharp. Original tool marks are also logical. An original carver, working by the hour or piece-rate, polished exposed surfaces, not hidden surfaces concealed from view. Surfaces of reworked or newly carved pieces are sometimes completely polished on all sides, regardless if the surface is exposed to view or hidden. Grinding marks with a frosted, chalky appearance are also a typical sign of a recently carved or reworked surface.

One of the more obvious signs that a piece could not possibly be a piece of Bakelite is a mold seam. Authentic hand-finished Bakelite jewelry never has a mold seam. Modern hard plastics produced in a mold, virtually always have a mold seam. No original Bakelite will warp or bend under heat or exposure to moisture. Any warped or distorted piece is not Bakelite but some other material such as modern hard plastic or 19th century celluloid.

When testing Bakelite, always use safe, nondestructive tests like those described here. Never use a heated pin or open flame. And always ask the seller's permission before making any tests.

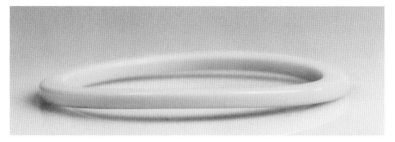

No authentic Bakelite will warp, bend or lose its original shape due to heat or moisture. Any warped or misshaped piece like the bangle above cannot be authentic Bakelite.

Plastic bangles from the 1960s, top, are frequently sold as Bakelite. These pieces fail the swab test and have an obvious mold seam, below. Vintage Bakelite never has a mold seam.

MARBLES

I n late 1993, sulphide marbles with previously unknown single figures and double figures began appearing in the market. Some of the marbles with sulphides were made with latticino swirls, which is also a previously unknown combination. A number of those marbles with previously unknown figures sold for several thousand dollars and more. There are various explanations of the sudden appearance of the previously unknown sulphides: One seller said the marbles were found in the former country of East Germany; another seller said his marbles were found in California while digging for other artifacts.

Laboratory testing found all the suspected marbles examined contained three to five times the sodium of known original sulphides. Why is that significant? Increasing the level of sodium generally lowers the temperature at which glass

Original packaging increases the value of most vintage collectibles especially marbles. Clever forgers are using digital image editing software to make fantasy packages like this example. Differences in how new and old plastic bags are manufactured can help you catch most fakes (see pages 258-261).

becomes elastic and workable. This means glass can be handled longer by less skilled workers. The cost of ingredients is also reduced. Glass with high sodium is used extensively in all types of reproduction glass including pattern glass, Depression glass and art glass. Substantially increased sodium is not by itself positive proof a piece of glass is a reproduction, but it is a strong clue that the glass is at the very least modern.

There are several features of the new marbles, though, that can be observed without laboratory instruments. The most obvious of these are clouds and swirls of tiny bubbles in the glass, unusual black hairlike shapes throughout the glass, open pits across the surface, pronounced surface swirls and crude remains of pontil and tool marks. Which features you find will vary on the state of the new marble. Originally, all the new marbles have a cloudy frosted appearance, which makes the clay figures seem blurred and cloudy. The blurring is caused by tiny broken bubbles and raised swirls at, or just under, the surface. These disturbances catch and refract rays of light. Some sellers try to improve the marbles by polishing out the broken bubbles and swirls but this has limited success. Bubbles and black hair-like inclusions appear throughout the entire glass body. Polishing one surface only exposed flaws in lower layer. No matter how much glass is ground away, the surface of the fake sulphides still have an overall dull speckled or pitted look and feel.

The dull, pitted surface created by broken bubbles and swirls of new marbles should not be confused with dull spots in old marbles caused by normal wear. Under magnification, normal wear appears as irregular random lines and fractures. True wear marks are absent from the polished fakes. The bubbles and swirls show up in the new sulphides whether they are polished or found unpolished. Pontils on old 2-inch sulphides are virtually never more than 1/4 inch across and are polished. Pontils on the new 2-inch sulphides are 1/2-inch across with obvious grinding marks.

Any sulphide, especially those with multiple figures, with hair-like lines, rough obvious pontils, clouds of bubbles and swirled surfaces should be purchased with extreme caution. Get the advice of experts before you make a decision to buy and if you buy, insist on a written guarantee that includes the general date or period of manufacture.

A new sulphide-styled marble with a figure of an angel. No documented vintage sulphides have ever been found with this figure.

NEW

A new sulphide-styled marble with two cows. All sulphides with multiple figures should only be purchased with a written guarantee including the date of production.

NEW

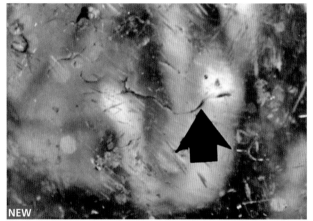

NEW

The surface of a new sulphide seen under 10X magnification. The black hair-like lines and swirls on the marble's surface are a clue to detecting the new sulphides.

Another view of the swirls and hair-like structures through the glass of the new sulphides. See photo below for comparison to normal wear lines on vintage sulphides.

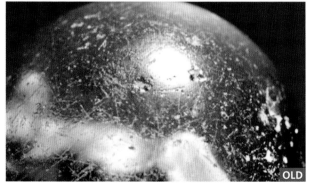

OLD

The random straight lines and irregular pits on a vintage sulphide marble, shown here, is unlike the black lines on the surface of the new sulphides.

Bags of marbles

Bags of new marbles with faked paper headers first began appearing in the market during late 1990s. When I first became aware of these fakes, there were thought to be around 50 different new bags. Since then the number of new bags in the market has probably tripled or quadrupled. New bags appear each month.

The most frequent victims of these new bags are buyers interested in the subject matter shown on the new paper headers. Disney collectors, for example, are more likely to buy a bag of marbles with Mickey Mouse on the header than a marble collector. Fishing lure collectors are more likely to buy a bag of marbles featuring Winchester sports gear than a marble collector.

The great majority of new bags are fantasy items; there never was a vintage bag like the new piece. So far, only a few original headers have been copied, primarily those of soft drink makers such as 7-Up, Pepsi and Coca-Cola. Most new headers are made from old advertisements or other images, which are scanned into a computer, manipulated and printed out as a bag header.

The new bags are fairly well known among marble collectors but often go undetected by other collectors and general line dealers. Marble collectors aren't generally duped by the new paper headers because they recognize the marbles are new. The following guidelines will help you identify the majority of bags with fake and fantasy headers:

- Virtually all full-color paper headers are new. If the header includes a complete range of colors like a color photo, it is almost certain to be new. Original headers were very rarely printed in more than one or two single colors.

- Almost all original plastic marble bags have a wide vertical seam up the center of the bag. New bags do not have the vertical seam. Generally, most old bags appear dulled, almost cloudy, from age. Most new bags have a bright, shiny surface that feels slick.

- Clear plastic bags were not used to package marbles until the early 1950s. In the 1940s, the great majority of bags used to package marbles were made of mesh, not a continuous sheet of plastic.

- Products, brand names, events or personalities of the 1930s or earlier years featured in packages which were not invented until 1950 are clearly illogical and should be viewed with suspicion. How could a header with a 1932 Mickey Mouse cartoon, for example, be featured on a type of packaging not invented until the 1950s?

- Most, but not all, vintage ca. 1950-60s headers are fastened with flat staples. Fake and fantasy headers are almost always fastened with round staples, not flat staples. Beware of artificially rusted new staples. Don't let new rusted flat staples persuade you into thinking the headers are old.

- Virtually all paper used in the new headers fluoresces bright white under long wave black light. Most paper in most vintage headers does not generally fluoresce. Many new inks used in inkjet and laser printers also fluoresce; most vintage 1950-60s inks do not fluoresce.

- The great majority of new headers are printed on inkjet and laser printers. Vintage headers were generally either silk screened or printed on a printing press. Full color images created on inkjet and laser printers are formed by a series of fuzzy dots of many colors randomly arranged. Full color images printed on presses are formed by equal-sized dots of only black, blue, yellow and red arranged in repeating patterns.

- Virtually all known new headers have been made on computers with image editing software. Artwork, trademarks and logos are generally scanned from old advertisements, catalog reprints or reference books. Those elements are sized, cropped and otherwise manipulated including adding or deleting text, changing color and other changes to make a digital image. Low-resolution digital images can often be identified by jagged, angular or ragged edges on letters and art work. Any of those features indicate a new header.

- Many new headers have obvious mistakes in spelling and grammar. Several new headers made by one forger-purportedly for giveaway bags-are marked "complements," spelled with an "e." The correct usage to indicate a giveaway is "compliments," spelled with an "i." Such mistakes are common in the fakes, but virtually never seen in vintage pieces.

New bags of marbles with faked headers feature highly collectible subjects such as soft drink manufacturers, tobacco products, sporting goods, movie stars, black memorabilia, transportation and other images.

New fantasy header with Babe Ruth and Beech-Nut chewing tobacco. "Babe Ruth says Chew Beech-Nut; Hit of the Day." No similar vintage bag was ever produced.

New fantasy full color header with logo of Chevron Gasoline, "Extra clean for fussy folk!" No similar vintage bag was ever produced.

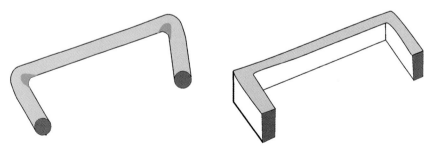

The majority of new headers are applied to new bags with new staples. Modern staples are round in cross section, left. The great majority of staples used in vintage ca.1950s headers are flat in cross section, right.

This is a typical new plastic bag made since the 1980s used for marbles. The new bags do not have a vertical seam up the center of the bag.

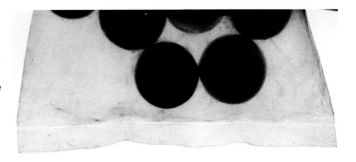

Plastic bags used for marbles before the 1970s almost always have a vertical seam up the center of the bag.

Jagged irregular lines in graphics or text are an indication of low-resolution digital images used in making the new headers.

Marble tournament medals

Original marble tournament medals date from the early 1920s to the 1950s. The medals were awarded to winners of school, city, state and national tournaments and are primarily of interest to marble collectors. Originals can sell for $400 to $800 depending on condition, material, and whether the original ribbon and box are present. Reproductions are generally available for about $30 each. So far, reproduction medals fall into two broad categories: 1) octagon and round National Marble Tournament medals with dates of the 1920s-30s; and 2) a variety of VFW (Veterans of Foreign Wars) sponsored medals with dates from the 1940s.

Most clues to the reproductions arise from the different ways old and new are made. Original tournament medals are die struck the same way coins are minted. A separate engraving of each side is forced against cold metal under great pressure. The result is a virtually flawless piece with very high detail. Reproduction medals are cast in molds taken from the original medals. In making the new molds, detail is lost. New lettering, for example, is often blurred, wavy, filled in and not of uniform height across the surface of the medal. The molten metal poured into the new molds virtually never cools uniformly. This creates obvious flaws and irregularities on the surfaces of the new medals such as pits, bumps or swirls. Most, but not all, reproductions also have a distinctive extra seam or line of metal around the rim.

The majority of original medals on the market are bronze. Although sterling silver original medals were made, the original silver medals are virtually never marked "sterling." Any marble tournament medal marked "sterling" is almost certain to be new. Another obvious clue to a reproduction silver medal would be a new shiny surface. Originals have a dull natural patina consistent with normal aging and wear. (Although an artificial dark black patina can be created with chemicals.) As a general rule, the color of original jump rings—the metal rings

Group of reproduction sterling silver marble tournament medals, copied from vintage

used to attach the medals to the ribbon—should match or be very similar to the color of the medal. If the jump ring is original to both the medal and the ribbon, it would logically have the same patina or surface finish.

Cast reproduction medals have virtually no details in faces such as eyes, mouth or nose. The heads appear as smooth featureless knobs.

The majority of die struck original medals have good facial details with distinct ears, eyes, mouth and nose. Heads are distinct and lifelike.

Winners' names and tournament dates are individually engraved on original die cast medals, right. Names and dates on the cast reproductions are not engraved. They are cast-in when the medal is poured, left.

Do let the presence or absence of a ribbon influence your judgment about the age of the medal. Genuinely old ribbons from other sources can be attached to new medals. Likewise, genuinely old medals may have a modern replacement added for display purposes.

Marbles with advertising, comics, and personalities

Virtually all marbles found in the market today with comic characters, brand names and products have been made since the 1970s. The only pre-1970 authentic marbles with a movie star or comic character were made by Peltier Glass in the early 1930s. The original marbles were 5/8-inch diameter and made on opaque white glass with one spot glass in a contrasting color. Line drawings and the names of the comic and cartoon characters were applied in one color. None of the images on the original Peltier marbles can be felt with your fingernail.

Peltier made only 12 vintage comic and cartoon character marbles plus one marble with Tom Mix, the only known movie star on an authentic vintage marble. Peltier also made one vintage marble advertising a bakery, "Cotes Master Loaf." The Mix and bakery marbles were made the same way as the comic and cartoon characters marbles. All other marbles with brand names, except for a few Akro Agate advertising marbles, are modern fakes, fantasies or forgeries.

Here are some of the general rules for advertising, comic and cartoon character and brand name marbles:

- If the marble is one solid color, it's new.
- If the marble is more than three colors, it's new.
- If the image, logo or words are full color, it's new.
- Any size other than 5/8" diameter is new.
- If you can feel the image, it's new.

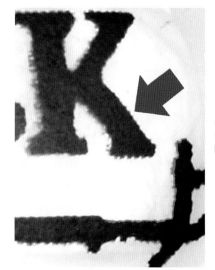

Under magnification, the letters on the "Buck Knives" marble, shown below, are ragged and blurred.

Four new 7/8" diameter marbles with advertising, a comic character and a movie star. All known vintage comic character marbles are 5/8" diameter, not 7/8".

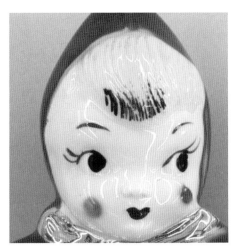

POTTERY

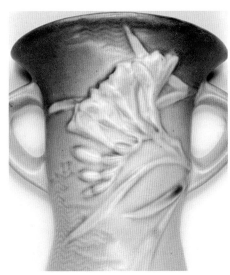

Y ou would think marking reproductions with the names of vintage companies such as McCoy, Roseville, Watt and others would be illegal, but that's not the case. Once a company goes out of business, there is no corporate legal staff to challenge the use of registered trademarks or brand names. If registration of a trade name expires, it can even be relisted under a new owner.

American Pottery in all its forms, from underglaze art pottery to folk art, is being reproduced more frequently. This example was seized in a police sting operation in Pennsylvania involving $23,000 of alleged fakes of Shenandoah pottery.

Unfortunately, this situation makes it difficult for collectors who previously relied on marks to date and authenticate items. Buyers must keep informed of the latest reproductions and how they differ from originals. Marks alone are not a reliable test of age for many areas of collectibles, but especially pottery.

One of the best ways to catch many new pieces of pottery is to simply measure a suspected piece. When molds are made from original objects, each step of the process reduces the size of the final product. The great majority of items made from new molds are substantially different in size from the originals. Although differences vary with overall size, it is not unusual for up to a one inch difference between new and old. Refer to reference books or catalog reprints for sizes of the originals. Measuring is particularly important when you buy without examining an item firsthand. Many Internet sellers as well as live-auction advertisements frequently round measurements in descriptions. If you choose to buy without a hands-on inspection, be sure to request exact measurements.

Review your reference books to verify which marks appeared on which patterns and lines. Reproduction manufacturers frequently use marks that never appeared on the shapes or patterns being copied. Next, double check colors and glazes. Many pottery reproductions are made in popular modern colors never made in the original vintage products. If a catalog reprint lists a particular vintage line in red, blue or green, any piece in purple would obviously be a warning sign.

Bauer Pottery

In 1999, the Bauer Pottery name was re-registered with the United States Trademark Office. Since then, new pottery has been made marked "Bauer Pottery." New products copy the so-called "ring ware" pieces originally manufactured in the 1930s and '40s using the original shapes as models.

The original company, "J.A. Bauer Pottery," was located in Los Angeles, Calif. It produced utility goods, dinnerware and art pottery between 1910 and 1962. The original Bauer is perhaps best known for a line of dinnerware with molded rings similar to the Fiesta line by Homer Laughlin. Although the official Bauer catalog name for the ringed line was "California Pottery," most collectors today refer to the line simply as "ring ware."

The first products of the new Bauer company had marks very similar to marks on pre-1962 vintage pieces. Almost immediately, the new pottery began to be sold as old in the secondary market. Bauer responded by adding "2000" to marks on most new Bauer beginning January, 2000. By early 2001, "2000" had been added to all but six of the 25 shapes being produced at that time. Marks were changed in the remaining shapes as those molds needed repair or replacement. Among the last pieces to have their marks changed were a tumbler and pitcher (shown on P. 269), two sizes of vases and two vases with a leaf design.

New Bauer 2000 ring ware pottery. From left: 7-1/2" dia. bowl, 4" tumbler, 7" vase.

New Bauer 2000 pottery: 8" tall flower pot, left; 6-1/4" saucer, right.

New Bauer 2000 pitcher, tumblers and dinner plates. New Bauer is made in bright bold colors similar to 1930s originals.

One of the raised molded marks on new Bauer Pottery before "2000" was added. All original Bauer marks are impressed, not raised.

Raised molded mark on new Bauer Pottery with "2000" added.

A paper label of the new Bauer Pottery. Gold with black lettering and a vase. Another version with a red vase is also used. Be alert for these new labels being removed and applied to genuinely old but unmarked pieces of low value pottery being offered as vintage Bauer.

Adding "2000" to new marks should be adequate for buyers who wish to avoid the new wares. Some collectors, though, may still be confused by new Bauer Pottery with marks that do not include 2000. Buyers should keep in mind that all vintage Bauer marks are *impressed*, or *incised*, into the clay. Any *raised* Bauer mark, with or without 2000, is new. Many, but certainly not all, vintage pieces of Bauer include an impressed model number in addition to the company mark. No new Bauer has an impressed model number.

The pottery body is also different between new Bauer 2000 and pre-1962 Bauer. New Bauer is much softer and more easily damaged than the vintage ware. Pre-1962 pottery was fired at a much higher temperature and is much stronger. Vintage pottery weighs more than new Bauer 2000 pieces. Color is not generally a reliable test of age. New colors are nearly identical to colors on vintage pieces.

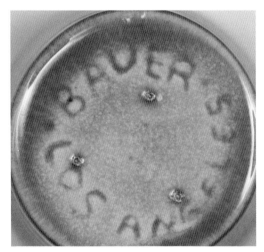

This new Bauer Pottery *impressed* mark without "2000" is confusing. It appeared on new tumblers made before the mold was updated. It's very similar to impressed marks on original Bauer.

This *impressed* mark on new Bauer Pottery has "2000" and is obviously from the new company.

Hull Pottery

Reproductions of Hull Pottery are becoming more common. Although not as widespread as new Roseville, additional patterns and shapes are constantly being added. Some of the patterns copied so far include Bow Knot, Orchid, Magnolia Matte, Woodland and many pieces of Little Red Riding Hood. Most new Hull, excepting some pieces of Little Red Riding Hood, is thought to be made in the United States, not overseas.

Many Hull Pottery reproductions have marks very similar to marks found on original pieces. Many marks on new floral patterns have an almost script-like appearance. Authentic marks on floral patterns are generally a block-style lettering, not script (see photos). Be sure to double check pattern and size numbers in marks. Sizes in several new pieces are different than the sizes in original marks for the same shape.

Another helpful clue to a fake is size. Most new pieces are significantly smaller than the originals they copy. New Orchid and Magnolia pieces, for example, are about a half inch shorter than originals.

Reproduction Hull Pottery vase in orchid pattern, shape #304 shown at left; the original is on the right. The new vase is 10-1/4" tall; original is 10-3/4" tall. The new vase is marked like the original.

The mark on the Hull reproduction. Note the script style of lettering which is particularly evident in the word Hull. Also note that the size is 10 and *one-quarter*.

The mark on the original Hull. Note that the lettering is a block style, not script like the reproduction. Also note that the size is 10 and *three-quarters*.

NEW

OLD

A close-up view of detail in the new pattern; this is very close to the detail in most original orchid patterns.

A close-up view of detail in the original pattern; this original is a particularly sharp mold.

NEW

NEW

The raised pattern on the reproduction Magnolia is in a shiny high gloss finish. The raised pattern on the original is a dull matte finish like the background.

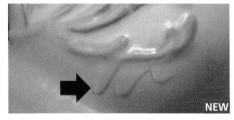

NEW

A reproduction vase in Magnolia Matte pattern. The new vase is only slightly over 8" tall; the original is almost always a full 8-1/2" or more. The new vase has a molded mark virtually identical to marks on original vases.

Drips and runs in the paint and glaze are common on the reproduction pieces. Such flaws are virtually never found on original Hull Pottery.

Little Red Riding Hood

The original Little Red Riding Hood design was created by Louise Bauer. Bauer assigned the design patent to Hull Pottery which sold Little Red Riding Hood pottery products between 1943 and 1957. While Hull Pottery has exclusive rights to the design, it outsourced almost all decorating and production to Royal China and Novelty, a division of Regal China Corp.

Many, but not all, original Little Red Riding Hood is marked with the Design Patent Number, 1#35,889, or the Hull Pottery name or some combination of both. Since many reproductions have look-alike marks, though, and originals may or may not be marked, marks alone are not a reliable test of age. The best test of age is to closely examine how a piece is decorated and formed.

Original Hull Little Red Riding Hood was made for functional, everyday kitchen and table use. Check the fit of lids, shapes of spouts and the fit and placement of handles. Ask yourself, "Could this piece be used for the purpose it was intended?" Reproductions are made as "antiques" and many new pieces cannot function in a practical, logical manner.

Original faces have lifelike eyes and facial expression. Eyes of the reproductions stare zombie-like straight ahead. Eyes of originals are looking to the side. Original eyes are virtually always blue; new eyes are almost always pale green. Hair on reproductions is a thick heavy pale yellow with a few thick strokes of brown to suggest single hair strands. Original hair is a crisp sharp yellow with generally very fine brush strokes to suggest a few single strands.

New gold trim shows no normal wear; original gold trim almost always shows at least some normal wear around handles, knobs, rims and lids. New gold trim also tends to have a mirrorlike reflective surface. Original trim is softer in color and less reflective.

All authentic Little Red Riding Hood pieces were made by Hull Pottery. Pieces of Little Red Riding Hood in today's market with McCoy marks are fakes (see McCoy Pottery on P. 278).

Size is one of the best clues to a Red Riding Hood Hull Pottery reproduction. So far, all the reproductions are considerably smaller than originals. The new cracker jar, left, is 7-1/2" tall; the original, right, is over 8" tall.

NEW OLD

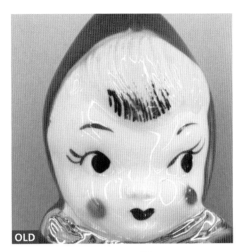

Typical reproduction face: small green eyes stare straight ahead; no spots of blush on cheeks. Poorly molded mouth and lips lack detail.

Typical original face: large blue eye in the corner of the eye, look to figure's left (viewer's right). Definite reddish-pink spots of blush on cheeks.

Smaller new teapot, left, 7-1/2" tall; original teapot, right, is almost 8-1/2" tall.

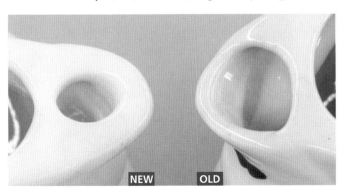

Many features on the reproductions are not functional. The very small new spout, left, wouldn't allow much tea to pass. The original spout, right, was made for daily use.

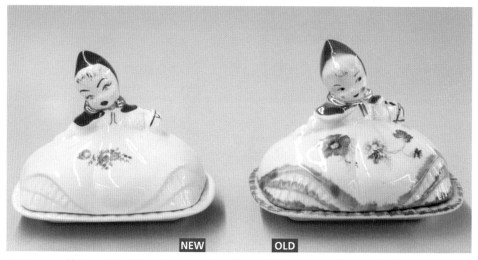

New covered butter dish, left; original butter dish, right. The base of new is 6-1/2" left to right; the original, 6-7/8". The opening in the bottom of the new cover is 6" x 4-1/4"; the opening in the old cover is 6-1/4" x 4-1/2".

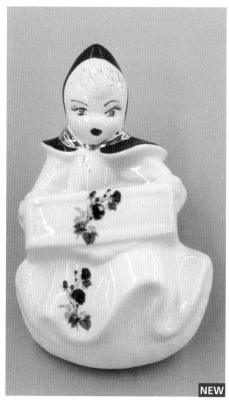

New wall hanging planter, about 8-1/2" top to bottom.

Original wall hanging planter, about 9-1/2" top to bottom.

NEW

New coin bank. About the same size as the original. Gold trim, crude hand-painted details. No mark.

OLD

Original coin bank, 7" high, 5" dia. at base. No mark. Gold trim and hand-painted details.

NEW

The casting holes in the new bank are so big a dime will slide through, which is not very logical for a bank.

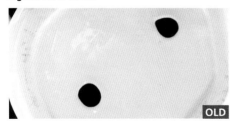

OLD

Casting holes in the original bank are only slightly larger than a wood pencil, about 3/8" in diameter at most. Bottoms were broken out to get the coins.

A new stringholder, made from the same mold as the new bank.

McCoy Pottery

New vases, wall pockets, bookends, pitchers and other shapes marked "McCoy" have been increasingly common in the market. Fake McCoy marks appear not only on products made by the McCoy pottery company, but on copies of pieces originally made by other potteries such as Shawnee and Hull. Unfortunately, this situation makes it difficult for collectors who previously relied on marks to date and authenticate items. Buyers must keep informed of the latest reproductions and how they differ from the originals. Marks alone are not a reliable test of age.

One of the best ways to catch most new pieces marked McCoy is to simply measure a suspected piece. Most McCoy copies are smaller than the originals. The new Uncle Sam vase, for example, is 6-1/2 inches tall; the original is 7-1/4 inches, a 3/4-inch difference. If you choose to buy without a hands-on inspection, be sure to request *exact* measurements. Many Internet sellers as well as live-auction advertisements frequently round measurements in descriptions. The 6-1/2-inch Uncle Sam vase could easily be listed as 7 inches.

Next to size, color is probably the next best test to catch McCoy copies. Many new pieces are made in colors never used in original production. The authentic standard McCoy mailbox, for example, was made only in green. New mailboxes are made in five colors. Most painted trim on vintage McCoy was applied over the glaze in unfired, or cold, paint. Many reproductions, like the Mammy cookie jar shown on P. 281, have trim applied under the glaze.

Force yourself to get in the habit of confirming the original maker. Any piece offered to you as being McCoy should be listed in a McCoy reference book. If you can't locate the piece in a reference book, be wary. One of the reasons some new pieces marked McCoy can't be found in McCoy reference books is that the piece was originally made by another company. A number of new pieces marked McCoy were originally made by Shawnee Pottery and Hull Pottery, not McCoy. Obviously, products known to be made by other potteries should not be marked McCoy. And don't fall for any stories commonly offered to explain such pieces as being made with "loaned" or "experimental" molds or "unsold warehouse samples" and other similar nonsense.

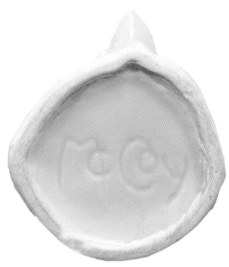

A new Uncle Sam vase marked McCoy. Originals were made in only three colors: aqua, yellow and white. New pieces are sold in aqua, yellow, white, pink, blue and green.

Both new and old Uncle Sam vases are marked "McCoy" in the base. Marks on new and old are virtually identical and not a reliable test of age.

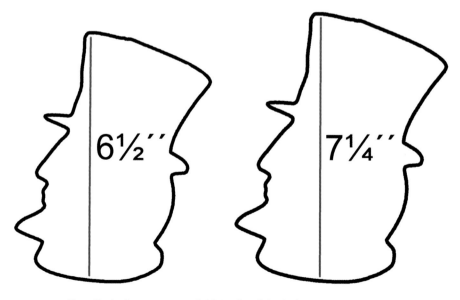

New Uncle Sam vases are 6-1/2" tall; original pieces are 7-1/4" tall.

A new Lady in Bonnet wall pocket marked McCoy. Virtually all vintage pieces were white. Reproductions are sold in cobalt blue, pale green, white and pink, shown here.

Both new and old Lady in Bonnet pieces are marked "McCoy" so marks are not a reliable test of age.

New Lady in Bonnet pieces are about 7-1/2"; originals are about 8".

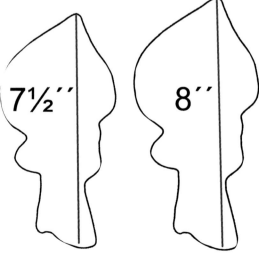

A new mammy cookie jar marked "McCoy." Decorations on many new jars are under the glaze. Hands, face, apron and scarf on originals are cold painted. Any jar with the trim applied under the glaze is new.

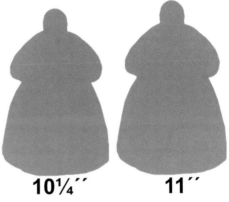

10¼˝   **11˝**

The original McCoy jar is 11". Reproductions, which can vary slightly, have never yet been found over 10-1/4" tall.

New fantasy Little Red Riding Hood head vase marked "McCoy." Vintage collectible Little Red Riding Hood was sold by Hull Pottery, not McCoy. No piece like this was ever part of the original Hull product line.

This is the fake "McCoy" mark on the fantasy Little Red Riding Hood head vase.

A new frog sprinkler marked "McCoy." The frog is a direct copy of a vintage original, but the original frog was made as a planter only, never as a sprinkler. Any piece like this with a handle is a fake.

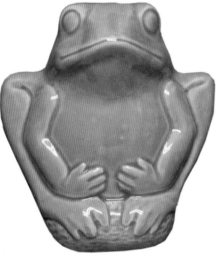

A new 6-1/2" frog wall pocket marked "McCoy USA." This is a fantasy piece; there is no old McCoy counterpart.

This is the fake mark on the new frog wall pocket shown above.

A fantasy 4-1/2" elephant bank with "GOP" on the side, marked "McCoy." There is no original vintage McCoy counterpart to this figure.

Red Wing Pottery

A new line of stoneware—from crocks to bean pots, pantry jars to planters—is being made by a firm using the name Red Wing Stoneware Company. This new company is located in Red Wing, Minnesota, and uses markings similar to earlier potteries from the same town whose products are widely collected. Unless you are familiar with the specific marks, it would be fairly easy to mistake the name and marks on new production for older collectible pieces.

Stoneware pottery has been manufactured in Goodhue County, Minnesota, since about 1861. At first, it was only terra cotta ware made with red clay. But by 1870, true stoneware was being made with a gray white clay with salt glazes. The first of the large potteries in the area was organized in 1876 and named Red Wing Stoneware Company. This was followed in 1883 by the creation of Minnesota Stoneware Company. The third large pottery was started in 1892 under the name North Star Stoneware Company. In 1894, Red Wing Stoneware and Minnesota Stoneware combined their marketing efforts by forming the Union Stoneware Company. The name was changed again in 1906 to Red Wing Union Stoneware Co. at which time the red wing trademark was adopted. The company continued with this name until 1936 when the name was changed for the last time to Red Wing Potteries (plural). It was under this name that the company started in the 19th century was forced to close in 1967. From the late 1940s, the main product was ceramic dinnerware. Production of stoneware was virtually over by the late 1930s and early 1940s.

The Red Wing Stoneware Company (RWSC) operating today is not a descendant of the original pottery of the same name. The current RWSC was gradually built up during the mid-1980s. According to company advertising, RWSC uses the same processes as earlier Red Wing potteries. New products may be slip cast, wheel thrown or ram molded. Clay for the stoneware comes from Roseville, Ohio.

RWSC currently produces many shapes similar to those collectors associate with late 19th and early 20th century production. These include bean pots, pantry jars, preserve jars, covered bowls, pitchers and crocks. Decorations include spongeware and molded designs like cherry bands.

Although markings on new RWSC items are similar to marks on older pottery, it is easy to separate modern stock from vintage pieces. The original pre-1900 Red Wing Stoneware Company never used a blue ink oval mark and never used a wing as a trademark. The original wing trademark was not used until ca. 1906 by which time the original RWSC pottery was known as Red Wing Union Stoneware Co. Original blue ink ovals and the authentic red wing trademark first appeared together ca. 1906-1930s. The ovals from this period read "Red Wing Union Stoneware Co., Red Wing, Minn." Ovals on new RWSC items with new wing trademark read "Red Wing Stoneware Co., Red Wing, Minn." All new products also have a circular ink stamp on the base with the full company name and wing trademark. No ink stamp on any original pre-1930 Red Wing pottery includes a wing.

New two-gallon crock made today by Red Wing Stoneware Company of Red Wing, Minnesota.

NEW

OLD

Two-gallon crock by Red Wing Union Stoneware Company Pottery of Red Wing, Minnesota, made ca. 1906-1930.

NEW

New oval mark, blue lettering. No original pre-1900 Red Wing Stoneware Company mark was stamped in blue ink in an oval.

Blue oval mark of Red Wing Union Stone ware Company. This is the original mark that appeared with the red wing, ca.1906-1930s.

OLD

NEW

Dark blue ink stamp on bottom of each new Red Wing Stoneware Company product. No wing appears in any ink stamps of original pre-1967 Red Wing potteries.

The only original ink stamp used 1906-1930s with the full company name spelled out. This is usually medium to dark blue ink and only appears on some pieces.

OLD

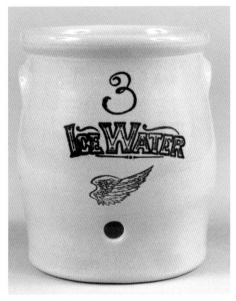

New half-gallon covered storage jar. Company name is in blue; wing trademark is in traditional red. About 6" x 6".

A miniature 4-1/2" version of a classic three-gallon water cooler. Don't mistake it for a "salesman's sample."

Original Red Wing Potteries

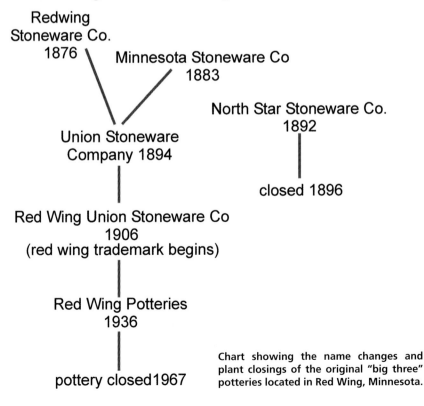

Redwing
Stoneware Co.
1876

Minnesota Stoneware Co
1883

North Star Stoneware Co.
1892

Union Stoneware
Company 1894

closed 1896

Red Wing Union Stoneware Co
1906
(red wing trademark begins)

Red Wing Potteries
1936

pottery closed 1967

Chart showing the name changes and plant closings of the original "big three" potteries located in Red Wing, Minnesota.

The most likely new pieces to be offered as old in the secondary market are the unusual shapes such as covered jars, pitchers and pots, some of which have sponged and molded decorations.

Rookwood Pottery

There are two types of new Rookwood circulating in today's market. The first group consists of unauthorized fakes and copies having no connection to the original company. These pieces are usually individually made to intentionally deceive or are made in limited numbers in imitation of original patterns and shapes. The other pieces are legitimate contemporary products from the "new" Rookwood Pottery, which owns the trademarks and molds from the original Rookwood.

The original Rookwood Pottery was founded in Cincinnati, Ohio, in 1880. For 50 years, its products were considered some of the world's finest art pottery ever made. Then the Great Depression and shortages of material in World War II led to the company's failing. During the 1950s, the company passed through various owners and was moved to Starkville, Mississippi. The business completely shut down in 1967 under the ownership of Herschede Hall Clock Co.

The molds and equipment were unused through 1982. At that time, a group of investors began preparing to move what remained of the company to Korea, where production would be resumed. The move would have included the molds, company records, medals Rookwood was awarded, and all other physical assets.

Word of the move reached Arthur Townley, a Michigan dentist. Townley went to Starkville and made a deal to buy Rookwood and prevent it from going overseas. The remains of the original company were in 31 crates stored on a cotton plantation. Their contents included: approximately 2,000 molds, 13 medals won by Rookwood, original shape books with freehand drawings, about 1,200 master blocks (from which were taken master molds), and around 5,000 glaze and clay formulas.

Perhaps most valuable of all are the Rookwood name and associated trademarks. Along with the physical assets, Townley's purchase also included the rights to the reverse R and P mark, the name "Rookwood," and the RP mark with flames.

Townley and his wife Rita began making pieces from original molds in the mid-1980s. The Townley's new Rookwood had the same RP flame mark as the original but there are several major differences. First, all the new pieces are dated in *Arabic* numbers, not Roman numerals. The dates are *ground into the glaze* with a diamond drill, not cast into the ceramic material.

New Rookwood Pottery bodies are all stark white *porcelain,* not the softer Ohio clay used in the original pottery. The glazes are also different in color and finish from glazes used on originals. All new pieces are glazed only; no hand

Bases on new Rookwood Pottery include the impressed RP and flames mark. On new pieces, though, the year of production (1989) is *engraved* in *Arabic* numerals, not impressed with Roman numerals.

Typical vintage impressed mark with the year of production impressed, not engraved, in Roman numerals, LVI.

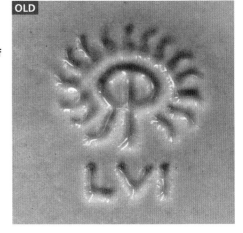

New Rookwood Pottery honey bear paperweight, 4-1/4" high. The year of production is engraved in the mark.

New Rookwood paperweight; 4-1/2" iridescent glaze. Year of production is engraved in mark.

New Rookwood Pottery fish vases, about 3". Year of production engraved in marks.

Two new Rookwood Pottery tiles. Year of production is engraved in the marks.

decorating is applied. Townleys limited production to 500 pieces of each mold number. Total production ran about 1,000 pieces per year.

In July 2006, the Townleys sold the company to a group of investors in Cincinnati, Ohio, which will be bringing the company back to Cincinnati. The new owners plan to expand and further develop production beginning with architectural pieces.

Rookwood fakes and forgeries

The new 5-3/4-inch tile in the photo of the rabbit tile on P. 291 is typical of many new pieces copied directly from Rookwood originals. Without copyright protection, a vintage Rookwood design is simply appropriated and put into production. Most of these products, like the tile, are sold in pottery gift shops and have relatively limited distribution and go largely unnoticed. They inevitably drift into the antiques and collectibles market where they can cause problems.

The majority of the pieces sold as new rarely have permanent marks. The only mark on the rabbit tile, for example, is "North Prairie Tileworks" rubber-stamped in black ink. Marks like these are not permanent and could be removed with acetone, fine sandpaper or other means. If the tile were mounted in a frame or if the tile were backed with cork or felt, the new mark also might go unobserved.

Riley Humler, gallery director of Cincinnati Art Galleries, a leading auction firm of American art pottery and Rookwood specialist, said the original Rookwood rabbit tile is scarce and rarely seen.

"The last one we sold was in 1996," Humler said. "It was a trivet form, in a single matte-color made in 1918 and brought $375. A multicolor original would easily be worth $400 to $600 or more."

Humler said the vast majority of original Rookwood tiles have permanent impressed marks. The exact mark found on tiles depends on when the tile was made. Before the tile division was combined with the overall operation, tiles were marked "Rookwood Faience," plus the date and various shape and production codes. Later production would be marked with the reversed R and P with flames mark, along with the date and various production codes.

Individually made fakes intentionally made to deceive are hard to categorize due to their one-of-a-kind nature. As a general rule, the RP mark with flames must always be accompanied by a model number. Another good indication of an authentic mark is to look for the small "hooks" that appear on the ends of authentic flames surrounding the RP. Most faked marks don't include this small detail. Original Roman numeral year dates are about one-third the size of the RP and flames. Roman numerals on the fakes are frequently much larger or much smaller than original year dates.

The rubber stamped mark on back of new rabbit tile is not permanent and easily removed.

Reproduction 5-3/4" Rookwood tile with high gloss glaze. This sample was purchased through a gift catalog for $50.

Forged impressed RP mark with flames. No hooks on tips of flames; no model number appears with the basic mark.

NEW

Typical authentic impressed RP mark with flames. Note the hooks on the flame tips and the impressed model number, "1222."

OLD

Roseville

The original Roseville Pottery Co. was founded in 1892 in Roseville, Ohio. In 1898, the pottery relocated to Zanesville, Ohio, where all the art pottery was made. The business closed in 1954. Commercial reproductions of Roseville Pottery began appearing in the late 1990s. Most reproductions are made in China but some patterns are also made in America. Many reproductions have virtually the same shapes, patterns, colors, and molded marks as original Roseville.

New Chinese Roseville copies originals from two style periods. The vast majority of reproductions are copied from Late Period patterns, those originally made 1935 to 1954. The balance of reproductions copy original Middle Period patterns made from about 1910 to 1934. Reproductions sell for $5 to $25 each, depending on size.

Late Period reproductions fall into two groups: Group A is marked exactly the same as originals; Group B is marked nearly the same as originals. All original Late Period pieces were marked on the base in raised letters, "Roseville U.S.A.," followed by a shape code and size number. The only exceptions are a very few creamers, sugars, flower frogs, candle holders, and other small pieces where part of the mark is omitted for lack of space.

Group A reproductions are marked exactly like originals with the raised "Roseville, U.S.A." and shape and size numbers. To detect these fakes, you need to reach down inside the suspected piece with your fingers. The group A reproductions are glazed on the inside only around the top few inches of the piece (see photos on the next page). The remaining inside surface is unglazed in a biscuit finish. All original Roseville is glazed completely on the inside because it was sold as practical functional flower holders that held water.

Reproduction importers countered within a few months by introducing group B with the insides of pieces completely glazed. Although the glaze clue was lost, another change in group B pieces proved an important help to collectors. According to the McKinley Tariff Act of 1890, all objects sold in the United States must be marked with the country of origin. Group A reproductions met this requirement with a removable "Made in China" paper label. However, U.S. Customs ruled that "U.S.A." in the mark implied the reproductions were made in the United States. Chinese manufacturers were ordered to remove it, and marks on group B reproductions no longer include the raised "U.S.A."

All letters of original Late Period raised marks—"Roseville, U.S.A.," shape code, and size number—are an equal height above the surface. Some Group B marks are still found with a very faint or very unevenly formed "U.S.A." If you find "U.S.A." in weak, shallow letters but with Roseville and shape numbers sharp and clear, it is from a new mold where the "U.S.A." has not been completely removed. The absence of the "U.S.A." is now an important clue to the detection of the group B reproductions.

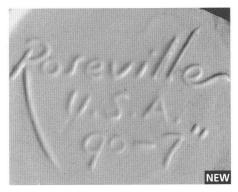

The mark on the first Group A Roseville reproductions. The new mark includes raised "Roseville, USA" with shape code "90" and size number "7"." The new mark is identical to the original mark.

The original raised molded mark on an authentic 7" Magnolia vase, "Roseville U.S.A. 90-7."

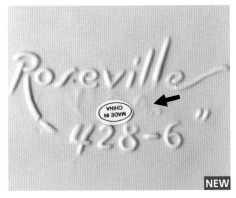

The new Group B mark with raised "USA" very faint (see arrow). The USA is either very faint or completely removed from Group B reproductions. If the "U.S.A." isn't in the mark, it's almost certainly a reproduction.

Another typical Group B mark with barely visible "USA" in mark. Except for a handful of very small original shapes, "USA" is the same height as all other molded raised lettering in authentic Late Period Roseville marks.

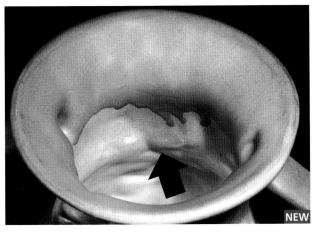

Group A reproductions which include "U.S.A" in the marks are not fully glazed on the inside. The glaze stops a couple of inches below the top rim (see arrow). Interiors of all original Roseville is fully glazed to protect the pottery from water and other liquids. Interiors of Group B reproductions are also glazed but marks on those pieces are missing "U.S.A."

Chinese reproductions of the Middle Period can also be identified by looking at the mark. Original Middle Period patterns—Luffa and Jonquil for example—are never found with a raised molded script mark. The vast majority of Luffa, Jonquil and other Middle Period pieces were marked with paper labels only, not raised molded marks. When an authentic Middle Period piece is found with a permanent mark, it is the single word "Roseville" only, *impressed* into the clay, not raised. Almost all Chinese reproductions of Luffa and Jonquil, are permanently marked with the "Roseville" in raised cursive letters.

Roseville copies have also been made on a more limited scale in the United States. American reproductions include a Rosecraft (Nude) Panel wall vase, La Rose vase, and various early pitchers in Tulip, Wild Rose, and Landscape. Many of the American-made fakes have "Rv" marks stamped in ink. Fake stamped ink marks of "Roseville Rozane" have also been found in blue ink under new glaze. Roseville reproductions are not limited to pottery. A reverse painted glass "dealers sign" with "Roseville Pottery Sold Here" has been in the market for about 10 years. It is about 16 inches by 8 inches with gold lettering on a black background. All of these signs are fantasy items; no vintage counterparts exist.

Most new Roseville has poor detail and bad paint but some pieces are the equal of originals. Quality is not always apparent, though, especially when viewing an online image. Study original marks and learn how they were applied and on what patterns they should appear. If bidding online or buying over the phone, be sure to ask very specific questions about how the piece is marked and glazed. Insist that a written receipt include the approximate year of production. "Roseville vase" on a receipt is not a statement of age or authenticity.

This new fantasy raised script mark appears on reproductions of Middle Period patterns such as Luffa and Jonquil. Original Luffa and Jonquil were marked with paper labels, not raised molded marks.

New Luffa pattern 7" vase marked with the raised molded mark in the photo above. No raised molded marks were ever used on authentic Luffa.

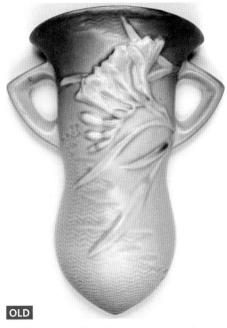

NEW **OLD**

Reproduction Freesia wall pocket marked Roseville, made in China.

Original Roseville wall pocket in Freesia pattern introduced in 1945.

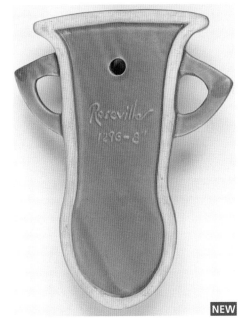

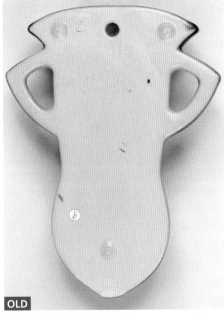

NEW **OLD**

The back side of the reproduction Freesia wall pocket. Note raised rim around edge, which is not on originals. Also note that the back side is painted; the original is not painted. Fake raised molded mark does not include "U.S.A."

The back side of the original Freesia wall pocket is left unpainted; no raised rim around edge. Note the three raised bumps. The original raised molded mark is hidden by thick glaze but clearly includes "U.S.A."

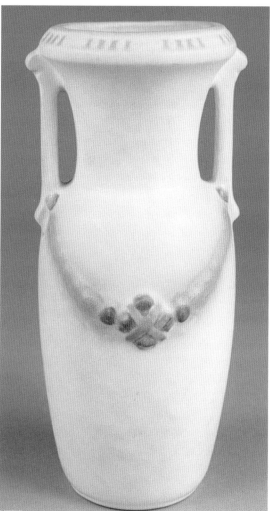

Reproduction La Rose pattern 9" handled vase with fake Rv blue ink mark. The shape is a copy of the original La Rose catalog #242.

The new ink stamp on the reproduction La Rose vase is pale blue like faded denim. Original Rv ink stamps are almost always dark navy blue or black and are thicker in width than the new stamp.

Royal Doulton

Fakes of Royal Doulton's Babes in the Woods ware with fake marks began appearing in early 2003. The most common shape is a plate sold already mounted in a frame. The new example shown on P. 298 was loaned by a buyer who purchased it at an auction.

The pattern collectors today refer to as "Babes in the Woods" originally appeared as the "Blue Children" line in Royal Doulton catalogs. Royal Doulton made 24 different Blue Children, or Babes in the Woods, scenes. All the scenes are done in blue and white and feature children, usually small girls, children with women, or a single woman, placed in naturalistic or "wooded" surroundings. The decorations appear on a variety of shapes including plates, oval and round plaques, a variety of vases, biscuit jars, jugs, pots and toilet sets.

All Royal Doulton Babes in Woods decorations were applied as printed transfers with hand-painted details and backgrounds. The series was made from 1890 to 1930. Pieces made before 1902 are sometimes, but not frequently, signed by the artist who painted the background. Earlier pieces generally have more handwork than later examples.

The most obvious problem with the fake plate shown on P. 298 is the mark. Virtually all original Royal Doulton Babes in the Woods pieces are marked with a transfer under the glaze. The only exceptions are wall plaques, which were generally unglazed on the back. The bisque surfaces of plaques were typically marked with an ink-stamped mark, not a transfer. The most common color of transfer mark found on authentic Royal Doulton Babes in the Woods is probably green but authentic transfer marks are found in a variety of colors. The typical Royal Doulton underglaze transfer mark is virtually without exception well defined and perfectly legible. You should see a crown on the lion's head and there are globes on the prongs of the crown on which the lion stands. The lettering of "ROYAL DOULTON" and "ENGLAND" should be well formed and uniform in height.

By contrast, the faked plates have crude, poorly formed, deliberately illegible marks. What passes for "England" in the new marks, for example, is completely smudged and distorted. Like other faked marks, this example is carefully crafted to suggest a famous mark without being an exact copy. If "England" was clearly legible, it would legally represent the country of origin. Assuming the new plates are made either in Asia or America, the use of "England" would be a violation of U.S. customs laws. This way, Customs rules can be met by listing the true country of origin on removable paper labels. The ceramic bodies of new and old are also very different. Original Royal Doulton Babes in the Woods decorations are on a hard dense earthenware body fired at high temperature. The new plates are made of a soft-bodied slip similar to the lightweight bodies used in hobby-grade ceramics classes.

Another unusual feature is how the fake plates are mounted in the frame. New plates are permanently attached to the frame with a wide bead of glue. Plates and plaques of any quality, new or old, are virtually never permanently attached to a display frame. The most practical, and logical, way to secure a plate or plaque is with a mechanical fastener to allow easy removal. Most buyers assume the frames were wood, but they are not. The frames on all the new plates found so far have been cast resin, or plastic, carefully molded with wood "grain" to resemble painted wood. Examine the frames carefully, and you'll see various pits, holes and casting flaws typical of molded plastic, not painted wood.

This new piece is being sold as Royal Doulton Babes in the Woods. It has a forged Royal Doulton mark on the back.

NEW

This vintage 8" plate in Royal Doulton's Blue Children line is commonly called Babes in the Woods by collectors. The original title of this scene is "Two girls talking to a tiny witch."

OLD

NEW

This is the faked mark on the new Babes in the Woods plate. The lion's body is badly distorted and the crown is poorly shaped. Also has meaningless symbols at the bottom rather than "England." This new mark is cobalt blue, the only color of the mark found so far on the new plates.

OLD

This is a typical authentic Royal Doulton mark found on an original Babes in the Woods plate. The lion is wearing a crown and standing on a crown. "England," the country of origin, is very distinct. This mark is green, which is the usual color for authentic Babes in Woods pieces, but colors of old marks may vary.

OLD

This is the original "Babes in the Woods" pattern as shown in a Royal Doulton pattern book. Most American collectors, though, commonly use "Babes in the Woods," to refer to Royal Doulton's "Blue Children" pattern, a line decorated with Victorian-era dressed girls and women.

NEW

NEW

Most new plates are permanently attached to new gold plate frames, left, with glue. Backs of new framed plates are covered in paper, right.

Shawnee Pottery

Shawnee Pottery corn ware, Corn King and Corn Queen, has been reproduced since the late 1990s. Two new pieces, the #73 casserole and #70 cream pitcher, here and on P. 302, are both marked the same as original pieces. Original Shawnee corn ware was introduced in 1941 and remained in production until Shawnee closed in 1961. The source of the new corn ware is unknown.

Husks, or leaves, on original Corn King/Queen are shades of green. Husks on the new pieces are a dark mottled brown-green. The corn kernels are about the same color on both old and new. But color is not a reliable way to separate old from new. Now that new molds have been made, the color can easily be changed. A better way is to look at how the color is applied.

Note that the insides of the creamer and both the casserole base and casserole lid are *white* or *uncolored*. In original Shawnee corn ware, the insides are *colored yellow*. Another key difference is that original pieces have unglazed standing rims. On new pieces, the glaze continues right over the rims on the pitcher and the casserole. Dimensions on old and new are virtually the same; they differ no more than measurements among original pieces.

Some pieces of new corn ware have what appears to be hand inscribed initials on the bottom of both pieces. The letters look like either "U K" or "V K" (see photo on P. 302). These hand-made marks are not found on original pieces.

Confusing new labels may pose another potential problem with Shawnee Pottery. The new labels are virtually identical at first glance to an original label. Look closely, though, and you'll see that the original label has an *arrowhead* in the upper left hand corner. The new label has a *tomahawk* on the left side. Otherwise the shape and lettering are virtually the same.

The new labels appear on new pottery made by Cecil Rapp of Ohio. Some of Rapp's new pottery is also marked with "Shawnee" in raised letters on the bottom. Rapp began selling the new pottery in the mid-1990s. Rapps has made miniature a variety of shapes including banks and cookie jars based on original Shawnee figural characters.

NEW   OLD

Reproduction #73 Shawnee corn ware casserole is on the left; the original is at right.

The bottom of the reproduction #73 corn ware casserole has the same raised mark as the original shown below.

The bottom of the original #73 casserole. Note the original standing rim (arrows) is *unglazed*; fake is glazed.

The interior of the new casserole base, left, is white. The interior of the original casserole base is yellow, right.

Interior of new casserole lid, left, is white. Interior of original casserole lid is yellow, right.

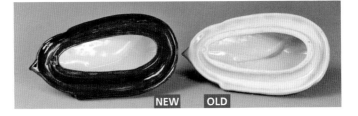

The new #70 creamer on the left is white inside (arrow). The original cream pitcher on the right is yellow inside.

NEW   OLD

NEW   OLD

The bottom rim of the new creamer is glazed over. The rim on the original creamer is unglazed (black arrow). Note the U K or V K initials at the white arrow.

NEW

The label on new pottery by Cecil Rapp, with the tomahawk on the left hand side.

OLD

Detail of the arrowhead on the old label.

NEW

Detail of the tomahawk on the new label.

OLD

The original Shawnee Pottery label has an arrowhead, not a tomahawk, in the upper left hand corner.

Shenandoah Pottery

Shenandoah Pottery is a type of folk pottery named after the Virginia valley in which it was developed in the 19th century. Authentic examples are among the most expensive pieces of American country pottery. Dog figures have brought over $13,000; lamp doorstops have brought $38,000 to $54,000. With demand pushing prices of originals so high, reproductions are becoming more widespread.

It is difficult to lay down specific tests to catch the fakes. Such high prices justify a forger's time to make carefully constructed one-of-kind works with great attention to details. Since different forgers use different techniques, clues to identifying Shenandoah fakes vary from piece to piece.

One of the most common mistakes forgers seem to make is with glazes and paints. The fake ewe and lamb piece in the photo below, for example, is glazed. All known originals are painted, not glazed. Similarly, the whippet figure in the photo on P. 304 is also glazed. All but two known originals are painted, not glazed. While glazing is wrong for these pieces, that is not a strict rule. Glaze does not always mean a fake. You need to consult auction catalogs and reference books to know which finish and technique is correct for any particular form.

Marks also need particular scrutiny. Sizes of many forged marks are different from authentic marks. Some forgers also apply the same mark to all their forgeries, regardless of form and decoration. It is very important to know the sizes of each original mark, how original marks were applied and what specific marks were used on which forms and shapes.

High prices of originals have encouraged very sophisticated fakes. You simply can't assume a piece is authentic. On every purchase, insist on a written guarantee that clearly states an estimated date of production, who will determine authenticity in the event of a dispute and how a return or refund would be handled.

A forged "John Bell" stamped mark on the ewe and lamb figure.

A fake ewe and lamb figure marked "John Bell." The original figure is painted; the fake shown here is glazed.

These are three pieces from among $23,000 worth of alleged Shenandoah pottery fakes Pennsylvania police say were sold as vintage originals.

This forgery is a copy of a vintage "S+S" mark that appears on vintage Shenandoah pottery.

Two alleged Shenandoah pottery fakes sold to Pennsylvania police in a 2004 sting operation.

Sleepy Eye Pottery

Old Sleepy Eye collectibles are primarily premiums, advertising items and promotional pieces from the Sleepy Eye Milling Company of Sleepy Eye, Minnesota. The town's name and the company's distinctive trademark were taken from a Sioux Indian Chief, Old Sleepy Eye. Founded in 1883, the company continued in operation till 1921.

Among the more popular Sleepy Eye collectibles is a series of blue and white pottery consisting of pitchers and accessories. This pottery was the second major ceramic line used by Sleepy Eye Milling as premiums. The first line was a blue and gray (Flemish) *stoneware* made from about 1899 to 1905 by the Weir Pottery Company of Monmouth, Illinois. The later blue and white *pottery* series was made from about 1906 up till 1937 by the Western Stoneware Company of Monmouth, Illinois.

Original pitchers were made in five sizes. Here are the original sizes by volume followed with the height of the pitcher measured from the lip to the base: a 1/2 pint–4 inches; pint–5-1/4 inches; quart–6-1/2 inches; two quart–8 inches; and gallon–9 inches. It is common for the old pitchers to vary slightly in size so not all old pitchers will be exactly the heights listed. Some new pitchers are close in size to the originals but others are not so size is not a reliable test of age.

The best test of authenticity is to look at details in the molded designs. Original pitchers, for example, were made as two separate pieces. First, the body of the pitcher was molded. Then a solid handle, which was molded separately, was applied to the body. This two-step operation left the inside of original pitchers smooth. In contrast, the body and handle of reproduction pitchers are molded in one piece to speed up production. The one-piece mold used in reproductions produces a hollow handle. This leaves a "dimple" or hole on the inside of the pitcher where the hollow handle meets the body. Another characteristic of the new pitchers is a raised ridge running around the lip. Old pitchers have smooth lips. New pitchers are also much lighter in weight than the originals.

On all the new pitchers, the decoration is the same on the front. The chief's head is in the center with a tree to the left of the bust and two teepees to the right of the head, between the head and handle. No original pitchers have two teepees between the chief's head and the handle. Original pitchers had either one teepee or one tree between the head and handle. A simpler easy-to-remember test for pitchers is to look at the teepees on the back side. A tree branch partially covers one or more teepees in new pitchers. Tops of teepees on original pitchers are not hidden by tree branches; there are distinct gaps between the tops of tepees on original pitchers.

Other new blue and white pottery shapes include a toothpick holder, salt and pepper shakers and a sugar bowl. There never were any old salt and peppers or toothpick holders in original Old Sleepy Eye pottery. Those three shapes are all fantasy items and exist only as modern reproductions. There is, however, an old sugar bowl. New and old sugar bowls can be separated by shape. The reproduction sugar bowl is curved at the base; the shape of the original sugar bowl is nearly straight-sided.

Various other pottery fakes appear from time to time. Beginning sometime in the 1980s, new reddish-brown clay paperweights were made. The tops are molded with the profile of Chief Sleepy Eye. Teepee designs are impressed around the sides. The reverse of the weight is marked "WSWCO" (Western Stoneware Co) Monmouth ILL." Similar fake paperweights are also known in blue and gray. All the paperweights are crudely made. Testing has proved the pieces are made of cast resin rather than true pottery or earthenware.

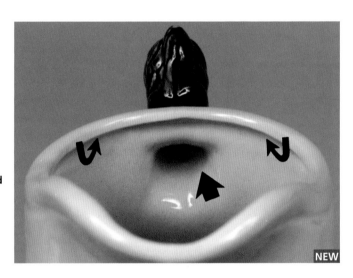

New pitchers have "dimples" or holes where the handle meets the body. Old pitchers are smooth sided where the handle joins the body. Note rolled edge at curved arrows.

All new pitchers have two teepees between the Chief's head and handle as shown by the arrows in the new pitcher above, left. Old pitchers have only one teepee or one tree between the Chief's head and the handle. This old 1/2-pint pitcher on right has one tree.

All new pitchers have three teepees on the back, at left. The top of the third new teepee is partially covered by the tree branch, (arrow). Old pitchers, at right, have either two or three teepees. There are distinct gaps between the tops of the teepees on original pitchers.

The reproduction sugar bowl, left, has bulging curved sides. The original sugar bowl, right, has straight sides.

The box from an antique reproduction importer with the Sleepy Eye name. Prices from this source for new pitchers range from $10.50 for a 9", to $7 for a 6-1/4" size.

This new ceramic "toothpick holder" is a fantasy item. No toothpick holder shape was ever made in vintage Sleepy Eye pottery.

Van Briggle

Van Briggle Pottery was founded by Artus Van Briggle in 1901 in Colorado Springs, Colorado. Before moving to Colorado for health reasons in 1899, Van Briggle was a major decorator for Rookwood Pottery in Ohio.

After Artus died in 1904, the business was taken over by his wife Anna and was renamed the Van Briggle Co. The business was reorganized again in 1910 as Van Briggle Pottery and Tile Co. Anna's involvement ended about 1912. Various managers and owners ran the business through the 1920s. In 1931, the name was changed back to Van Briggle Art Pottery, which remains in production today. Current products, although made in original shapes, are generally made in different colors and don't present a major problem to collectors.

Unauthorized fakes and reproductions, however, of original pre-1931 Van Briggle Pottery have been an increasing problem since the late 1990s. These new pieces are intentionally made to deceive and include what appear to be original company and finisher's marks. These false marks appear on three types of wares: reproductions of original Van Briggle shapes; new fantasy shapes never made by Van Briggle; and, some genuinely old pottery by other manufacturers to which forgers have added a Van Briggle mark.

Despite operating under various business names over the years, words and symbols on genuine Van Briggle Pottery have been fairly consistent. Authentic marks can be divided into two broad categories: those from 1901 to 1920; and those after 1920. The vast majority of authentic marks from both periods include a monogram consisting of two letter As and "Van Briggle." Pre-1920 marks usually included a date and often had a design or glaze number. After 1920, pieces were rarely dated and Colorado Springs was added, usually abbreviated as "Colo Spgs." There is considerable variation among authentic marks because marks were inscribed by hand, rather than molded or stamped. Marks used on Van Briggle made today are very similar to marks on vintage pieces from the 1920s.

Since original hand-inscribed marks vary so much, it is somewhat difficult to detect the fakes by marks alone. Most fakes with forged marks so far have been shapes never originally made by Van Briggle. Unfortunately, unless you are very familiar with the large number of original shapes, you'll probably have trouble recognizing fantasy shapes.

At this time, there is no single test or clue to catch the fakes. Other than finding two finisher monograms on the same piece, forged marks are virtually identical to original marks. Here are some suggestions to help you catch most of the fakes:

• Almost all original Van Briggle Pottery had a highlight or accent color applied over the main body color, i.e. dark blue over light blue, dark blue over

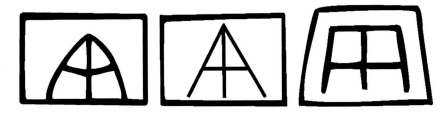

The AA monogram, which stands for Artus and Anna, appears on virtually all Van Briggle pottery. It is hand-inscribed and can appear in a number of different styles; no one style is right or wrong. Several typical original versions are shown here. This mark also appears in forged marks.

A fake 6" bowl with American Indian designs. Fantasy piece, no original was ever made. Reddish brown glaze, no highlight color. Mark on fake is shown in the photo below. *Fake courtesy of William Schultze.*

A typical fake Van Briggle mark. This is hand inscribed in wet clay on fakes like the one shown in the photo above.

maroon, etc. So far, all of the fakes with forged marks have been solid, single colors with no highlight colors.

• Experienced Van Briggle buyers say that colors of fakes do not match colors of original glazes. However, colors are subjective and may change. What may be obvious to an experienced eye may not be noticed by a general or beginning buyer.

• The most common original shape reproduced seems to be the 8-inch Columbine vase. The reproduction has good detail and a convincing bottom mark. All the fake Columbine pieces reported have a forged finisher's mark of the letter "K" joined with the letter "V." There is no record of any vintage KV mark.

• Beware of any unusually rough or crude bottom marks. Be especially suspicious of flat-sided "trench-like" lines in marks. Such marks may have been engraved with rotary tools after the clay has been fired. Also be wary of any marks with the clay raised along the lines of the mark.

A fake 9" vase. Brownish red glaze, no highlight color. The mark is shown in the photo right. *Fake courtesy of William Schultze.*

The fake mark on the fake vase at left, showing finisher number "28" and finisher initials "AO." Two different finisher marks never appear in original marks.

Chief Sitting Bull 10" one-piece bust, not a jar. Issued in 1984 by Van Briggle Pottery.

A fake 6" jar, no highlight color; marked with "AA" monogram and "Colo Spgs." No authentic piece like this was ever made by Van Briggle. It is somewhat similar to a limited edition series of busts of famous American Indians Van Briggle Pottery issued in the 1980s (see the photo of Chief Sitting Bull above). Those pieces were 8" to 10" tall; no jars were made. *Fake courtesy of William Schultze.*

Some Van Briggle pieces, like this Butterfly bowl made in 2000, have been in continuous production since the business was founded. It is virtually identical to the same piece shown in the 1907 factory catalog in the photo below.

Van Briggle

661

Rabbit L____ with shade

385

690

684

Lamp G

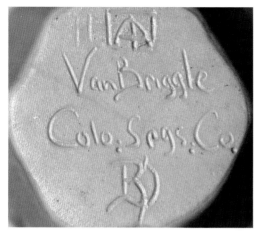

Typical hand incised mark found on current production like the Butterfly bowl shown.

A modern special production piece with a rubber stamped "VB 100." No vintage mark was ink stamped.

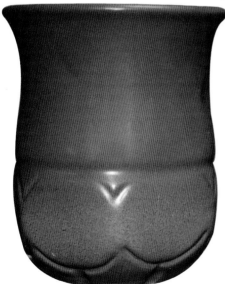

Pieces like this made after regular working hours in recent years have been marked "Original" (illustration at right).

This mark appears on the Original vase shown. No vintage Van Briggle pieces with this mark were ever made.

Wedgwood Fairyland Lustre imitations

Several new pieces have been found which loosely imitate the iridescent glazed fantasy designs introduced by Wedgwood 1915 as Fairyland Lustre. The characteristic fairyland themes painted in bright colors outlined in gold was developed by Wedgwood artist Daisy Makeig-Jones. Original vintage Wedgwood Fairyland Lustre was produced from 1915 through 1932.

The new ware features a variety of fairy-related scenes similar to the new jar shown below. A pearl-like iridescent glaze similar to original Fairyland Lustre covers the new pieces. New ware is a fairly heavy thick pottery. With the exception of some earthenware plaques and juvenile breakfast pieces, virtually all original Wedgwood Fairyland Lustre was painted on bone china blanks. Almost all bone china pieces are marked with the Wedgwood's Portland vase mark stamped over the glaze in gold. Some authentic earthenware pieces may have impressed marks, but the bone china was stamped in gold.

Although the new ware is made in China, it has fantasy marks suggesting it was made in England. The new jar shown here, for example, is marked "Braithwaites Fairy Lustre Ware Cumbria." Original Wedgwood Fairyland Lustre is hand painted. Decorations on the new jar are applied as transfers, or decals. No biscuit jar shape appears in Wedgwood's list of the 72 shapes most frequently decorated with authentic pre-1932 Fairyland Lustre.

Wedgwood's Fairyland Lustre was also widely imitated by other makers in the 1930s. Be particularly alert for rubber stamped fake gold Wedgwood marks applied with to the lustre wares by other 1930 makers.

A new 6" square biscuit jar with iridescent lustre glaze. The fairy decoration is applied as a transfer, not hand painted.

A close-up of original hand-painted detail in original Wedgwood Fairyland Lustre. The entire design is outlined in gold.

The new biscuit jar in the photo on P. 314 is made in China but the blue mark under glaze on its base implies it was made in England. The mark is "Braithwaites, Fairy Lustre Ware, Cumbria." Mark appears blurred due to glaze.

WEDGWOOD

MADE IN
ENGLAND

Almost all original bone china Wedgwood Fairyland Luster has the Portland vase outline mark in gold shown here.

Silver

Articles marked "sterling" in America must contain a minimum of 925 parts silver for every 1000 parts of material. This ratio is called the "sterling standard" which was adopted in the USA in the mid-1860s. The vast majority of 925 sterling silver made in America, from the 1860s through the 1970s—especially items made before 1940—is marked "sterling" or "sterling silver." These vintage American marks are almost always accompanied by a company name, patent date or number, shape or model number or other marks and symbols. Very rarely are pieces of American sterling silver from those years marked "925" only. Rarer still are pre-1940 American marks which include "sterling 925" only without additional marks and symbols.

In the 1970s, the same standard, 925/1000, was also adopted by the European Community (now called the European Union). Unlike America, though, the EU adopted the numeric "925" as the official standard mark, not "sterling," which is understood in only English-speaking countries. In 1999, England also

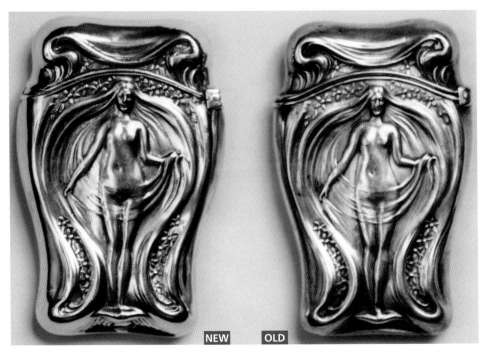

NEW   OLD

Without careful examination, both of these Art Nouveau-styled match safes appear to be old. One is an original made by R. Wallace and Sons, ca. 1880-1910; the other is a fake. See P. 318 for the details that separate old from new.

began to accept "925" as a standard mark with only slight variations from the EU mark. England accepts 925 as a standard mark only if it accompanied by separate stand-alone "control" mark. The control mark is always a balance-type scale accompanied by "925" which is always in the middle of the scale. The control mark signifies a piece was made in a country which signed a treaty certifying that the silver content has been tested. In addition to the control and standard marks, silver made for sale in England may or may not also include a maker's mark.

For all practical purposes, 925/1000 is now a globally accepted silver standard and "925" appears on most of the world's new silver including reproductions. Although a mark of "sterling" alone doesn't guarantee a piece is old, it is generally true that virtually all silver marked "925" only or "sterling" and "925" has been made since the mid-1970s. All marks with "925" within the image of a scale are also new, probably no older than 1999.

NEW

In the authentic mark on the vintage match safe, bottom, "sterling" is flanked by a company trademark (Wallace & Sons) and catalog model number "379." The reproduction, top, is marked "sterling" only. "Sterling" rarely appears on vintage American silver alone.

OLD

This is a 925 standard mark on a typical sterling reproduction made since the mid-1970s. The PAJ is an unidentified maker's or importer's mark.

Since the mid-1970s, the 925 standard mark may appear alone or with "sterling."

The 925 standard mark on new silver may appear with sterling and various other symbols such as the "G" in diamond marks on this new example. Virtually no silver before 1976 was marked with "925" and "sterling."

The most common convention hallmark is the balance scale control mark with 925 standard mark. This mark is required on sterling silver imported into England. It may also appear on silver exported from England to other countries.

This English convention hallmark includes an optional registered maker's mark, the letter "J." Optional maker's marks may be any type of symbol and can be placed to the right or left of the control and standard marks.

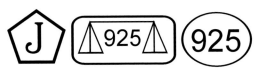

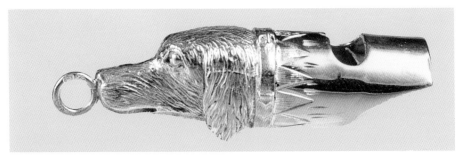

Reproduction sterling silver 2" figural dog whistle. Marked with the scale-925 convention mark and 925 standard mark indicating a modern piece made in England.

The use of "925" in a mark, however, does not preclude the use of other potentially confusing symbols. Marks on some silver antique reproductions deliberately include symbols easily confused for vintage hallmarks. As a general rule, it is usually safe to assume all marks including "925" are modern regardless of how many additional letters or symbols may be included. Ask the seller to prove any exceptions.

Deliberately forged marks

The best way to catch most deliberate forgeries is to become familiar with how marks were applied to vintage silver. Most intentional forgeries can be detected by learning how original marks were applied. Marks on almost all

This reproduction silverplated napkin ring has a forged Meriden mark including the original model number.

The forged Meriden mark is molded, not stamped. It lacks detail and is slightly blurred.

Meriden's original silverplated boy feeding dog napkin ring.

The original Meriden mark is die stamped, not molded. It is sharper and has more detail than the molded forgery.

New sterling silver match safe, marked with G in diamond hallmark, 925 and sterling.

New sterling silver match safe with G in diamond mark purporting to be associated with the Benevolent and Protective Order of Elks (BPOE).

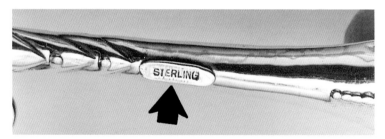

If a mark appears on a separate piece of metal, it should generally be considered a sign of a potential forgery or reproduction (see exceptions described in the text).

antique and collectible silver and silverplate were applied with punches or stamps, either hand-struck or machine pressed. Many of the most common forgeries in the market today are molded, not applied by stamping. In other words, the mark is created when the entire figure is cast, not applied after the piece is made. Molded marks almost always lack the detail found in stamped marks. Cast marks tend to be shallow with ragged or blurred edges and are uneven in depth of impression. Original stamped marks are just the opposite: clean sharp edges with an almost perfectly uniform depth of impression.

All marks on a separately applied piece of metal, such as a tab, disc or other shape, should also be considered as warning signs of a potential forgery. Many reproductions have these odd bits soldered to the main body in odd and illogical locations. The new silver baby rattle on P. 321, for example, has such a piece. A small oval tab marked "sterling" is soldered in the middle of the handle. Although a handful of authentic Victorian-era silverplated pieces are marked with applied pieces of metal, any piece with applied marks should be examined very carefully. Many genuinely old applied marks have been removed from inexpensive pieces and applied to originally unmarked more expensive pieces.

Considering construction

Many silver reproductions and fakes can be detected by examining how the pieces are constructed. About half of the sterling silver reproductions in the market today are made by casting. That is to say the pieces are made as one entire piece in a mold. The great majority of sterling silver and silverplate made before the 1950s was made from multiple pieces soldered together to form the finished product. The body and handle of the new sterling tussy mussie in the photo on the next page, for example, is one single piece of silver. Similar vintage originals would typically be formed from a number of smaller pieces, such as handle, body and top rim, and joined together with solder. The reproduction silverplate toothpick holder also on the next page is also one solid piece. A similar vintage piece would be made of at least three pieces: the base, the figure and the holder, which would be soldered together before silverplating. Although not a guarantee of age, multiple pieces joined by perfectly made and finely finished solder joints are generally a positive sign of age and correct vintage construction.

Other than the three-dimensional figures used in pieces like figural napkin rings, toothpick holders, compote stems and similar pieces, most mass-produced vintage sterling and silverplate was formed by die stamping. Die stamping, the technique used to mint coins, is a precision process requiring great human skill and costly machines. It is the die stamping process that gives vintage original flatware, match safes, sewing notions, pins, watch fobs, napkin rings and other pieces their great detail. Many silver and silverplated pieces, which were originally made by die stamping, are reproduced as single piece castings.

The back sides of most die stamped vintage sterling pieces will follow the contour of the design on the front side. Backs on most cast sterling fakes are smooth and flat. Most vintage die-stamped pieces used to assemble original sterling silver products are relatively thin and lightweight, rarely thicker than the cardboard used in cereal boxes at most. Modern castings tend to be quite thick, often 1/8 inch or more in thickness and two to three times the weight

A new sterling tussie mussie. The body and handle are cast as one single piece of silver. Originals are assembled from several separate pieces soldered together.

A one-piece cast silverplated toothpick holder. Similar vintage pieces would have been assembled from several separate pieces, not cast as one single piece.

of the die-stamped originals. Cast reproductions frequently have crude obvious molds seams often with coarse grinding marks. Seams on die-stamped originals were carefully fitted together by skilled artisans with virtually never any tool marks.

The previous discussion of die stamping and casting should be used as a general guideline only. Some sterling reproductions are being made with original dies used for vintage pieces. Be sure to use several tests for age including marks as well as construction techniques.

Confusing new marks

Occasionally, the legitimate marks of contemporary silversmiths are mistaken for old. Silversmith James Mackie, for example, clearly marks his very accurate copies of Victorian figural napkin rings. Many collectors don't bother searching for the hallmark in a reference book and simply assume the mark is from a vintage manufacturer. Marks of vintage silver manufacturers are well documented. If a particular mark can't be found in a reference book, you should at least consider the possibility that it could be new. The hallmark of contemporary English silversmith David Bowles is frequently assumed to be Victorian even though it usually appears with an obvious date letter. Be sure to carefully look at all the features of a mark before forming a conclusion about age and authenticity.

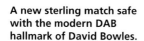

Hallmark on a new piece of sterling by English silversmith David Bowles. The DAB maker's mark is on all of Bowles' new pieces.

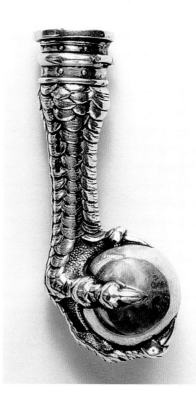

A new sterling match safe with the modern DAB hallmark of David Bowles.

A new napkin ring made by James Mackie, a Portland, Oregon silversmith. Mackie currently offers 20 new copies of vintage figural Victorian napkin rings.

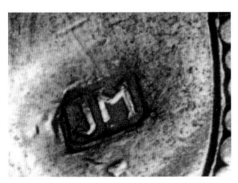

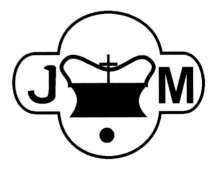

Mackie permanently marks his copies with one of two hallmarks. The letters "JM," above, or "JM" with a crown, right.

TOYS

Cast iron was the 19th century equivalent of today's plastics: the raw ingredients were cheap, it could be made in almost any shape, and identical pieces could be mass-produced in molds. It was the perfect material for inexpensive toys. Those are the same reasons cast iron is so widely reproduced today-it's extremely cheap to make, especially overseas.

There are so many cast iron reproductions, it is impossible to learn specific differences between all the new and old cast iron toys. It is better to learn and understand how to evaluate cast iron in general and then use those general rules during your routine inspection. Handmade individual forgeries, of course, cannot easily be categorized, but the following guidelines will help you avoid the majority of factory-made reproductions currently in the market.

Old cast iron, for example, almost always has a much smoother surface than new castings. New cast iron generally has small prickly bumps that rise above the surface and holes or pits that go below the surface. The rough texture is the most obvious on unpainted surfaces, so try to look on the inside or underside of toys.

Old castings almost always have sharper detail; new castings are generally less sharp, blurred, and lack fine details found in old pieces. Most new molds don't fit together very well and molten metal runs out through gaps where mold halves meet. This is called "finning," which is seldom found on old pieces but is common among reproductions.

Wheels are a particularly good place to inspect for casting quality. The many slender spokes in most wheels are difficult to cast correctly and are almost always subject to crude joints and finning. Original cast iron wheels rarely show finning and typically have smooth surfaces on the running rims. Obvious mold seams on running rims are a common warning sign of a reproduction.

Joints of original cast iron toys were often fitted together by hand filing or at least had the edges tumbled smooth. This extra attention produced very tight joints in original cast iron toys. Seams in new cast iron are typically very loose and carelessly made; gaps in seams are frequently one-eighth inch and more in width. What little finishing work is done on reproductions is usually performed with modern high-speed production tools. Any visible grinding marks are usually positive proof a piece is a reproduction.

The unpainted surface of new cast iron is virtually always rough and pitted, left photo. Look inside banks and under toys to find unpainted areas. Grinding marks, right, are common on new cast iron, but rarely seen on old.

New molds seldom fit properly. The metal that runs through the gaps is called a fin or finning. Finning is rarely found on originals, but is typical of most cast iron reproductions. Finning is a particular problem with new cast iron wheels, as seen here.

 **NEW** **OLD**

The running rims of wheels are a good place to check for casting quality. Note grind marks, misaligned mold seams, and roughness in new wheels, above.

Running rims of old wheels, above, have relatively smooth surfaces, no mold seams, and no flaws.

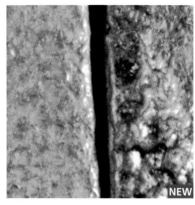

Reproduction cast iron almost always has wide, poorly fitting joints where pieces meet. The gap, at left, is nearly one-eighth inch. The gap, above, while not quite one-eighth inch, is still substantial and very noticeable.

Original cast iron was usually hand fit and has very tightly fitting joints. Many joints in original cast iron toys, like this example, are too tight to pass through a piece of paper.

Old iron usually was decorated with fairly heavy paint, most frequently some type of oil-based enamel. New pieces are typically decorated with a much thinner paint that is usually a water-based acrylic. Old and new paints were also applied differently. Many old pieces were dipped in paint, not painted with a brush (although details may have been added by a brush). Many new pieces are painted with spray guns to speed production. Dipping deposits paint on inside surfaces like hidden angles and along the edges where seams meet-spots usually missed by spraying. Toy banks, for example, should usually show paint on both inner and outer edges of the coin slot.

Normal wear in original heavy enamel paint is characterized by sharp-edged paint chips. New, thin paint on the reproductions seldom produces chips (even if you deliberately gouge it). If you look at the chips in the photo, you'll see a lighter inner ring (arrows). This is another sign of the older, thicker paints; most chips reveal one or more additional colors underneath the top layer of paint.

Old unpainted iron usually looks dark brown or even black; new cast iron is typically gray or a dirty silver color. Rust on old cast iron is dark brown or black. Rust on new iron is red or reddish brown. Be wary of any painted pieces with an overall uniform appearance. High temperature can turn the surface of a new piece into a uniform dull brown or darker color. Burying a new piece or soaking it in chemicals can also change the color.

Old paint should logically show natural wear. Natural paint wear is characterized by scratches of random width and direction, varied length, and irregular depth. Artificial wear, applied with sandpaper, files, etc., is characterized by parallel lines in a regular, repeated pattern all aligned in the same direction.

Many new paints used on reproduced cast iron, especially red, fluoresce under long-wave black light. Black light is also helpful to detect repaints and repairs. Check for hidden repairs by going over the entire piece with a magnet. Many repairs and replacement parts are made with epoxies, brass, and aluminum, which have no magnetic attraction.

Fasteners are also important clues to age. Many cast iron reproductions are joined with modern Phillips head screws and hex head bolts and nuts. Vintage cast iron was typically held together by peened or hammered steel rods. The only screws that should appear in vintage cast iron, if used at all, have flat slotted heads, not a Phillips head. The only exceptions would be if modern fasteners were used to make a repair to an old piece. In any case, the appearance of modern fasteners is a warning sign of either an outright reproduction or at the very least a repaired or altered original.

Some vintage toys originally made of cast iron have been reproduced in brass. These new brass pieces have occasionally been offered as mold "masters," the pieces used to made the sand molds in which most cast iron was produced. The so-called "masters" suffer the same problems as new cast iron. Poor casting detail, modern fasteners, misaligned mold seams and wide gaps in joints.

Artificial vs. Natural Wear

Scratches produced by natural wear are random in direction and vary in width and length. Artificial wear created with sandpaper, files, wire wheels, or other abrasives and power tools, generally leaves an evenly spaced pattern of parallel lines of almost identical width in the same direction.

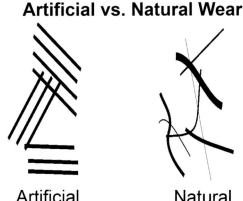

Artificial

Natural

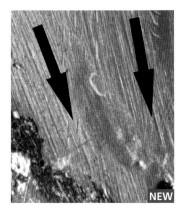

NEW

NEW

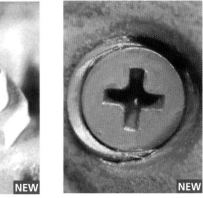

NEW

A typical example of artificial wear. Regularly spaced lines of wear oriented in the same direction.

Hex nuts and Phillips head screws are used to join about 99 percent of cast iron reproductions. These fasteners are almost a guarantee of a reproduction.

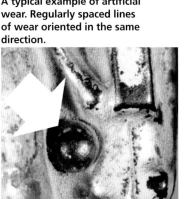

OLD

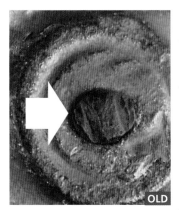

OLD

The majority of original pre-1930 cast iron was joined by peened or hammered steel rods. In vintage pieces which did use screws, only single flat slotted heads were used, not Phillips heads.

NEW

Reproduction cast iron goat pulling steel cart with cast iron wheels. This is copied from an early 20th century original by Hubley. Finning in wheels, wide gaps in joints and obvious grinding marks are all clue to its recent manufacture.

Disney Windups

New Disney character metal windup toys which copy vintage 1930s originals have been imported from China since about 2001. All the Mickey and Minnie figures in the new windups have the so-called "pie-eyes," eyes with wedge-shaped gaps in the black pupils. This is important because collectors generally associate pie-eyes with the very earliest Mickey and Minnie faces used on toys made ca. 1930-1935. In this case, eyes are NOT a reliable clue to age because they have been copied on the new figures.

One of the most obvious clues to these toys recent manufacture is the word "China" included in the mark. No 1930s Disney pie-eyed Mickey and Minnie windups were made in or were marked "China." The vast majority of authentic metal windup Disney toys from the 1930s were marked Japan, USA or Germany, but never China.

Another easy way to date the toys is to keep in mind the various changes in how the Disney name appears on licensed products. Licensed products up to 1939 generally include "Walt Disney Enterprises", often abbreviated as WDE or Walt Disney Ent. After 1939, the name in marks is generally "Walt Disney Productions" or the abbreviation WDP. The copyright symbol, ©, may or may not appear with any of these early marks. The mark on the new windups shown here is "© Disney" only, which is not a mark commonly found on genuine pre-1950 officially licensed Disney toys.

New metal windup Pluto pulling Mickey in cart, 6″ overall. Available August, 2001. Wholesale $30 each.

New Mickey Mouse metal windup, 5" tall with "pie-eyes." Retail price around $20.

New metal windup, Mickey and Minnie dancing figure.

© Disney
YOUNG EPOCH
MADE IN CHINA

Mark on new metal windups. Vintage 1930s Disney character toys were never made in China. Any Disney toy marked "Made in China" has almost certainly been made since the 1980s at the oldest.

New metal 5" windup Pluto; head wags from side to side as toy moves forward. Marked Made in China like the other toys from this group.

The new windup Disney toys come in vintage-style boxes. Choking warning label has appeared on toys only since the mid 1980s-early 1990s. These labels are an obvious clue to a modern product.

Hubley-Marked Racer

Copies of classic 1930s Hubley cast iron toys with fake Hubley marks are among the most confusing reproductions. When they first appeared several years ago, they fooled even experienced buyers. This includes the race car shown on the next page. Just like the scarce original, this reproduction features 12 exhaust flames which move up and down through the hood as the wheels turn. Originals bring $2,500 to $3,500. Hubley produced two sizes of the original racer, one 7-inch and the other 10-3/4 inch. The reproduction is of the larger 10-3/4-inch size.

Unlike most new cast iron, new Hubley racers are well made. The casting quality is generally very good, very close, if not equal, to original quality. Paint is thick and heavy, also very similar to original paint.

Marks on new and old are virtually identical. The "Hubley" mark is cast in raised letters on the bottom of the left rear frame on both new and old. Mold or part numbers are cast below the surface on the bottom of the car's steps on both new and old. As a practical matter, there is no difference between new and old lettering and marks in size, location, or sharpness.

The new paint is also very convincing at first glance. It is thick and heavy like the enamels used on originals. Because it is thick like the original paint, it produces the deep irregular chips that buyers normally look for to authenticate old cast iron. This test, which has been used for many years to separate new from old cast iron, does not apply to the new Hubley racers.

Unpainted surfaces of the great majority of cast iron reproductions are shiny silver or red with rust. In the new Hubley racers, unpainted metal-like axles and exposed metal under paint chips-appears a dark brown, almost black, color. These dark colors have traditionally been found only on originals, not reproductions. Like paint chips, the dark patinas and colors previously used as a test for old cast iron do not apply to this reproduction.

Separating new and old racers requires attention to some very small details. First, look at the front axle. The exhaust flames are raised and lowered by bends in the axle. Look closely and you'll see dents and flat spots in the new axle. New front axles have been hammered into shape. Old axles are smooth without dents. They were made in a power fixture by bending, not hammering.

Next, use a 10X loupe to examine areas of paint wear. Under the loupe, you'll see that every spot of bare metal resembling paint wear on the reproductions is surrounded by regularly spaced parallel scratches. Such marks indicate the wear is artificially created, most likely by sandpaper or a wire wheel. Normal wear appears as scratches of irregular width and random direction. Any patches or groups of evenly spaced parallel lines of regular width are virtually always a sign of artificially applied wear.

A reproduction 10-3/4-inch cast iron race car marked Hubley. Exhaust "flames" in hood rise and fall as the car wheels turn just like the original car.

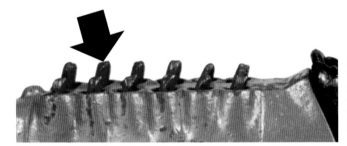

Close up of exhaust "flames" on the reproduction. One side rises as other falls which is the same action on the original.

Bottom view of the new cast iron Hubley racer showing the location of the Hubley mark at white arrow. The bend in the front axle, blue arrow, acts as a cam to raise and lower the flames in the hood.

Close up view of the front axle in the new Hubley racer. shows distinct hammer marks not found on original front axles.

Kitahara Reissues

A number of confusing replicas of early 1950s Japanese tin windups were made in the 1990s. Probably the most accurate copies, and now the most easily mistaken for vintage pieces, were new toys produced by Teruhisa Kitahara. Kitahara, who had one of the largest collections of Japanese toys, is a well-known expert and author of a number of books on the subject.

During the mid-1990s, Kitahara created a line of limited edition reissues that were virtually exact copies of vintage originals. Original dies and molds were used to make the reissues so new and old are, for all practical purposes, virtually identical in shape. There were at least five different windups issued including, using the original 1950s names, Circus Boy, News Cub, News Dog, Santa Claus and Rabbit Drummer.

Dating the new pieces may be especially difficult because the copies have what at first glance appear to be vintage marks. Both new and old Circus Boy figures include the Japanese Patent Design Number and the trademark of Nikko Kogyo, the Japanese manufacturer which made the vintage version of this toy. If you looked at the Patent Number and trademark alone, you would naturally conclude both toys were pre-1960.

In this case, you need to look for a third mark to separate the old toy from the 1990s reproduction. The new Circus Boy toys include Kitahara's own trademark, a crown enclosing the initials "TK" surrounded by a banner with the word "Toy." Regardless of any other symbols or names, any mark which includes the crown trademark of Kitahara cannot have been made before the mid-1990s at the earliest.

Kitahara's reissues were expensive at the time they were produced and made in fairly limited numbers. Each reissue originally retailed in the mid-1990s for $150 to $200 each. It was claimed only 1,000 of each reissue design was made. Although the Kitahara copies may become collectible in the future for their own merits, they should not be confused with vintage 1950s originals.

Teruhisa Kitahara's mark on 1990 reissues of vintage 1950s Japanese tin toys.

Marks of the original Japanese toy maker, Nikko Kogyo, and pre-1940 patent number on Kitahara's 1990s Circus Boy.

NEW

OLD

A 1990s reissue of Circus Boy tin windup.

The original ca. 1950s Circus Boy tin windup made in Japan.

All the reissued toys were sold in vintage-styled boxes. This is the new box of the reissued Circus Boy.

Three other tin toys reissued by Kitahara in the mid-1990s. All are nearly identical copies of 1950s originals. From left: News Cub, News Dog, Santa Claus.

The largest of the Kitahara reissues was this 8" Rabbit Drummer.

Marx

Original Marx playsets were produced between 1949 and 1976. Many were based on popular television shows and movies from the 1950s and 1960s like "The Untouchables," "Yogi Bear Jellystone Park," "Zorro," "Ben Hur," "Davy Crockett," and "Robin Hood." Other popular sets included gas stations, farms, airports, military themes of all kinds, and cowboys and Indians. Most sets from the 1950s and 1960s originally sold for about $5 to $10. Today, original playsets sell for $300 to $2,000, depending on title, number of original pieces, and condition.

Separate groups of plastic figures from Marx playsets have been reproduced since 1995. Complete boxed playsets including metal buildings, plastic figures and accessories, have been reproduced since 1997. At least four new sets were in production in the late 1990s, including: Davy Crockett at the Alamo, Fort Apache, Sears Service Station, and Cape Canaveral. Sets reproduced in the early 1990s included: Lassie's Heartland America, The Flintstones, Battle of Navarone, The Gold Rush Western Frontier, The Jetsons, and The Great Chariot Race.

The new Davy Crockett playset shown on P. 339 and 340 highlights basic differences between new and old metal in all the sets. First, look for the original Marx trademark on the metal. Virtually without exception, the lithographed metal used in original pre-1970 playsets should include "Made in United States of America." Most, but not all, trademarks on metal also include "New York, NY." All the metal pieces in the new playsets so far are made overseas primarily China. So far, all the pieces of new metal playsets I have seen have the new circular trademark which does not include Made in United States of America like the old marks. Metal pieces from many vintage playsets are also marked with the names of additional license or copyright holders such as Walt Disney, MGM, ABC, etc. Although not an absolute guarantee of age, the printed name of an additional copyright or license holder such as Disney, Hanna-Barbera or others, is a positive sign of age. Keep in mind that not all metal pieces in original playsets were marked. The best pieces to examine for marks are the larger more important metal pieces such as buildings.

Marks can reliably be used to evaluate metal pieces of playsets, but not the plastic figures and accessories. Many plastic pieces appearing with the new sets are made from original Marx molds and include old-appearing dates and trademarks. Several manufacturers have sold new unmarked figures designed to be used with Marx playsets such as the Civil War and Alamo since the mid-1900s. Although some of these figures may be marked "China," importers could legally mark only the packaging with the country of origin and not mark the individual pieces. Many of the new plastic pieces which are marked have marks that are very small and difficult to see especially if figures are in bags or boxes. In addition to common figures which formed the bulk of Marx playsets, the harder to find licensed character figures are also being reissued.

Generally, figures from the Marx molds, both reissue and old, have more detail than lookalike pieces made by other manufacturers. Colors of the look-alikes are also different but color can be confusing. Some pieces from the original Marx molds have been made in original colors. While the plastic in authentic original playset figures and accessories varies from later look-alikes and the modern reissues, it can be very difficult to use plastic alone to separate new from old. As a broad guideline, most original human figures and larger original accessories such as horses and trees, are made of a soft plastic which has a dull finish. Most, but not all, lookalike and reissue human figures, horses and many accessories have a shiny, not dull, finish.

Since a complete playset with most of its contents is worth about two to three times that of a set with only half or fewer of its pieces, there is also strong temptation to mix in new plastic figures and accessories to round out incomplete original sets. Just because the metal parts are authentic, don't automatically assume all the plastic figures are vintage pieces. Examine all the parts and pieces before making a judgment of age and authenticity. Many variations of original sets were made. There were at least 40 versions of authentic Fort Apache playsets, and 12 or more authentic Cape Canaveral sets. Study and learn what markings, pieces, and assortments of figures were offered in the original playsets.

This new playset titled "Official Davy Crockett at the Alamo" includes metal buildings marked Marx Toys.

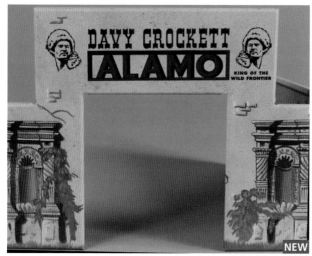

The metal gate in the new Davy Crockett Alamo playset does not include the name of Walt Disney.

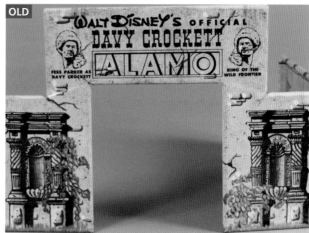

The metal gate in the authentic playset is marked "Walt Disney's Official Davy Crockett at the Alamo."

This revised Marx trademark appears on new metal buildings made overseas. It does not include "Made in United States of America."

The original Marx trademark on original metal buildings includes "Made in United States of America, New York, NY." Marks on new plastic figure and new playset boxes may include "United States of America" but no new metal pieces so far include Made in USA.

The new metal Alamo building is 12" x 4" x 4", one full inch shorter than the original Alamo building which is 12" x 4-1/4" x 5". (Measurements do not include the domed top). This original building shape was used in many original Marx sets. Only the printing on the metal was changed.

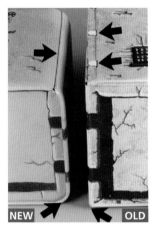

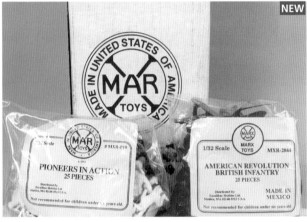

The new metal buildings, shown above, have rolled seams and rounded corners to meet new child safety standards. Original metal buildings, above, were made with exposed slots and tabs and sharp, square corners.

New plastic accessories are packaged in boxes and bags which may have the original Marx trademark including "Made in United States of America, New York, NY." The figures inside the bags and boxes may or may not have the original Marx trademark.

New lookalike Alamo Mexican Soldier, left, compared to an original Marx Alamo Mexican Solider, right. The original Marx figures were sold with Zorro and Alamo playsets.

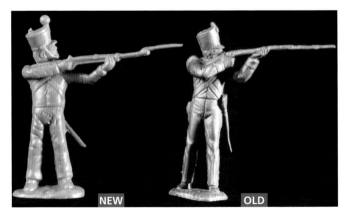

Some new plastic pieces made in original molds are marked with the original dates. The base of this new plastic figure made from an original mold is dated 1965 in Roman numerals, the same date as on originals.

Mark on the base of a new lookalike Mexican Soldier.

Examples of character figures from new and old playsets. From left: reissued Bullet figure; reissued Dale Evans figure; reissued Davy Crockett statue; original Friar Tuck figure.

Saddle horses from original Marx molds. The reissue is on the left; the original on the right. The reissue has a very shiny slick surface. The original has a dull matte surface with virtually no shine.

Paya Reissues

Since 1985, Paya, a Spanish toy maker, has been reissuing metal toys it originally made in the early 20th century. The new toys are made in the same molds and dies from which originals were produced.

The Paya company dates back to 1902. Emilio, Pascual, and Vincente Paya expanded the business into the company called Hermaños Paya (hermaños means brothers in Spanish). This name is represented by the trademark monogram "HP" used from 1906 to 1910. By the 1920s, Paya's mechanical toys were competing with the established toy companies of Germany and France.

Like the rest of the European toy industry, Paya essentially shut down during World War II. Following the war, it struggled financially. In 1985, a decision was made to reissue the early 20th century toys. According to a present day Paya sales brochure, 2,000 different toys were made between 1906 and 1940. Currently, 50 toys are being made as reissues.

Many original Paya toys are in the $200 to $2,000 price range in today's antique market. One of Paya's most sought after toys, a Bugatti race car from the 1930s, has sold for more than $10,000.

The new reissues are produced with the same trademarks that appeared on original pre-1940 Paya toys, so marks alone are not a test of age. Marks found on both new and old include the "HP" mark and a stylized version of the word "Paya," in which the "P" forms the body of a locomotive. Both old and new marks are in various sizes and color combinations.

Since old dies are being used, reissues appear to be identical with originals. Although there are slight differences in paint and the way the metal is finished, these clues are not easily recognized. Fortunately, Paya markets the new reissues as "limited editions" and permanently marks each piece by stamping an edition number into the metal.

Unfortunately, if unethical sellers want to misrepresent pieces, most buyers don't know what the stamped numbers mean; new numbers look like old model numbers or production codes.

New Paya reissues have an edition number between 1 and 5,000 stamped into the metal. The location of the number varies and is not always obvious. Numbers are slightly more than 1/8" high.

A new 11" windup metal motorcycle. The original was first made in 1936. The new reissue price is $350; the original sells for $1,400 to $2,200.

 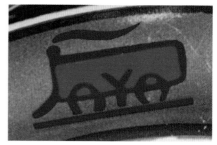

Hermañose Paya trademarks: "HP" monogram mark, left, and locomotive logo, right. The letter "P" forms an engine, other letters form wheels. Both marks appear on both old and new toys so marks alone are not a reliable test of age.

Reissue windup rowboat by Paya, 14". This is the same as the original, made in 1923.

Schylling Toys

Schylling is a present-day toy maker/distributor specializing in "nostalgic" products. Its product line includes many character toys and copies of toys originally made during the 1930s through the 1960s, many of which are character toys based on figures from comics, cartoons and movies such as Dick Tracy, Felix and Popeye. Many of the toys being copied are virtual clones of originals made by well known American makers such as Marx and Chein, as well as important toy makers from Japan.

One of the clues to identifying new Schylling toys, which copy vintage American toys, is to look for the phrase "Made in the USA" or "Made in America." As far as is known, all Schylling toys are made in and are marked "China." Marks of original toys by Marx and Chein, by contrast, are almost always marked "Made in America" or "Made in the USA."

In at least one case, Schylling is known to have purchased the original vintage molds and dies of American toy companies no longer in business. Original 1930s tooling for the tin windup classic Crocodile and Native Rider are now owned by Schylling Chein. The company has been using the tooling to make reproductions since 2003. Schylling is also producing a series of metal cars virtually identical to a series made by Marx. The graphics, names on the cars and the car body shape are all direct copies of the Marx originals.

Although the majority of the lookalike toys by Schylling are clearly marked China, this is not always apparent if you're looking at the toy online. Don't assume you're looking at the original. Be sure to ask the seller very specific questions about all markings and whether the seller will guarantee an approximate year of production.

The Schylling logo as it appears on a key from a new windup metal toy. Schylling marks may include additional marks and symbols.

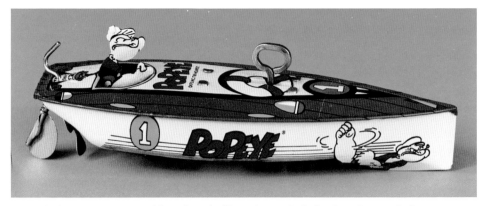

New windup Popeye 7" speed boat by Schylling. The toy includes licensing marks by Hearst which are similar to marks appearing on vintage character toys.

New 12" metal windup toy made by Schylling from the original 1930s tooling. The original toy and tooling were made by J. Chein & Co of the United States in the middle of the 20th century, ca. 1930s-40s.

New Dick Tracy Riot Car made by Schylling. This is a very close copy of the original Dick Tracy Riot Car made by Louis Marx & Company, ca. 1946.

Dr. Seuss Items

Theodor Geisel, better known under his pen name of Dr. Seuss, was both author and illustrator. Although his main characters, including The Cat in the Hat, Grinch, Horton and hoards of other strange creatures, were originally designed to interest children in learning to read, the weird creatures also formed the basis for colorful and unusual collectibles.

Vintage Dr. Seuss pieces have been rising rapidly in price since the death of Seuss in 1991. Unfortunately, a flood of reproductions released since then far exceeds the amount of original ca. 1950-1970s collectible material.

How do can you separate new from old? Many collectors think overall quality of an object is one test. This is largely due to Geisel's insistence on quality. While he was alive, Geisel was very selective about the number and nature of items that were licensed. After his death, there was less control. Today, at Seuss Landing at Universal Studios in Orlando, Florida, for example, you can now buy everything from silk pajamas to a full set of drinking glasses with Seuss characters. While the huge numbers of Seuss reproductions make it difficult to list all the new materials, there are a few general guidelines.

The great majority of vintage pre-1970 Seuss items were made in America. Most of these pieces are marked with the name of a 1960-1970s American manufacturer or toy company, such as Mattel, and some reference to being "Made in USA." Most current Seuss products, with the exception of books, are made almost exclusively overseas, particularly in China, India, and Indonesia, and are marked with the names of those countries. If those countries appear in the mark, it's very likely that the item has been recently made.

Certain company names and marks appear only on modern post-1991 products. "Seuss Landing," the theme park begun in Orlando by Universal Studio, for example, was first registered with the US Patent and Trademark Office in November of 1997. No piece marked Seuss Landing could have been made prior to 1997.

Here are some additional names of some of the largest licensees and manufacturers which appear only on new, never vintage, Seuss products.

- Esprit de Corp—cannot be earlier than 1995 when Esprit acquired all apparel licensing rights in America and Canada.

- Schylling—Any item with the name Schylling cannot be old. Schylling is an American toy distributor specializing in nostalgic and vintage appearing toys (see photo on the next page). Schylling's first Seuss metal toys are scheduled for release September of 2002.

- Manhattan Toy—distributor and licensee for many of the soft character toys made since 1999.

- University Games—on new games based on Seuss characters and stories.
- Hallmark—variety of ornaments, novelty and gift items.

Many vintage pieces are generally very simply marked, usually with just the word or symbol for copyright and the words "Dr. Seuss" such as "© Dr. Seuss" or "Dr. Seuss, Copyright." However, this is far from a guarantee of age; many new products may be similarly marked.

You need to be very cautious of using dates on Seuss products as your only test of age. Most dates in marks on Seuss products indicate the year a design, character or book was copyrighted or registered as a trademark, not the date of production. Many dates on currently manufactured pieces, for example, include trademark and copyright dates from the 1950s and 1960s.

Some would argue that present-day Seuss items are collectibles in their own right. After all, it's the novel artwork that makes Seuss pieces so attractive to many collectors, not necessarily the age. That's fine if all sellers honestly represent new merchandise as new and not vintage. But with the huge price differences between modern and vintage, there is bound to be some mistakes in descriptions, either honest or deliberate. Just be aware that there is a tremendous amount of new Seuss items in the market and many more likely to follow.

OLD

NEW

The lid of the vintage Cat in the Hat jack-in-box above is marked with multiple images of the Mattel Toy Co. logo. Other markings on the old jack-in-box include "Mattel, Ind., Hawthorne, California 90250, Manufactured for Mattel, Made and Printed in USA." A new jack-in-box on the market is marked "Schylling" and "Made in China." The front of the 1970 box at right shows the cat only from the neck up. The front of the new box shows a full length image of the cat.
Photos courtesy Connie Swaim.

New metal dome-top lunch box with character from Cat in the Hat. 8" x 4-1⁄2" x 8", average retail price $14.95. All original vintage boxes were flat topped like the original shown below.

NEW

OLD

Vintage 1970 Cat in the Hat metal lunch box. Original boxes are marked Aladdin Industries Inc. and USA. Vintage boxes can sell for up to $150 and more.

The Cat in the Hat is one of several figures available as a hanging ornament or brooch in sterling silver. Ten other Seuss characters are also sold as sterling silver charms. Retail prices range from $45-$49 for ornaments and brooches; charms are $24 each. No comparable pre-1970 products are known.

New 10" waste basket with illustrations from One Fish, Two Fish, Red Fish, Blue Fish. Average new retail price, $10-$15. No comparable vintage product is known.

Some new Seuss items, like this 12-piece Cat in the Hat cube puzzle, have no mark. Unmarked pieces can often be difficult to accurately date without additional research.

Many marks on new products have what appear to be dates associated with original production items. The new puzzle box, left, for example, includes a 1960 copyright date. A second copyright date of 2000 finally appears about 4" away from the first date. If the early date is included in a photo in an internet auction and bidders don't ask specific questions, the item may be assumed to be vintage, not new.

TM & © 1960 Dr. Seuss Enterprises, L.P.
University Games Corporation, San Franci

$14.00 U.S. $18.00 CAN.

51400>

9 780394 800929

ISBN 0-394-80092-3

Very few vintage Seuss products have Universal Product Code (UPC) bars. The majority of Seuss products with UPC bars are made after the 1980s. The absence of UPC bars does not mean a product is necessarily old, though. Many UPC codes are on throwaway packaging, not the actual products. This UPC appears on a new Seuss book.

The choking hazard warning, as shown on this new Seuss product, virtually never appears on vintage Seuss products.

⚠ WARNING:
CHOKING HAZARD - Small parts.
Not for children under 3 years.

Copyright, 1938, by Dr. Seuss

Copyright statements in Dr. Seuss books become progressively more complicated and lengthy over the years. Compare the 1938 example, right, to the 1993 example, above.

Space Toys

Among the most popular vintage tin toys are those with a space theme. Rocket ships, robots and spacemen were perfect subjects to implant battery and friction motors to give the toys of post war Japan action, sounds and lights. Naturally, the popularity of space toys has not been overlooked by reproduction manufacturers who have copied many of the most famous vintage originals.

One of the very earliest and rarest toy robots, Atomic Robot Man, for example, has been reproduced for about 10 years. Originals can sell for $500-$1,000 and more; the reproductions retail for about $20. The original Atomic Robot Man is thought to be one of the first tin robots made in postwar Japan. It is tiny compared to later toy robots, measuring only 5 inches tall. One of the most interesting features of this robot is its distinctive way of walking. Rather than shuffle along on wheels like later battery-powered robots, ARM's windup mechanism drives a pointed spike hidden under each foot. The spike jabs down and completely lifts the legs on each step producing a Frankenstein-like side-to-side shuffle. A removable key fits into the robot's left side of the body. Originals, made immediately after the war, are sometimes, but not always, marked "Made in Occupied Japan." The original manufacturer is unknown.

Both old and new robots are virtually identical in mechanical operation, size and general construction. A quick glance in a book and both versions would appear to have an almost identical appearance as well. There are several details, however, which you can use to separate old from new.

First, the majority of known original Atomic Robot Man robots are made in two colors. The body and legs are one color; the arms and head are a second color. Almost all originals have khaki brown bodies and legs with gray arms and heads. So far, the new 5-inch Atomic Man robots are one color only: blue, silver or red. Although some promotional literature shows new robots in two-tone color schemes, I have seen new robots in anything but a single color.

Next, look at the gauges and dials on the robot's body. The original Atomic Robot Man has only three dials on the chest; the reproduction has five. Also note the large circular dial is on the left chest of the reproduction; it is on the right chest of the original. Be careful, though, that you compare the gauges on the robot itself. The gauges appear correctly on the new box in which the new robots are packaged although they are incorrect on the robot itself.

Boxes should be examined as closely as the toys because original boxes can often double or triple the selling price. New Atomic Robot Man boxes are easy to spot: they are printed with a UPC bar code and modern safety warnings for small parts. Bar codes and safety warnings are never found on original Atomic Robot Man boxes.

Keys sold with the original Atomic Robot Man are plain cheaply stamped sheet steel similar to those found with other inexpensive Made in Occupied Japan toys. The new keys sold with the reproduction is cast pot metal and embossed with the toy distributor's name "Schylling." It's common practice, though, to discard new keys and replace them with old keys from cheaper toys.

About 5 years after the original 5-inch size of Atomic Robot Man was reproduced, a larger version was brought out. At 11-1/2 inches tall, it is more than twice the size of the original. Any Atomic Robot Man this size is automatically new and no closer examination is required.

The reproduction 5" Atomic Robot Man tin windup robot. New robots are sold in facsimiles of the original cardboard box.

The new Atomic Robot Man box has a child warning label and UPC code which do not appear on the original box.

OLD

OLD

The original late 1940s early 1950s Atomic Robot Man robot, left, and the original box, right.

11½"

5"

NEW

OLD

Around 2002, an 11-1⁄2" reproduction of the Atomic Robot Man was produced. All 11-1⁄2" versions are fantasy pieces; 5" is the only size in which originals were produced.

The large round gauge is on the new robot's left chest as shown here. The round gauge is on the original robot's right chest.

Size is also important when evaluating another rare 1950s tin space toy collectors know as the X-9 Robot Car. The original was made by the Japanese toy company Masudaya in the 1950s. Original X-9 Robot Cars rarely appear for public sale, so it's difficult to estimate their value. Other original vehicles with robot bodies, though, are among the most desirable and highest priced space toys. Similar originals with robots mounted in space vehicles like the Mechanized Robot by TN Co., for example, has sold for over $25,000. The Space Robot Car by Yonezawa, which has a plastic dome similar to the X-9 Robot Car, sells for $2,000 or more. By contrast, the reproduction X-9 Robot sells for around $25 or less through mail order catalogs.

Looking at only a photo or an image on a computer monitor, new and old look virtually identical. But unless you ask careful questions and read an honestly written description, you might not be able to separate new from old. It's only when you set new and old side by side or carefully read a reference book on toy robots does the difference become apparent. The reproduction is only 4 inches long; the original is almost 8 inches long.

This is more of a problem than it first appears because many of the toy robot reference books, including Japanese tin toy expert Teruhisa Kitahara's books, generally only list dimensions in millimeters (190mm long). American readers need to convert the metric dimensions into equivalent inches before realizing the actual size. While that is not a huge chore, it is an extra step that may be overlooked in the hurry to place a last minute bid in an online auction.

Another significant difference not readily apparent in photos alone is that the original X-9 Robot Car is a battery-operated toy; the reproduction is powered by a windup mechanism, not batteries. There is a knob on one side of the reproduction to wind the mechanism. If only one side of the original toy is shown in a photo or image, the knob will not be visible. This information is not generally included in photo captions of many toy reference books. In Kitahara's *Robots-Tin Toy Dreams*, for example, the photo of the X-9 Robot Car appears on P. 31, but the text describing the toy as battery operated doesn't appear until an entry in the appendix on P. 101. Since only the left side of the original is shown in that particular book, you wouldn't know that there should not be a wind up knob on the right side as found in the reproduction.

The craze for robot toys during the 1950s and early 1960s led vintage manufacturers to experiment with many different designs. No only were robots attached to other machines such as vehicles and rockets, but other creatures were converted into robots. One of the most unusual, and much sought after original examples, of an animal-turned-robot is the tin Space Dog made by Yoshia of Japan in the late 1950s. As originals began bringing up to $600, reproductions soon appeared.

Reproduction X-9 Robot Car tin toy.

The reproduction, shown here, is powered by a spring mechanism wound by this knob (arrow). The original X9-Robot Car toy is powered by batteries, not a windup mechanism.

The original 1950s X-9 Robot Car, shown here in outline, is nearly 8" long. The reproduction is only 4" long.

The reproductions are usually, but not always, marked "Made in China." Originals, made in Japan, would never be marked China. Most originals are marked with the Yoshia trademark and "Made in Japan." All the Space Dog reproductions I have seen have included a nameplate, or dog license, with the name "Rover." No original Space Dog has ever been found with a similar "Rover" nameplate.

The Space Dog reproductions are all powered by windup mechanisms. Original Space Dogs may be found with either windup mechanisms or friction motors, with friction motors being the most common. Both originals and reproductions are made in all red and all chrome finishes.

The popularity of vintage space toys has inspired many new fantasy knockoffs. That is to say, manufacturers have adapted and blended themes and subjects of vintage toys to create new products with no old counterparts.

One of the most obvious examples is a new marble game which looks, at first glance, like it's straight from a baby boomer's toy box. The game's graphics are based on well known space toys originally manufactured and sold in the 1950s and 1960s.

New tin Space Dog, available in red or chrome. The reproduction has a "Rover" name tag on the front and is marked "Made in China" on the base. The reproductions are driven by windup mechanisms.

The original tin Space Dog made ca. 1955-60s by Yoshia in Japan. No originals were ever marked "Rover." Most originals are usually marked only with the Yoshia trademark and "Made in Japan." Originals are most commonly found with friction motors but were also made with windup mechanism.

In the lower left of the new marble game, for example, is the Space Dog robot toy discussed earlier. Towards the top center is the toy known as Rocket Racer by Masudaya; at the bottom center is Gear Robot by Yoshia. Other well known space toys appear throughout the background. No old counterpart to this game was ever made. This is just an attempt of marketing a new toy that takes advantage of the widespread interest in vintage space toys. The new marble games are 10 inches long and retail for $5 to $10 each.

Another new toy without any old counterpart combines a typical space toy theme with a distinctly non-1950s material, wood; the result is a strange 6-inch pushup toy with a dancing robot. Pushups, very popular in the 1930s, feature a jointed figure connected by elastic cords running through a hollow body and limbs. The elastic cords are attached to a wooden disc in the base. Pressing the base tightens or loosens the cords causing the jointed figure to extend or relax the various body parts, or dance.

The red and white paint on this example fluoresced brightly under long wave black light, but you don't need a black light to confirm this piece is new. While it might be theoretically possible to find a folk art robot toy made like this, no 1950-1960s factory-made examples of this pushup toy are known.

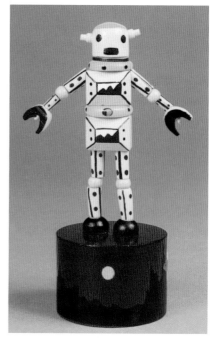

This new marble game features many well known vintage 1950s space toys such as the Space Dog, Rocket Racer, Gear Robot and others. No old counterparts to this toy exist.

New 6" painted wood pushup toy with a robot. No factory-made toys from the 1950s-1960s like this example have ever been documented.

Wood, Paper, Cloth

When many people think of reproduction toys, they often limit their concerns to the most expensive examples such as early cast iron, tin wind ups, character toys or complicated space toys. But while those toys certainly are widely copied, buyers often forget to be wary of simpler toys made of paper, wood and cloth.

Many original toys in those materials are often sought after as folk art because of the great amount of hand work required in their construction. For years, poorly made mass-produced reproductions of originals were relatively easy to spot when compared to authentic American folk art originals. Now, however, reproductions are also being made one at a time by hand in China, India and other countries in which hand labor paid a very low wage. As a result, many reproductions now include hand-stitched fabrics, hand-carved wood, hand-brushed paint and other hand-crafted details. In other words, many clues previously used to authenticate originals—such as random length stitches, tool marks, brush strokes and other signs—are now found in modern copies.

Here are some broad general guidelines to help you avoid most of the toys made of wood, paper, and cloth.

Wood: Hand-carved and hand-worked wood is widely used in reproduction toys. It appears in copies of toys originally made in small factories to reproductions of folk art pieces originally made at home. What makes the new wooden pieces so confusing is, like the originals, most are made entirely by hand. This means the wooden reproductions have the same tool marks and irregularities found in most originals.

One of the best ways to catch a great many new wooden toys is learning to recognize so-called Philippine mahogany. This wood can range from almost white to dark reddish brown and has dark brown or black pits in the grain. Other common woods used in reproductions are pale wide grained wood and extremely light weight woods from India and China. Learning the grain patterns of only a few American woods such as maple, pine, hickory and ash will help you avoid most wooden reproductions.

Another much simpler way to catch many wood reproductions is the "sniff test." Virtually every wood reproduction is heavily finished with paint or varnish. Many wood reproductions that are over five years old still have a strong paint or varnish smell. Obviously, if a piece was made 50 to 150 years ago, there should be no present trace of odor. Many reproductions made of painted wood may also be detected by a heavy coating or primer paint. This is usually a dark red color and is frequently visible through chips and scratches in top coats of paint. True wooden folk art was rarely primed before painting. Red-colored primer is primarily a modern product and should be considered a warning sign of a reproduction.

Paper: The most commonly reproduced paper-related toys are copies of "litho over wood," a general term for vintage wooden toys decorated with colorfully lithographed paper. You can detect virtually all new paper litho toys with two simple tools, a 10X loupe and a black light, or ultraviolet light.

In modern color printing, colors are formed by printing dots of the primary colors, red, blue, yellow plus black. Varying the proportion of dots printed in only those four inks—red, blue, yellow, black—create all other colors. Blue dots mixed with yellow dots, for example, makes green; blue and red dots make purple, and so on. The human brain blends the dots into solid colors. You can practice identifying modern color printing by using a 10X loupe on the color photos you find in current magazines and books. You'll see that the primary dots are arranged in a specific repeated pattern. These dot structures will be the same as you'll find in recently printed reproductions including books, novelties and paper pasted over wood.

The majority of color printing on paper before 1920, especially on paper decorated wood toys, was produced by lithography. Generally, each lithographed color required a separate plate. Fourteen colors required 14 impressions by 14 different printing plates or stones. The colors in lithography are produced by areas and patches of solid color, not a regularly repeated pattern of tiny dots as in modern color printing.

While most paper reproductions are mass produced on large printing presses, you also need to be wary of new paper images printed by inkjet and laser printers. Anyone with a scanner and home computer can duplicate almost any color image. Laser and inkjet printer generally create images by printing rows of dots. Most inkjet and laser images show obvious streaks of parallel lines when viewed under 10X. Similar rows of dots and parallel bands are never found in vintage lithography. Such patterns are almost always warning signs of a recently created image.

Regardless of the printing technology, the paper itself can also be used to detect new images. Modern paper, especially white paper stock, has been extensively bleached with chemicals. These chemicals almost always fluoresce a bright white or bright blue under long wave black light. The best area of paper to examine under black light is a surface without ink. If the paper is pasted down or entirely covered with ink (printing), look at the very edge of the paper. If the edge fluoresces, the entire piece is new. Black light is especially useful to detect new images made with laser and inkjet printers which are some of the most extensively bleached and treated papers. Black light is also useful to detect modern glues used to attach new paper. Old animal, or flour based, glues rarely fluoresce; modern synthetic glues almost always fluoresce.

Cloth: Many buyers are fooled by reproductions in cloth because they assume these new pieces will be machine stitched. That would be wrong. The majority of reproductions made of cloth today—made in China, India, Indonesia, etc.—

are almost always hand stitched. Looking at stitching alone is not enough to identify the new products.

The Topsy Turvy rag doll shown on P. 364 is a good example. All seams are hand sewn and the facial details are hand embroidered. There is a functional hand-sewn pocket on each side of the doll's dress. All the fabric is natural cotton printed with a small floral pattern and small geometric shapes very similar to vintage fabrics.

If you're very experienced in old sewing, you might observe that the new stitching is not as close and small and fine as good quality original home work. But to general buyers, those details are probably not known and easily overlooked. Stitching, therefore, should be one test of age but not your only test. Buyers inexperienced in textiles and sewing might be better off to use a black light to detect cloth reproductions. Virtually all new white thread, whether made of natural or synthetic fibers, fluoresces bright white under long wave black light. Many colors of new synthetic thread, especially red, also fluoresce.

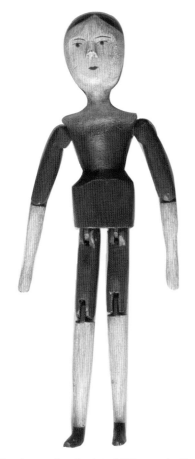

Hand carved and painted 15" reproduction of a mid-19th century peg doll.

Detail of the new peg doll. New red paint on lips fluoresces under long wave black light.

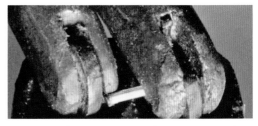

The joints of the new peg doll are hand carved and pegged just as original peg dolls.

Dark red primer showing through a chip in the surface paint on a reproduction. The red primer is a warning sign of modern mass production.

Reproduction child's pencil or trinket box, 8" long, made of Philippine mahogany. The recently applied finish on the wood has a strong odor of paint.

A detail view of the locomotive knob on the pencil box. Note the "antique" finish applied at the factory with simulated edge wear, dents and other distressing.

Regular repeated dot pattern of modern color printing. Shown about 10 times actual size.

A reproduction farm set. The 12" x 4" x 9" painted wood case (closed) has new paper "lithos" pasted on the top. The edges of the new paper fluoresce under black light.

The new wood case opens into a "barn" with stalls. The set includes nine animals covered in pasted paper.

Reproduction farm animals with paper pasted over wood. The new paper has been produced on a laser printer which shows a series of horizontal bands under magnification.

Modern hardware is often used to assemble reproductions of litho over wood. Hinges on the new wood case, for example, are fastened with Phillips head screws, a sure sign of modern construction.

This new farm animal has decorative paper on only one side. Original litho paper over wood pieces have paper on both sides.

This is a new base which holds the new animals shown on P. 363. With the animal figure removed, the groove is bright and fresh with no sign of age or use.

Children's books are widely reproduced, especially late 19th century examples with die-cut pages like this new Mother Goose book. The full color imitates old lithography but shows the dot pattern of modern color printing.

The new Topsy Turvy doll is very similar to vintage originals including a period looking fabric with a very small floral pattern. The new thread fluoresces under long wave black light.

INDEX